THE MELGHAT TRAIL

Walking the Wilds with a Forester

Prakash Thosre

PARTRIDGE

To order additional copies of this book, contact
Partridge India
000 800 10062 62
orders.india@partridgepublishing.com

www.partridgepublishing.com/india

CARACAL CARACAL   PC:DHARMENDRA KHANDAL

This book is dedicated to the fond memory of CARACAL, the lightening quick wild cat. In mid-1940s it adorned the durbars of Maharajas from western Maharashtra where leashed specimens would be kept on display. During a special show, to entertain their guests, a Caracal would be unleashed on a flock of feeding pigeons. This super cat with extra ordinary agility would kill 9-10 pigeons before they could take off the ground. On the afternoon of 1st December 1994, I saw the 'gymnastic event' of this beautiful animal on Dhakna-Dolar road in Melghat forest. Its athletic, arched body like a bow, trying to ambush a peacock, is a sight that I will never forget in my life time. It has recently disappeared from Maharashtra's wilderness forever. After ruling its grasslands for thousands of years, this acrobat is on its way to extinction from India's wilderness too. In India last few specimens survive in the States of Gujrat and Rajasthan. Its distribution coincided with that of Cheetah and both of them basically survived by feeding on the small gazelles. The last Cheetah was shot in India in early 1950s. When do you think would it be the turn of Caracal? Let's strive to ensure that this beautiful creation of God survives till Homo sapiens (humanbeing) survive!................ Prakash Thosre

BLURBS

Honest, lucid and graphic portrayal of the life of a forester-wild-lifer. One who lived, observed and learnt the hard way, throwing aside his ego, opened up ears and eyes to the wisdom and knowledge of jungle craft regardless of whether it was from a modest jungle dweller or a lowly staff member. Blessed with an avid and alert mind Prakash thus embellished his ecological knowledge with how Nature actually works it out in the field. Son of an illustrious forester father of yester years from whom he inherited a spear-headed jungle walking stick that came handy in treacherous terrain, Prakash claims to have imbibed a lesson in 'peaceful coexistence' from a leopard and a tiger and eventually got baptised by a 'bhaloo' on hind legs, while he kept up his legging the sheer Melghat wilderness.

Such a person with a powerful pen can but roll out true stories of experiencing the ways and happenings in raw wilderness abounding in deer, gaur, wild pig, tiger, leopard and the omnipresent bhaloo. The narration is succinct, thrilling and more gripping than a brilliant spy fiction. For example Prakash, having perched himself in the wait of wild animals coming to a waterhole, on a makeshift low machan, after long and quiet wait, eventually switches on the probing spotlight only to find the leopard just six feet underneath his machan. The resulting commotion, compounded by the waiting driver switching on headlights and approaching for sahib's rescue, ends up normalising the heartbeats of the sahib and the leopard alike. Sketches accompanying several stories are communicative merrily hanging between the graphic and the comic.

Genuine appreciation of sincere, intelligent and brave wildlife researchers like Prachi Mehta, with stories to back, clicked my memories of her as WII's genuine research scholar while I was Director of the Institute. Prakash also tries to delicately balance the deprivation and hardships that a jungli's family has to contend with against Nature's gifts to the Jungli, but in the end it is a price that he and his family ended up paying."

H S Panwar IFS (Retired)
Two decade long Director, Kanha National Park and Tiger Reserve
National Director Project Tiger 4 years
Founder Director Wildlife Institute of India (WII), Dehradun 9 years
First recipient Rajiv Gandhi Wildlife Conservation Medal of GOI
Duke of Edinburgh Conservation Medal of WWF International, (Only IFS)
World Conservation Union's highest Fred M Packard Parks Merit Award
President of India Padma Bhushan in Civil Services category (Only IFS)

"Prakash Thosre takes us to an unhurried world where the animals make the rules. The stories bring to life the magic of the Indian jungles".

Sathya Saran,
journalist, biographer, author, critic.

"Mr Prakash Thosre's insightful knowledge told in a easy narration - story form is amazing - so are the experiences and sketches depicting it in a lighter vein. The experience of so many years put in such lucid way is an asset for the nature lovers".

Pullela Gopichand
Padma Shree, Padma Bhushan ,Arjuna , Dronacharya awardee
World badminton Champion in 2001 at All England Open Championship

"We met in 1982 on the beaches of Alibag. Even in those early years Prakash's affinity with the jungle was evident. I envied the harmony between the man and his profession. While others sat behind desks plotting their careers, Prakash chose the jungle trails of animal inhabitants, mostly untrodden by man, to uncover and show us another world.
In his stories he has synthesized the significance of the environment, the forest and its treasure of animals, plants and humans. Profound issues emerge with an appealing simplicity
The most unique and fascinating feature of his work, never captured before, is the understanding of animal psychology - often quite contrary to prevailing notions of animal behavior.
Many incidents from these pages will never leave the reader."

Arun Bhatia IAS (Rtd)

"Prakash Thosre's book gives a deep insight into forests & the real life experience with animals in their natural habitat. Wonderful reading it!"

Chandu Borde
Former Captain of Indian Cricket team and
Former Chairman of Selection Committee for Indian Cricket team, Life time Member of MCC, Lords, Arjun Awardee, Padmashri, Padma Bhushan

"Thosre closely follows the footsteps of Jim Corbett. Passion, riveting stories and great narrative skills .Here is your post shikar-era narrator"

Ms Vandana Chavan
Member of Parliament, (Rajya Sabha) India

"This book gave me the feeling of Jungle book; based on real stories with wonderful characters inhabiting the Rudyard Kipling's same historic forests of Satpuda Landscape".

Kishor Rithe
Former Member National Board for Wildlife and President, Satpuda Foundation, an NGO working in Melghat for last three decades in the field of Wildlife conservation

"The thick jungles of Melghat, full of wild animals, beautiful birds, and some really interesting people come alive through every story that Prakash Thosre narrates. What adds to the magic of his amazing experiences is that he uses simple language to share his treasure of knowledge on what to and what not to do when in the field. This, and the fact that it leaves the reader richer in information while discussing human traits without actually intending to do, is pure class."

Uma Karve Chakranarayan
Journalist, entrepreneur, publisher and a pet parent.

"This book will take you along the jungle trails and the quiet places. It will bring you face to face with the incredible wildlife while you sit in your sofa and enjoy your coffee. Prakash has this amazing ability to transport us to places we always wished to go and to experiences we always wished to have."

Hrishikesh Kanitkar
Ex Indian International cricketer and coach

"Biodiversity is a lifeline to our future.
If we break the line, we are doomed for ever
If we nurture and love it,
We will live to see a bright future
We can make it happen, the choice is ours."
Prakash Thosre's book signifies that life line.

Dr Erach Bharucha
Director, Bharti Vidyapeeth Institute of Environmental Education
And Research, Former Chairman, Maharashtra State Biodiversity Board and
Former Medical Director of Jehangir Hospital, Pune.

CONTENTS

FOREWORD

Prakash Thosre's book is a delight to read for anyone. The extraordinary tales are narrated in an inimitable style reminiscent of Corbett and Anderson. He shares his deepest insights into wildlife, the people who live in the forests, mans conflicted approach towards the forests, the animals, the attempts at understanding the eco system and pressures that man exerts on the forests. The insights come to the reader, not as boring statistics and analyses but as wonderfully narrated stories of situations and events,that the author has been through. The words jump out of the book. It starts with a faint sound, followed by the scent, waking you up to the invigorating sensations of the forest. One moment you are reading the book, the next moment you are in the forest.

Thosre has converted a sidelined posting into an opportunity of great learning and a brilliant career giving him a unique position as a forester, an officer, a naturalist and now, a good writer. His description of the forests, its large variety of animals, the tribals who live there, is enthralling and beautiful. Thrilling accounts of confrontation between man and the animals that haven't been narrated before; like the Korkoo tribal who tripped and stumbled over a leopard; the dak runner who climbed a tree to protect himself from a tiger- soon joined by the tiger who climbed up the same tree to protect himself from wild dogs!

One doesn't know of anyone who has written about one of the most interesting and little known sanctuaries in India- The Melghat Tiger Reserve. The sanctuary is vast about 1700 sq kms and has a core area of over 350 sq kilometers. It's located in one of the most ancient parts of the country - Vidarbha, *darbharahitpradesh* which means a region where the *darbha* grass doesn't grow. The unique landscape here is very different from other places like Tadoba, Kanha and the other famous ones. The book transports the reader to these forests. It talks of the flora and the fauna. It uses the local names and the Latin names along with the common names. It has stories-terrifying ones and comical ones and true to how things happen there; the stories of courage, of bravery, of danger and of survival. There is the story of a Korkoo's combat with a leopard and the story of a tiger who out of gratitude, followed tribal maidens that had protected him from wild dogs.

The book is delightful, educative and much needed- The Jungle Book of recent times. May we see more coming from Prakash Thosre

(S A Bobde)
Chief Justice
Supreme Court of India

PREFACE

Octber 1976 was an eventful month for a typical bureaucratic family as ours. It was the month in which we had witnessed a seamless changeover of the baton of the Indian Forest Service from father Jagannathrao Thosre to his son Prakash Thosre. It was indeed a dream come true for a nature lover like me (as well as my father). About seven to eight decades ago, *shikar* (hunting) was legal, and authors like Jim Corbett and Kenneth Anderson wrote thrilling accounts of their experiences. Times have changed since then, perspectives have changed, and values have changed. Hunting down wild animals is no longer a macho sport, and crowing about one's machismo with a gun will only bring opprobrium today – and rightly so.

The wilderness provides plenty more excitement than bringing down ferocious cats. I had learnt this lesson as a forester's son, and the lesson got hugely reinforced during my own career as a forester. I began looking for opportunities for sharing these thrilling, seminal lessons with as many people as I could. I began to give talks on the subject at every available opportunity. I started contributing articles to newspapers and magazines. This book is a compilation of all those talks and writings and quite a bit more. It is an effort at sharing with my readers the awe and wonder that the wilderness has always inspired in me.

My first posting in Melghat was followed by two more. During these three postings, spanning over six years, I travelled about 150,000 kilometres, often on foot. Besides camping in century-old forest rest houses (FRHs), I also camped in the bamboo huts constructed for patrolling in the core area of Project Tiger. As I lay stretched out in these huts, I would imagine that the ancient sages of India would have been absorbing nature in quite the same way. Occasionally, a stay on a machan (platform) constructed in a tree, hideout, cave, tent, or vehicle added variety to the experience.

During my ramblings in Melghat, I got first-hand information about the behaviour of wildlife. Many of my myths vaporised when I encountered first-hand the unheard-of and unseen personality of the forest and all its inmates. As I remained busy reaching out to the nook and corner of Melghat, my home front was ably looked after by my wife, Deepti. She played the role of a perfect homemaker and attended to the difficult task of grooming our children in their tender years. It was difficult to quantify, but your role was most precious. Hats off to you Deepti ! She along with my sister Mrs Chhaya Landge would often keep enquiring about the progress of the book. This pressurized me and made me work harder. Thanks Chhaya and Deepti for the positive nagging.!

My posting as conservator of forests (CF) and field director (FD) of Project Tiger gave me the opportunity to study from close quarters the flora and fauna of a region noted for its abundance of both. I was rather lucky that even as I had joined, my predecessor, Mr Gogate, took me to the field and explained various water conservation initiatives taken by him. These initiatives were immensely important for the wild animals to tide over the pinch period comfortably. That very night, as we were returning along a narrow walking trail, we were smartly dodged by a leopard with whom we would otherwise have collided head-on. As stated earlier, I began by giving talks and doing slide shows for a variety of audiences right from schoolchildren to Rotarians to senior citizens. A journalist friend, Uma Karve, persuaded me to write a regular fortnightly story for a children's magazine of the *Sakaal* group of newspapers called *Young Buzz*. I am grateful to her. Later on, Mr Vijay Darda of the *Lokmat* group of newspapers found the stories interesting enough to have them appear as a weekly feature in Marathi, Hindi, and English.

Thus, fifty stories appeared in all the editions of the *Lokmat Times*, the *Lokmat Samachar*, and the *Lokmat* in Maharashtra and Goa. The response from the readers was very encouraging, with many of them suggesting that these stories be put together in a book. I am indebted to

Mr Vijay Darda for his constant encouragement and support. I also owe thanks to my readers for expressing their views through their mails – all this while my friend Nadeem Khan looked into my English critically and gave very useful tips. This manuscript would not have seen the light of day but for his support. Not only while the book was being written but also through the entire process of a mere forester evolving into a writer, Nadeem has been by my side, guiding me at each step with a smiling face. A big, big thanks to you, Nadeem.

This manuscript was given to my friends Rajan Mulani and Sundaram Srinivas Ranjan, who invested their precious time and suggested a ruthless pruning of about 20 per cent of the fat and to come out with a slimmer version. I am thankful to them for this voluntary service. The communication between the writer and the reader became clearer thanks to the sketches drawn by the artist Viji Paul for this book. Thanks, Viji, for capturing what was in my mind and producing it for the readers. Mr Sharad Bobde, Chief Justice of India, has written encouraging words in the foreword for this book. I am obliged.

Looking at my affinity for jungles in general and Melghat in particular, my friends sometimes addressed me as a *jungli* and forest colleagues as a *Melghati*, respectively. *Jungli* is also a quite loosely used term meaning 'uncultured'. I took these two terms as compliments. Irrespective of whatever the term may mean, a forester or a researcher or a student of nature, what you need most of all in the jungles is a strong pair of legs. The more you walk around in the forest, the clearer your understanding about wildlife and their habitat becomes. Your eyes, ears, and nose need to stay on 'high alert' all the time. Even if you are on official work, you cannot merely be passing through the forest doing your assignment. You have to pause and soak it all in. You have to learn to appreciate the minute facets of nature's personality, thank your stars for the opportunity of being in the wilderness, and share your happiness with as many as you can. Some such minute facets of nature's personality that I have observed in Melghat are shared in the form of four stray cases with you. They appear as 'That's Melghat for you!' in the following four paragraphs.

My wife, our five-year-old daughter, and I were relaxing in the veranda of a century-old FRH located in a dense forest miles away from civilisation when the generator was switched on. Suddenly, we saw a full-grown female sambar (deer) emerging from the neighbouring forest, running towards us, and stopping just about three metres away. My immediate reaction was to check whether it was being chased. There was nothing there. To my amazement, I found my daughter and wife playing with the 'wild' animal. Later, I learnt that the sambar doe was Sonu, which would come over to greet the guests in the FRH on hearing the sound of the generator. That's Melghat for you!

Before I joined, the local staff had seen a leopard as well as a tiger within the premises of an FRH. I had not seen any of the big cats in those premises. But they had not only seen me but also left their visiting card. In the summer, I would often sleep out in the open. A well-tucked mosquito net was fixed on the bed to provide security from a wide range of life forms ranging from mosquitos to large carnivores. I remember one morning getting up and seeing a collage of pugmarks of a leopard near my cot. It had obviously been curious of the screen and all that the screen concealed. That's Melghat for you!

The surrounds of most of the FRHs are excellent for birding. One winter morning I was walking around Hatti-kund, a spot near the FRH where the water in the river was as deep as an elephant. A major fire line passed near this *kund* (deep pool). Suddenly, all the birds started giving alarm calls as the tiger of the sky, a crested hawk eagle, was on wings. It swooped down at the fire line and killed a big male grey jungle fowl. Holding the fowl with its claw, it gave us a look, felt threatened, and tried to fly vertically up to a *haldu* (*Adiana cordifolia*) tree. It could not bear the weight (about two and a half kilogrammes) and lost grip. It sat on a lower branch of the tree, keeping a sharp eye on its prized possession. As we moved a little away, it came down and began its meal. That's Melghat for you!

FRHs and ghost stories go hand in hand. The ones with the best stories are Rangrao, Rangubeli, Hathru, and Belkund. Koktoo was never in the list till one night something unusual happened. The kitchen call bell was a metal bell, the kind one sees in temples. A string was stretched across two poles to reach the rear veranda. Anybody desiring to call the attendant had to go to the back veranda and pull the string, and that would bring the attendant waddling in. Once, around midnight, on a moonless night, the clang of the bell woke the attendant up from deep slumber, and he rushed to the rear veranda. But not a soul was there. He returned to his room, wondering whether he had imagined it all. But the bell kept chiming off and on. Once, on hearing the bell at midnight, the guests pushed all panic buttons, seriously shortened their travel plans, and left Koktoo in the early hours, talking in excited voices about the 'unseen hand'. The brave attendant was keen to locate the 'unseen hand'. One day he hid himself in a room and, with the help of a torch, tried to spot the 'hand' in action through the window. As soon as the bell rang, he flashed his torch on the string of the bell, and there it was! A big fat owl was perched on the string. The flash of the torch sent the bird fluttering into the dark, and with that disappeared the only chance of Koktoo redeeming its honour among its brother FRHs. That's Melghat for you!

Melghat literally means 'confluence of *ghats*' (undulating terrain). The Melghat forests are some of the last few glorious congregations of plant communities which have survived the onslaught of the axe-wielding man. Extending over three thousand square kilometres in the Dharni and Chikhaldara tehsils of the Amravati district, Maharashtra State, India, they have had a long history of scientific forest management going back to the mid-1860s, when the labour camps were established in the Melghat forests. With the passage of time, the labour camps near *padao*s in Melghat grew into the villages of today. Ironically, efforts are now on to prise these villages out to create a human-interference–free habitat for the tiger.

In the summer, these labourers would eat local mangoes and throw the seeds near their camping place, almost always located near a waterhole. Some of these seeds germinated and created an orchard, which, in local language, is called *amrai*. These orchards later got christened by their unique features and became important landmarks and reference points. They had *aam* (mango) as a prefix, as in Aamadoh or Aambeda or Aamzari, or as a suffix, as in Dunda-aam (mango tree with a branch broken), Dokra-aam (old mango), Banaam (mango tree in the forest), Chikhal-aam (mango in the slush), Dhondriaam (a mango tree with fire in it), Gadu-aam (mango tree shaped like a *gadwa*, a metal vessel for water), and so on.

In 1973, the Melghat Tiger Project came into existence, followed by the birth of the Melghat Tiger Reserve (MTR). A frontline staff of about one hundred was sanctioned initially, which later increased to around five hundred. Initially, Project Tiger was totally in charge of the core area of 361 square kilometres. Now it has gone up to 1,500 square kilometres. The two highways – namely, Nagpur–Indore (Paratwada–Dharni) and Akot–Harisaal – pass through it. A drive on these roads, especially in the monsoons, is indeed a pleasant experience. Semadoh, Harisaal, and Shahanoor have nature education centres and a safari drive available for the ecotourist.

The book is divided into seven chapters, namely, 'Habitat', 'The Wily Leopard', 'The Royal Tiger', 'The Lesser Mortals', 'The Bravehearts', 'The Sahibs', and 'Unique'.

A. Habitat

'Habitat' includes stories related to the places where I stayed, travelled, and toured. They broadly cover Chikhaldara, where I began my service, Tarubanda, the place where I did my range charge, and FRH Dhakna, where I enjoyed staying and frequently touring the Dhakna–Dolar road. These are the venues with which my everlasting memories are attached. Such memories include my first six hours in Chikhaldara, where I met my first boss, met a loner wild boar at attackable distance while walking alone through the fog, met a speechless watchman who had, moments ago, seen a sloth bear in the FRH premises, and received a nasty welcome bite on the bed in FRH Chikhaldara.

The FRH Tarubanda stay was more memorable because it happened to be my solo stay for about a month in an FRH that was located away from the village, in the midst of forest, with not a single soul around at night. Dhakna, I remember from the story narrated by a Korkoo woman who, as a ten-year-old kid, had gone fishing with an English madam and had come across a tigress with cubs at the Siddukund. As far as DD Road is concerned, it was a daily new show in store for me: watching the antics of an intoxicated bear feeling tipsy because of an overdose of stale *mahua* (*Madhuca indica*) flowers or watching from a conked-off jeep with a non-functioning starter a loner gaur at handshaking distance or a pair of biped bears chasing my vehicle at full speed.

B. The Wily Leopard

This bunch comprises seven exciting encounters with leopards in MTR. The thrill of releasing a trapped leopard in the wilderness, the leopard and tiger coexisting in the same patch of forests, a leopard coming head-on along the same footpath as mine, and a leopard trying to ambush a sambar and taking position under my very low machan are the first four stories. An unusual experience of my unknowingly travelling on the same path, in the same direction, as the leopard's and coming so close that my companion was about to stumble upon it is the penultimate story of my experiences with leopards. The fifth story speaks about the extreme courage shown by a Korkoo boy while single-handedly combating a bear and then a leopard.

The last article 'Mother's Instincts' is a bunch of incidents highlighting the role of a wild mother in grooming the young ones and among these is an interesting story regarding reunion of mother leopard with cubs after a long separation.

C. The Royal Tiger

The first story is about an unusual case where a tigress with cubs kills a man. This incident happens on the eve of the chief minister's (CM) visit to Melghat. The sequence of events, the follow-up, and, overall, how the situation gets handled should make interesting reading. A look into the well-maintained in-use tiger cave is my next story.

Joining as FD of Project Tiger and positively trying to sight a tiger in Melghat but remaining luckless for one and a half years prompted me to write my next story, 'The Elusive Melghat Tiger', which is a lesson in a textbook for eleventh standard students of English literature. How a tiger behaves when sensing an imminent threat to its life from a large pack of wild dogs can have comic elements, and that is my next story. Then there is a story titled 'Moonlight Tryst' in which I outline the steps I took to sight a Melghat tiger and the kick I got out of it. The last story in this group is titled 'The Camouflaged Cat', where I managed to get a good sighting of the tiger, shot a few wonderful pictures, and even followed the tiger on foot.

D. The Lesser Mortals

This bunch contains stories of wild animals other than the high-profile tiger and leopard. It comprises four stories, including 'The Dirty Dozen', where a dozen wild boars land up very close to my patrolling party and about the poor eyesight of wild boars, which fail to recognise us at close quarters. It looked as if their survival depended on their sense of smell. Then there are two stories about the gaur, one discussing its spirit of brotherhood and the other one the overdependence of a herbivore on its olfactory sensation and totally missing out on living objects like me who happened to be very close. The last story is about the attack of a sloth bear on my team while we were patrolling in the vicinity of FRH Koktoo.

E. The Bravehearts

It comprises four stories which highlight the extraordinary level of sincerity, hard work, and courage shown by the persons connected with the MTR. The role played silently behind the scenes by these gems earned goodwill for the MTR. They also worked as mentors to motivate others. The first story is regarding Chau the watchman who was instrumental in searching out a party of our field staff lost in jungle and had rescued the FD PT from a precipitous slope. Next story is about Surajpal, a daredevil tracker. Third one is regarding Prachi, a courageous girl and the last one is about 'unsung heroes' who silently toiled hard for earning a good name to MTR by themselves remaining in the background. This story includes brief information about Somji, the master night walker, Neemkar the multifaceted driver with excellent eye for minute observation, courageous Jaju who risked his life for reuniting leopard cubs with their mother and Ajay Pillarisett who did an excellent job of trust building.

F. The *Sahibs*

The stories in this chapter can conveniently be appreciated in pairs. The first pair is 'Maa Said So' and 'Being a Forester's Son'. These articles are dedicated to my parents. My mother briefed me about the days around the time that I was born. My father was a *chhote sahib* (sub-DFO or sub–divisional forest officer) at Allapalli when I was born in 1952, and my interaction with wildlife started right away. The sub-DFO of Allapalli's official residence was and is still located at the edge of the forest. There is a stream that flows behind the bungalow and has a *doh* (deep water spot) where the water is perennially available. Wildlife would turn up there on summer evenings to quench their thirst, including an occasional tiger. A leopard, tempted by a dog or a calf, would sometimes jump the fence and enter our premises. A couple of Madia (local tribal) boys would be summoned to shoo it away. The second story deals with my memories as a child who remembers the tiger *shikar* done by the collector uncle from Melghat.

The second pair is '*Chhote Sahib*' and 'The Shoe Size Turns Larger (*Chhote* Becomes *Bade Sahib*)'. These articles explain the basic hierarchy as also some personal responsibilities. 'Both Chhote as well as Bade sahib experienced certain maiden events which are penned here as 'Maiden Experiences'. The next pair is 'Of Dreams and Nightmares' and 'Rebuilding Trust'. The former story is a dream in which one goes back to the 1960s, and the entire story depicts how happy a local inhabitant was. Then many systems and laws change, which makes the local inhabitant unhappy. He gets a feeling that there has been a breach of trust. The story 'Rebuilding Trust' is precisely an effort to provide answers and do trust-building activities.

'A Ramble through the Core', is an article which talks about trekking/patrolling in the core area of the MTR. As there were no villages in the core, there was no place for staying for the staff in the core, and hence, proper patrolling was not possible there. So huts were constructed at strategic points, and the problem was tied over.

G. Unique

This chapter includes eight stories related to certain unique characters of Melghat. The annual feature of devastating forest fires, certain rare birds and animals, the snakes, the flash floods caused by the undulating terrain, the unusual floral diversity, and the gods and god-intoxicated persons unique to Melghat, appear in the form of individual articles. The experience of swimming in a water-body gathered under a waterfall and realising that there was a huge python also swimming there was a spine-tingling experience related in the article. Another hair-raising experience that I had was at Jinbaba, where, on a foggy night travelling alone on the Akot–Harisal road, I heard some whisperings. The penultimate article in this chapter is titled 'The Price of Progress'. It basically talks about the ill effects of electrification and the intensive agricultural practices respectively often misused in Melghat for the electrocution and poisoning of wild animals. We end the stories with a unique article about the Wednesday weekly market at Harisal.

***

In the end, I will say that all my stories are true stories and are narrated as they really happened on the ground. Hence, they may not be as 'spicy' or 'juicy' as many wanted them to be. Also, I have not been maintaining a detailed personal diary for refreshing my memory.

Hence, except on a few occasions, I have not been able to quote the exact date when an incident occurred. If a little bit of blandness and some amount of approximation in the time frame is tolerable for you, then please go ahead.

After you are hooked onto the book, you may feel tempted to visit Melghat. Please implement your plan. But remember, you should not go there with 'tiger-obsessed eyes'. For various reasons, the tiger is a difficult animal to sight here. But there are plenty of other marvels of nature to feast your senses on. They could be the nests of various birds, the footmarks of wild animals on the ground, the claw markings of tigers, leopards, or sloth bears on various trees, or the burrows of porcupines, spiders, or ants. Any one of them can set the adrenaline racing through your system if you have primed it well.

Literally walking through the clouds, showering under a waterfall, stretching out in an *aaraam-kursi* (lounge chair) in the veranda of a century-plus-old FRH, reading the 'visiting cards' of a variety of wild animals (in the form of footprints, spoors, wallows, barks, antler-rubbed stems, or droppings), listening to the alarm calls of various herbivores, eating local wild vegetables or a roti roasted in a big leaf of *mahul vel* (*Bauhinia vahlii*) – all these things add up to give you a wildly satisfying experience.

The experience could become unique for the few who have time and the aptitude to visit my 'encounter' locations, preferably in the right season – for example, FRH Chikhaldara, with my baptism story, or the Memna graveyard, where a tigress with cubs had killed a drunkard, or the *palash* (*Butea monosperma*) tree at Tarubanda, to which bullocks were tied and one of the bullocks tied next to my cot was killed, or the Hathkua waterhole, where a leopard was sitting under my machan, or Dolar-deo or Jinbaba or my favourite Dhakna–Dolar road or Pipalpadao, where a head-on collision with a leopard was avoided, or at Kuapati, where a bison challenged a pair of tigers to protest the killing of his friend, or the Siddukund, where a British lady had fainted after seeing a tigress with cubs.

Wherever needed, please ensure that due permission of the FD is taken. My hope is that this book works as a teaser, a trailer for enticing you into the wilds and experiencing first-hand the pleasure of walking the Melghat trail. A book can never be a substitute for the real thing. But till such time as the real thing comes along, happy reading!

Prakash Thosre, IFS
Retired Principal Chief Conservator of Forests, Maharashtra State, India
Mobile Nos.: 9422314360; 8055755655
Email: pjthosre@hotmail.com

Melghat Tiger Reserve
Maharashtra

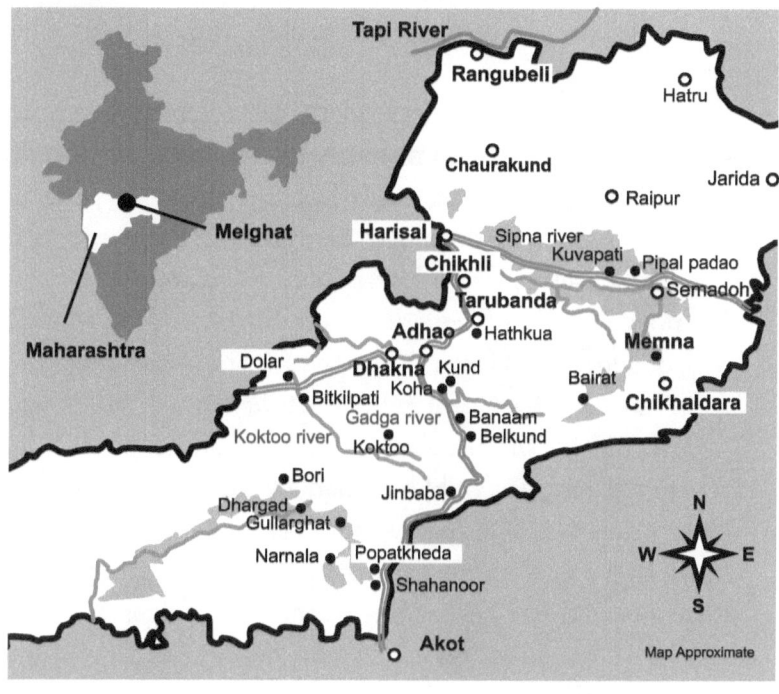

O Prominent Towns ● Places ═══ Roads ～ Rivers ● Tourism Zone

Melghat is well-known for its natural beauty. Hugeness of area, combined with undulating topography,scarcity of drinking water, the presence of undergrowth and other limiting factors make sighting of large mammalian wildlife in Melghat rather tough. So do not go there with the tiger-obsessed eyes lest you may be disappointed. However there exist numerous amazing creations of the Almighty such as the nest of a Baya bird or that of a Creasted hawk eagle, a porcupine burrow ,claw marks of a tiger or that of a sloth bear found on the bole of a tree, variety of birds, insects or the floral species and so on.All this needs your appreciative eyes.

Melghat has three Nature Education Centres namely at Shahanoor, Harisal and Semadoh. Some accommodation and transport facility is available at the Forest Rest Houses too. Pl check up online.

Story-locations in the sketch

1. Chikhaldara the only hill station in Vidarbha. Reached Chikhaldara on 30th June 1979. Baptism by fire. Joined as a probationer on 1st July 1979.
2. On Chikhaldara-Semadoh road 5-6 km down from Chikhaldara is Memna, where during a VIP visit, a drunkard got killed by a tigress with cubs.
3. Continuing on the same road before reaching Semadoh, in Comptt no.103 reunion of mother n cubs of a leopard after a gap of 3 days. Jaju is the unsung hero.
4. 3-4 kilometres ahead we have Semadoh on the banks of Sipna river. It houses a Nature Interpretation Centre..
5. On northern side of Semadoh is the comptt. no176 where Pipal padao is located. Hasan driver from inside a car saw a leopard from our parked car, following the footsteps of Mr Gogate and myself. But for the alertness on the part of the leopard, on our return journey we would have had a head on encounter with it.
6. Comptt no. 163, Kuvapati where a bison, whose companion was killed by a pair of tigers, first paid respects to his friend and later displayed extreme anger towards the pair of tigers.
7. In C 241 we three (myself, Hasan driver and Gannu budha) followed a tiger.
8. Harisal haat on main road going to Dharni. Drunk youngsters, walking as a chain in comptt no. 648 were enlightened about the lurking bear on their way back home. Tigress with cubs came to see us in C 578 sitting on ground in a dilapidated cage.
9. Chikhali C 749 cobra around the cycle of a Ashram school boy.
10. Tarubanda my Range charge. C 766 leopard killed a bullock near my cot.
11. Adhao C 839, stayed in a school building on a rainy night and ate rotis made from elephant ration.
12. Siddukund C 856 where a Britisher lady went angling . FRH Dhakna. D D Road A pair of bears chasing my jeep.
13. Koha C 814 experienced flash floods.

14. Ban Aam C 812 Wake up call (by Gaur).
15. Jin Baba on Akot Harisal Road C 963 Scary experience.
16. Vairat-Koha Road C 821 Dirty dozen (wildboar) sighting from close quarters.

NB-The sketch is drawn under my guidance by Mr Viji Paul my artist. The story locations shown and the distances mentioned in the sketch are very approximate. They are meant to give a very rough idea to the readers about story locations mentioned in the book.

Prakash Jagannath Thosre

A

HABITAT

The literal meaning of *melghat* is 'confluence of *ghats*' (undulating terrain). It is a compact block of deciduous forest in Central India, predominantly of teak. It abounds in a variety of mammalian wildlife. The tiger is the flagship species here. I had three postings in Melghat, namely, at Chikhaldara for the probation period (including Tarubanda for the range charge), as sub-DFO at Dharni, and as FD of Project Tiger, initially at Paratwada and later at Amravati. During these postings, I toured intensively in the nooks and corners of Melghat forests, travelling about 150,000 kilometres, often walking through the area. In this opening chapter, I introduce the Melghat habitat to my readers and take them through the exciting days I spent at Chikhaldara, Tarubanda, and Dhakna and on the Dhakna–Dolar road. The stories related to the habitat are as follows.

1

GETTING BAPTISED

I t was the last week of June 1979. After having successfully completed my two years of professional training at Dehradun and four months of the foundation course at Mussoorie, I was looking forward to my first field posting in Maharashtra which the state allotted to me. My father had recently retired from the Indian Forest Service, and his colleagues were in top positions in the Forest Department in Maharashtra. Naturally, they asked him where I should be posted. Pat came the reply – 'Post him in the interior-most forest area, under a tough boss, where he can learn all aspects of forestry the hard way.'

The top bosses basically had two broad options for my posting: viz. the Allapalli and Melghat forests. The former was then the mecca of forestry in India and is presently notorious for the insurgency (Naxalite) activities in the newly formed Gadchiroli district. The Melghat forests too were a huge chunk of undisturbed nature and had a hard taskmaster as DFO. It was this factor that tilted the decision in Melghat's favour, and that's how I got my first posting in the West Melghat Forest Division. The headquarters of this division was at a hill station named Chikhaldara.

My baggage was very affectionately packed by my father. Besides the main trunk carrying my books and other personal belongings, he had given me a fully loaded ration box and a tiffin carrier to ensure that I did not suffer from the pangs of hunger that he himself had suffered while working in interior inaccessible forest areas, especially when heavy rains or forest fires cut one off from all succour. He had also not forgotten to pack an olive-green mosquito net in the holdall to keep me safe from malaria-carrying mosquitoes in the thick forest vegetation. This mosquito net, I used extensively later in Melghat to camouflage me while sitting on a machan for observing wildlife. He also parted with his prized possession, a multipurpose walking stick with a spear at one end, which indeed proved immensely useful to me during my wanderings in Melghat.

I was to join at Chikhaldara on 1 July 1979. Those days, there was no direct bus from Nagpur to Chikhaldara. Hence, I left Nagpur by the state transport (ST) bus early in the morning and landed up at Paratwada around noon. Armed with my spear in one hand and a big tiffin carrier in another, I landed up at the Project Tiger office along with two trunks and a holdall. There, I met Mr Vishwas Sawarkar, who had done some pioneering work in Project Tiger, for which he was felicitated at the hands of the then prime minister of India Mrs Indira Gandhi. He later quit the service and joined the Wildlife Institute of India (WII) and went on to become director there. Sawarkar prevailed upon me to travel up to Chikhaldara in a Project Tiger jeep, and I finally landed up at Chikhaldara on 30 June 1979 around four in the evening, along with my two trunks and a holdall.

I got down from the jeep, and as my baggage was being put inside the FRH, I looked around. Nothing really had changed from what I had seen as a kid. The ambience was as fresh as ever. It was a typical cloudy day at the hill station, with low clouds and a slight drizzle. The huge Indian holigay and silver oak trees could be seen hazily through the fog. So also were the moss-laden mango (*Mangifera indica*) trees. One *langra* mango tree in the vicinity was still in fruiting. A brief walk in the backyard revealed that the leftover red flowers of the summer bloom of the huge *gulmohar* were still visible on it. The thirty-plus-foot-tall wonder cacti were still decorating the four corners of the FRH. (The one in the south-eastern corner still survives!) The prospect of staying in this set-up alone for the next three months gave me mixed feelings of happiness, excitement, and fear.

The FRH I am writing about is Braeside (*brae* means 'a hillside, especially along a river'). Just opposite Braeside is Peach Grove, now the official residence of the DFO. Previously, Peach Grove was the FRH. I remember having stayed in Peach Grove as a kid and plucked raw peaches and eaten them too. Unfortunately, today the building is there, but the 'grove' that gave the name to the building has disappeared. Braeside was the better building of the two. It was the summer residence of the CF. I, as a school-going boy, had seen Mr Sarvate, the CF of Amravati, stay there and had envied him and wondered if I would ever get a chance of staying there. Today my dream was getting converted into reality. Both these colonial constructions have huge grounds that are planted with coffee. The British maintained these plantations, pruned them regularly, and earned revenue. Years of neglect and disuse have, however, converted them into a low-canopy forest under the shelter of huge trees, providing an excellent shelter for wild animals. Both these buildings are located on the upper plateau, whereas the entire village is on the lower plateau.

There is an interesting map of the upper plateau drawn in 1937 by a seven-year-old girl, Ms Ann Wright, daughter of the then divisional commissioner of Amravati. Besides sketching the important features, little Ann had also marked a location where a tiger had killed a bullock, also where their favourite dog was buried. When I was the FD of Project Tiger, Ms Wright herself presented this pencil-drawn map to me. This map was later put on display at FRH Chikhaldara.

I tried to recollect other important features of the upper plateau. There was the DFO office where I would be sitting from the next day. It had a more-than-a-century-old still-functioning rainwater-harvesting system. Sparsely located heritage buildings belonging to Christian missionaries, one of which was rented out to Project Tiger for their museum, a rest house belonging to the Maharashtra State Electricity Board (MSEB), the rangers' college, and Beer Tank nursery accounted for the other landmarks of the upper plateau. A beautiful forest park was a major attraction for the visitors visiting this hill station. I briefly visited the garden, which was just a two-minute walk. It had a perennial well with a marble tile reading, 'Constructed under the guidance of V. K. Maitland, Esq, IFS, DFO, Melghat, Chikalda, 1936.'

Another 'attraction' in the forest park was a cage in which a female leopard was housed. Interestingly, she had attracted not only the park visitors during the day but also a male of her clan from the wild and who would jump over the gate to say hello to her almost every night. (I had seen the claw marks on the pillars abutting the gate and pugmarks near the cage.) In olden days, this forest park boasted of the best collection of roses and delicious mango trees in the entire Central India. There was a dance floor, a tennis court, and a swimming pool in the garden. Unfortunately, then, it was open only to the whites.

After the park visit, I toyed with the idea of visiting Hurricane Point. It was the only viewpoint located on the upper plateau. From this point, one gets a view of the Gawilgarh fort and an aerial view of Paratwada and its surrounds. This point has known some tragedies. The son of one of my colleagues had fallen down from this point, and the then DFO, Mr Jagir Singh, an ex-army officer, had tied himself to a rope and lowered himself in the deep gorge in an attempt to retrieve the body. This point was also witness to a lady tourist losing her life to a bear attack. I had a mind to visit this point to kill time but soon realised that the fog was so thick that I would not see anything. Instead, I redirected myself to call on my boss, the DFO. I went to Peach Grove and met the DFO and invited him over to Braeside for dinner at eight.

As I relaxed in the *aaraam-kursi* kept in the back veranda of Braeside, Aziz, the *khansama*, came with a piping hot cup of tea. Sipping the steaming tea, I watched the clouds passing through the veranda and realised how fortunate I was to get to work at a place where I would come on picnics as a kid.

I had come to Chikhaldara from the Lal Bahadur Shastri National Academy of Administration, Mussoorie, where there were excellent sports facilities which I had used to the maximum. The training, yoga, gym, sports, and hobbies had kept me fully occupied during the preceding four months. So sitting at the FRH at five, engulfed by a thick fog, alone, waiting for dinner to be served, was a depressing scenario. Aziz suggested I go to the rangers' college, about a kilometre away, where there were sports facilities for the ranger trainees. I could kill time there. He also advised me to return to the FRH before it was dark as there were a lot of *bhaaloos* (sloth bears) lurking in the area, and they were prone to attack suddenly without provocation. As there was no transport available, I thought of going to the rangers' college by walking.

The outing to the rangers' college was exciting. An exhausting game of basketball was followed by a couple of 'singles' of badminton. The sweating out was really refreshing, but then it was soon getting dark, and I remembered Aziz's warning about *bhaaloos*. The rangers' college staff offered to drop me to the FRH by their truck – the only mode of transport they possessed then. The FRH, however, was just a kilometre away, and I insisted that I would sprint the distance in less than ten minutes. They reluctantly agreed but warned me to watch out for *bhaaloos* on the way.

Engrossed in my thoughts, I did not realise that I had already reached the road touching the forest garden and that my destination was just about three hundred metres away. Suddenly, through the fading light and the fog, I saw a rock-like structure abutting the road. A closer look from about five metres made it look like a huge pig. Then I noticed the big tusks jutting out, and it struck me that the motionless creature was a lone hundred-kilogramme-type wild boar. Such a big loner often proves to be a tough customer, even for a tiger. I knew that such an animal charges human beings without provocation and can kill, so crossing this fellow was out of the question. I slowly retraced my steps and waited till the 'rock' disappeared into the fog and then, taking a left turn, sprinted towards the circuit house and, in no time, reached there.

I had escaped the main danger but had now lost my way in the fog. It had become almost dark. So I started calling out loudly to the circuit house watchman. A window creaked open, and out came a hand to show me the direction to the FRH. I begged him to come out and show me the way. But he declined politely but firmly. He said after dusk, it was *bhaaloo* time, and he just could not risk stepping out. Based on whatever tips he gave, I sprinted through the fog with Olympian strides in the direction of the FRH.

At the FRH, Aziz was a worried man. What could have gone wrong with the new *sahib* (master)? Why was he taking so long to return from the rangers' college? He was indeed relieved to see me in one piece. Seeing me sweating and panting, Aziz offered me a glass of water. I cooled down and then briefly narrated to him my 'encounter'. Aziz quickly got me a cup of tea. I settled into a cane *aaraam-kursi* kept in the cloud-wrapped rear veranda of the FRH. Aziz made himself comfortable on the floor and narrated an incident to justify his worry about my safety.

Just a couple of days earlier, his close friend, a cook from the rangers' college mess, was badly mauled by a bear almost at the same spot where I had seen the wild boar. It seems that this cook was returning to the college at night after downing a couple of pegs at the lower plateau. When he reached the forest garden on the upper plateau, a bear suddenly appeared from nowhere and charged at him. It chased the poor chap, who made a futile attempt to climb a nearby banyan (*Ficus benghalensis*) tree. The cook survived the attack but lost most of the skin below his waist.

Tea and story over, Aziz got busy with the dinner preparations for my boss, the DFO, who was joining me at the FRH. It seems Chikhaldara had been in clouds with intermittent rains for the last fortnight. The heavy tapestry in the FRH was moist, and the rooms exuded a peculiar fungal stench. For the last couple of days, there had been no electricity either. The DFO arrived at 8:00 p.m. sharp, accompanied by an escort. My boss was an elder-brotherly figure for me, and the post-dinner tips he gave that night have been immensely useful to me in my service career. It was ten by the time my boss had decided to leave for his residence. Peach Grove was just across the road, a three-minute stroll. Hence, I was amazed to see Aziz arming himself with a *tembhal mashaal* (flame torch) for escorting my boss across. The torch, I understood, was less for light and more for keeping away the dreaded *bhaaloo*. I bade goodbye to the boss and turned towards my suite to retire to my loneliness.

Hardly five minutes had elapsed when I heard a loud SOS call just outside the FRH. I rushed out with my torch, but thanks to the thick fog, I could not see anything beyond ten feet. Soon, through the fog emerged Aziz, panting, sweating, and bleeding from the elbows and knees. Every time he attempted to speak, he only sputtered. It was my turn now to return Aziz's favour of a smiling glass of water. It had the desired effect on Aziz, and he narrated his experience.

Aziz…..dashed towards the Rest House

It seems that after dropping the DFO, when Aziz was entering the rest house compound, he saw a bear in the coffee plantation. The bear was busy digging up a mound, searching for termites, its favourite food. It had not taken any notice of Aziz. Aziz, however, was not taking any chances. He threw his *mashaal* away and dashed towards the rest house. He had taken a couple of topples running across those fifty feet and had grazed himself. Aziz indeed was not overreacting. A bear often stands on its hind legs to become a six-foot monster and shreds the upper part of the human body, leaving the victim disfigured for life. No wonder – and no shame – Aziz had panicked.

Aziz soon quietened down, brought me my water, placed a dim-lit lantern in my room, and proceeded to his outhouse, his transistor radio blaring loudly to shoo away any likely wildlife in the vicinity. Those days, the range forest officer (RFO) would disburse salary advance to class-four staff on the last day of the month, and those days, a priority purchase would be a new set of batteries for the transistor so that it could be played at its loudest. I returned to my suite. The fog, the bear on the campus, the creaking, whistling, whispering window, the sooty, dilapidated, dim-lit lantern, the civet cats romping on the roof, and poor me, alone in the sprawling old building – the setting was perfect for a horror film. But I am happy to report that I was not scared. As the son of a forest officer, I was to the spooky manor born.

As I lay reliving the 'encounters' of day (and evening) one, something bit me nastily on my thumb. In the dim light, I could not see the culprit. But by the time I could fetch more light, my white bed sheet as well as the floor was spattered with blood. Trying to stop the bleeding, I rushed out and called out to Aziz. But beating his radio was impossible. So I went out in the thick fog and fetched him from his outhouse. He inspected my room and my injury and suggested that the tiny two pricks on my thumb could be the fang work of a snake. *A snake?* I started feeling a little dizzy, my heart rate and sweating increased, and my throat went dry.

Aziz took on the doctor's role and I meekly listened and obeyed. He gave me neem (*Azadirachta indica*) leaves to eat and asked me how they tasted. 'Bitter' was my reply. Then he made me eat sugar, and I confirmed that it tasted sweet. A few more such tests, and he diagnosed it couldn't have been a snake. It should then be a rat. After biting, guilty rats generally hide themselves somewhere in the room. Saying this, he opened the drawer of an old table, and out jumped the culprit – a big fat rat. All my adverse symptoms just vanished in moments. Aziz gave a hearty laugh and left. I opened my holdall and took out the olive-green mosquito net that I had inherited from my father, fixed it on my cot, tucked it under the mattress, and then got back into bed, well and truly baptised for the thrilling life of a forester.

I had learnt three important lessons:

a. In a jungle situation, try to follow your timings; days are for citizens, and nights are for the denizens of the wild.
b. Be alert and save yourself from accidents by taking timely action in areas abounding in wildlife.
c. Mosquito net does excellent rodent proofing too.

2

GETTING TO KNOW TARUBANDA

I had stayed at Braeside, Chikhaldara, for barely a couple of months when I received my transfer order for Tarubanda. During my Chikhaldara stay, I would often visit Vairat, a *gawli* (a cow-herding community) village near the highest point in Melghat (four thousand feet above mean sea level) to spend a quiet evening. (The village at Vairat has now been shifted to provide an undisturbed habitat for tigers.) Of course, the major tourist attraction there was the spectacular sunset. From Vairat, one also got a panoramic view of the dense Melghat forests abounding in a variety of wildlife. The view was dotted with hamlets, which were originally labour camps established by the British for housing labourers on forestry work. One of those tiny dots was Tarubanda, where I was to stay for the next seven months of my life, actively supervising major forestry activities.

Looking back on my stay at Chikhaldara, I realised that it was indeed a soft responsibility, a kind of paid holiday in a FRH at a hill station. There were the early irritants: jungle rats feasting on my belongings, toddy cats creating a rumpus on the rooftop, creatures of the dark scurrying across the false ceiling, the whistling windows in the 'ghost house', and, of course, the fear of a *bhaaloo* lurking in the foggy surrounds of the coffee plantations. However, I had gradually overcome these factors and really settled down. I relished reading till well past midnight and finishing all books on wildlife by Jim Corbett and Kenneth Anderson. This activity was all the more enjoyable because sitting in my room, looking out of the glass door, I had seen several hares, toddy cats, wild boars, sloth bears, porcupines, and, yes, a leopard too. Reading *shikar* stories while actually seeing wildlife in the solitude of a century-old FRH always sent my adrenaline levels soaring.

Range Forest Office, Tarubanda

Tarubanda in the local dialect means 'a parasitic plant', something similar to a Loranthus shrub growing on a mango tree. Tarubanda was a small hamlet of about fifty-sixty households, including the staff quarters of the Forest Department. There were three other prominent buildings: a range forest office, a forest medical/health centre, and a wireless station on an adjoining hill. There was a small grocery shop too, selling the bare essentials, including tobacco. (Tobacco has been a big curse in Melghat. The story goes that these simple, innocent tribals often run up huge debts buying tobacco on credit from the local grocer. Some have even lost their lands!) The houses were located on either side of a dusty track. The Korkoos – the simple, peace-loving tribals – inhabited the hamlet.

The most conspicuous house in Tarubanda belonged to a tribal by the name of Somji Patel, who moved with a halo round his head. The title *patel* means village head/chief. He was dark and had big protruding teeth. The tribals were scared of Somji because he was known to be a *bhumka*, a tribal doctor, and they believed he could perform black magic. Somji's house was at one end of the village, and at the other end was the forest health centre. There was a nice bungalow for the doctor, but since no doctor had occupied it for a long time, I planned to move in after getting it done up. Just behind the health centre was a beautiful lake which abounded in big fish. The water was shared by the villagers and their cattle during the day and was used at night by the wild animals. About half a kilometre from Somji's house was the FRH, and I decided to stay here while the bungalow was being done up.

Nestled in dense forest and perched on top of a hill, this beautiful rest house commands an excellent panoramic view of about ten thousand hectares of dense forest area. The British foresters had an excellent sense of site selection, I must say. It was a two-suite rest house with a spacious veranda with a couple of old-style *aaraam-kursi*s for stretching out after a tiring day in the jungle. This veranda had also become famous after a pair of tigers had been sighted resting there. The electric supply was very erratic. As a routine, we had to make do with hurricane lanterns. In the rear part of the FRH was the dining room with large glazed windows all around, which allowed us the pleasure of admiring nature as we ate our breakfast or lunch. Each suite had huge king-sized beds and a functioning fireplace for winter. An interesting map called the 'shooting blocks map' adorned a wall of the rest house. In the olden days, this map indicated to the hunters the limits of the block reserved for their exclusive hunting on payment of some fees to the government.

I remember having visited this FRH as a kid. One thing that was missing from my earlier visits was the *punkhah*, a hand-pulled fan. This fan was a rectangular piece of thick cloth, about three by ten feet, attached at the top length to a raft and pulled high up into the ceiling. This contraption was swung to and fro by a rope-and-pulley arrangement. The rope was sent out through a hole at the top of the wall and pulled and released rhythmically by the *punkhah* puller. Every door and window of the FRH would be sealed with thick curtains of woven vetiver (roots of a fragrant grass called khus). The job of the fan puller was to sprinkle water on the *khus-tattis* (as they were called) and swing the fan. All this was officially provided to ensure the comfort of the officer and his family during the harsh summer days of Central India, when the temperature in the shade soars up to forty-six degrees Celsius. We kids used to sympathise with the fan puller and did his fan pulling during his lunch break. Another fixture of yesteryears found in all the FRHs in Melghat was the cool, cool thatched roofs. With the advent of electricity, the thatched roof and the hand-pulled fan system have disappeared. But the olfactory memory of the cool khus-scented breeze remains.

About a hundred metres down in the valley from the rest house was a place called the *masaan*, a corruption of the Sanskrit word *shmashaan* (cremation ground or graveyard), where a RFO was buried. Rumour has it that the RFO had died of cholera because he could not get medical care as the river Sipna (which means 'teak' in the local dialect) was in spate. A lot of ghost stories were built around this episode attached to the FRH. Fifty metres down from the FRH, on the other side of the Tarubanda hill, is a life-sized imprint of a tiger pugmark etched on a rock. This place is called Kula (tiger) Baba (holy man) and worshipped by the Korkoos. On the Tarubanda–Kund road (the inhabitants of Kund village have now been rehabilitated to clear the space for an undisturbed tiger habitat), about five kilometres away, is a spot called Kandri, where there is a Hanuman temple. I remember walking down to the spot late on the Dashera evening of 1979 with a couple of daredevils. On the Tarubanda–Adhao road is the monument of Dolar Baba. More about Kulababa, Kandri, and Dolar Baba in my story 'In God We Trust'.

Though a leisure walk from the village to FRH Tarubanda takes just about ten minutes, it passes through dense forest, and it requires courage to traverse the distance alone, especially at night. The walk involves a blind turn at which one can collide head-on with a wild animal. I remember the first time I walked to the rest house from the village with a city dweller, forester Mr Gawai, as my escort. It was night-time, and Gawai had lit a *tembhal/mashaal*, primarily to light the path but also to keep wildlife away. Intriguingly, Gawai punctuated his walk every few steps by suddenly pivoting 360 degrees (*pradakshina*) with the torch held high in his hand. He advised me to do the *pradakshina* too and offered me an interesting explanation for this strange manoeuvre. He said that if we didn't circle round, the wily wild animals would attack us from behind. So we had to be extra alert and keep a 360-degree vision. I wonder whether this friend exercises similar caution on city streets, which are a great deal wilder than any jungle patch.

3

RINGSIDE VIEW
OF DHAKNA

During my Tarubanda days, the Dhakna round was my important work centre where I would frequently visit for the inspection of fieldwork and for making payments. Dhakna continued to attract me even during my Dharni days and later during my days with Project Tiger. What attracted me to Dhakna most was the beautiful forest in and around it, with an unusually high density of wild animal population. It also had a beautiful FRH. This two-suite FRH, located on the banks of the Gadga, is more than a century old. In the early 1960s, this FRH was substantially damaged by the floods in the Gadga and required special repairs. I had the pleasure of occupying this place more frequently from 1979 to 1981. At that time, it had decent art-deco–style furniture and elegant crockery and cutlery dating back to the British raj days. Like other FRHs, it too had a beautiful veranda in front. The FRH register was a treasure of interesting remarks dating back to the 1920s. In the first half of the twentieth century, Dhakna attracted hunters from far-off places, especially from Mumbai and Pune (then, of course, known as Bombay and Poona). I remember one such excited hunter comment in the register, 'Very successful stay . . . Shooted (sic) 5 leopards, 3 tigers, and 2 sloth bears.' Unfortunately, this FRH was popular with our jungle brethren, and the space between the false ceiling and the roof was converted into a comfortable boudoir by the civet/toddy cats too.

Snow-white-haired Rehman was the custodian of FRH Dhakna. He was an excellent cook; non-vegetarian food was his area of specialisation. The specialty of the campus was that it had numerous fully grown lemon trees. Rehman looked after these trees very well and earned a good income from the sale of lemons besides his salary. Hundreds of yellow juicy lemons on these trees in the right season was a sight to remember. Two huge banyan trees – one near the FRH and one a little away from the FRH, in the direction of village – would be in fruiting a couple of times in a year and would invite numerous frugivorous birds, including the state bird of Maharashtra, the rather shy green pigeon. A nice stone-and-cement platform was constructed around the base of the banyan tree. Labourers coming to receive payment would be seen perched atop this platform, enjoying the cool breeze under the shade of the banyan tree. This huge evergreen, *akshaya* (one which has no death) tree provided nesting sites to so many birds and animals.

One late night I remember taking a small informal post-dinner training session at FRH Dhakna for my forest guards on how to identify and interpret various sounds in the forest. I was telling them about the calls of various carnivores and the alarm calls of their prey. There was rapt attention and pin-drop silence, nothing except the chorus of crickets, when suddenly, the silence was shattered by the loud alarm call of a barking deer from close quarters. Everyone was startled. Just to check how alert my trainees were, I asked a sleepy fellow what sound that was. Pat came a serious reply – 'It is the sound of the fat Ranger Sahib sitting in the backyard who has just sneezed loudly, sir.' It brought the house down.

In the summer days, the Gadga shrinks to a few small pools. One such *doh* or *kund* is diagonally opposite the FRH. All the major wild animals congregate at this pool, especially in the peak summer month of May. Gaurs, being shy, would approach the waterhole circumventing the FRH campus, but tigers often sauntered through. Even sloth bears were occasionally sighted. A post-dinner walk on the campus grounds, especially in summer, would give one a fair chance of encountering a wild animal as there was no fence around the FRH.

On the Dhakna–Adhao road, about three kilometres away from Dhakna is another deeper *kund* in the Gadga called the Siddukund. *Siddu* in the local dialect means 'liquor'. Perhaps with a perennial supply of water being essential for the brew, the local entrepreneurs of past times found it a convenient spot for setting up business. The Siddukund abounded in fish. For this reason, this spot was selected for the successful introduction of crocodiles in Melghat. In fact, during senior officers' tours, fish from the Siddukund was a mandatory item on the menu card. As it was the only source of drinking water in the area, all the wild animals in the vicinity would converge there. For this reason, the anglers used to wind up their activity around the Siddukund before the sun set. Anybody lingering on was only inviting trouble. Such trouble was invited once by a white lady in the mid-1930s.

A British forester (perhaps Mr Maitland) had come to camp at FRH Dhakna along with his wife. The conscientious officer would spend about twelve hours of the day in the forest, leaving his wife behind, twiddling her thumbs in the FRH. To kill time, the lady picked up the hobby of angling. The hobby is such that you get totally engrossed and often do not know when to stop. Once the harshness of the sun had abated, she would go angling to the Siddukund in the company of a ten-year-old Korkoo girl. One evening the lady got a little too greedy and stayed on till much beyond sundown. She also ignored the alarm calls of herbivores that the alert tribal girl brought to her notice. The result was that as the lady was about to leave the Siddukund, a tigress with a cub approached and made a mock charge at the lady, who promptly fainted. The girl ran back to Dhakna without once looking back and spread word in the village that the madam had been eaten up by a tiger. Quickly, the villagers gathered and rushed to the Siddukund and brought the swooning damsel home. This story was narrated to me by one of the two lead players in that little skit. She was not a ten-year-old anymore, naturally, but in her mid-fifties when she came to collect her daily wages at FRH Dhakna.

One important reason why the wild animal population suddenly disappears from some areas is the presence of wild dogs. They entirely terrorise the landscape and effect a temporary migration, especially of herbivores. Perhaps for this reason, I encountered one such dry run on the Dhakna–Dolar road. However, just before entering the gate of FRH Dhakna, we had a leopard sighting. Within seconds, that leopard too disappeared in the darkness. Hell-bent on sighting wildlife, we reversed the jeep, and I started searching for the lost leopard with the help of a searchlight in my hand. Soon, I located a pair of bright, shining eyes in a nearby fallow agricultural field. As we were starved of seeing wild animals that night, I instructed Hasan to leave the main path and get the jeep into the field to get a better view of the animal. Yes, the sighting was indeed clear in the open.

With the leopard on our left, we stopped about twenty metres away from it, and for a change, I switched off the searchlight and the headlights for about ten seconds. When we switched them on, voila! The leopard had disappeared from the spot to reappear on the right at a new spot some forty metres away. I switched them off again and experienced the same magic again. I have never seen such cunning and agility in any other wild animal except when I came across a caracal (*Caracal caracal*) on the Dhakna–Dolar road more than ten years later when I returned to Melghat as CF and FD of Project Tiger. It is this magic of appearing and disappearing that has ensured the survival of the leopard over every nook and corner of Maharashtra's wilderness.

THE VEGETATION

Aerial view of Melghat

The tiger habitat

Humanbeing making inroads in the tiger habitat

A machan located in the tiger habitat

THE VEGETATION
(CONTINUED 1)

The riparian zone

The Koktoo River crossing

Laxmi (elephant) making her way through elephant grass

The *Beheda* (Terminalia bellirica) tree which has become a waterhole for the bees, butterflies and birds in summer

4

WELCOME TO DD ROAD

Patrolling the vulnerable wildlife habitat had been an important part of my duty. Observing wild animals in their natural habitats was my hobby. I would combine my duty with my passion and often land up with the best results. During my Dharni tenure, almost every summer evening, I would step out and into the jungle. During those days, the Dhakna–Dolar road was my favourite haunt, and I did not miss out on any opportunity to travel down this road and observe wild animals. Normally, after sighting a large wild mammal, I would ask my driver to stop the vehicle, pull out my binoculars, closely observe the health and beauty of the animal, and then proceed. It was only on one occasion in my entire service that circumstances compelled me not to follow this routine . . .

One evening I was coming from Dolar to Dhakna. I was midway through, and it was almost dark. In the darkness, we totally missed noticing a pair of sloth bears just abutting the road ahead of us. As we were going past them, they suddenly let out a loud frightening call. Normally, on sighting wild animals, I would ask the driver to stop the vehicle to have a good look. I looked back to see which animal had given the call. But what I saw made my heart thump against my ribs, and I asked Hasan to seriously step on the gas. I had seen my most terrifying scene in the forest. Both the bears were on their hind limbs and were chasing the vehicle at full speed, almost catching up with us. The chase continued at full speed for about a hundred metres. I was very sure that had Hasan applied the brakes during the chase, the pair of bears would have crashed into the vehicle and caused all-round damage.

Both the bears were on their hind limbs and

DD Road often dished out to me such out-of-this-world experiences. It is said that happiness increases when you share it. Since I was keen on doubling my happiness, I always took my guests down my happiness street: DD Road. Guests were a rare commodity in Dharni, so when they came, I wanted to do my best to entertain them. The best place I could think of for entertaining them was to take them to my hangout – DD Road, to be more precise – in an open jeep. An hour-long drive on this road on a summer evening would mean seeing almost all the species of the major mammalian wild animals of the Melghat forests. But sometimes my idea of entertainment and theirs did not match, resulting in dark mutterings, even if under breath.

One such incident occurred when my friend Tasneem's mother, the hookah-toting lady, had come to Dharni, and I had to drop her off at her son's place at Chikhaldara. En route to Chikhaldara, I purposely took a detour and took her via Dhakna. Once we hit the Dhakna–Dolar road, the fauna closely stuck to the script. I felt proud as a circus ringmaster seeing his animals jump through the hoop. But Tasneem's mother's reaction was different. She presumed that we were entering some deadly area where her son would be mobbed by wild animals. Hence, every time we encountered a wild animal, rather than appreciating the animal, she would curse and murmur, 'Beta (son), you got a good posting in a big place like Dharni. My poor child Tasneem! How can he survive among such wild creatures?'

A couple of days after this incident, a businessperson from Nagpur came to Dharni to see if I could be a suitable match for his sister. The proposal materialised, and I married Deepti and brought her to Dharni. One morning I told her to be ready for going on an exciting outing in the evening. It was the month of May, five in the evening, and Deepti was all decked up for the outing: lipstick, high heels, and pink saree with a huge matching purse-cum-handbag. In about four hours, we were back from the Dhakna–Dolar road in an open jeep with our faces beyond recognition thanks to our dust bath. Was the young bride amused? Think again.

In a third incident, Deepti's brother Anil, along with his wife, Aarti, and little daughter, Payal, came over to visit us. Aarti was a dyed-in-the-wool Puneite who had never ventured out of the metropolis before her marriage. And here she was in the wilderness, stuck with a wild relative-by-marriage of a relative-by-marriage – wild to the point of actually finding life in a dense jungle exciting. As usual, I very proudly took these guests to FRH Dhakna and then to the Dhakna–Dolar road in my open 3913 Jeep to flaunt my wild friends. We were indeed very lucky ('Oh, really?') to see a great variety of species of wild animals. I remember we saw almost all the wild animals except a tiger. But the anticlimax was that every time I sighted an animal, Aarti would close her eyes tight and seek a whispered assurance from my wife that the animal had gone before she reopened them. Of course, barring these exceptions, an excursion on the Dhakna–Dolar road on summer evenings was almost always very exciting and sometimes funny too.

About seven or eight kilometres from FRH Dhakna on the Dhakna–Dolar road was a young teak plantation. As per the technical requirement, the plantation site requires a total clearing of the site. In such cleared sites, visibility is very good. Also, a lot of grass comes up in such areas, which attracts a good number of herbivorous animals, which, in turn, attract carnivores. So I used to make it a point to visit this plantation whenever an opportunity came my way. On the edge of the plantation abutting the road, on the right side was a lofty *mahua* (*Madhuca longifolia*) tree. This tree would bear succulent off-white flowers every year in April. *Mahua* flowers are used by the local tribals to produce an alcoholic beverage or are dried and sold in the market or powdered and mixed with dough to make local bread.

Sloth bears love to eat *mahua* flowers. It is said that in April, this tree belongs to the tribals during the day and to the bears during the night. On one such night, I saw a bear on this tree as we drove past it. I went ahead for some distance, took a U-turn, and came to the tree again after about an hour. I saw the same bear now gorging himself on the fermented *mahua* flowers on the ground. I went to FRH Dhakna, had my dinner, and drove back in the direction of the *mahua* tree. Before I could reach the tree, I came across the most comic scene I have ever seen in the jungle. The inebriated bear was stumbling all over! All it needed was a dopey smile and crossed eyes to become a Walt Disney character – Baloo the bear.

There were exceptional days when the magic of the Dhakna–Dolar road failed. One such day was when my boss, the DFO, came on tour to Dhakna along with his wife and infant child. Normally, he preferred staying at Tarubanda, but on my insistence, he came to stay at FRH Dhakna. I had more or less given a guarantee of showing him wildlife in its wildest avatar. We started on our evening drive around five but did not have any sighting. We gave up around seven and came back to FRH Dhakna. I was feeling embarrassed for our dry spell. So after a cup of tea, I suggested a different route for another excursion. DFO Sahib agreed. He took the steering wheel; his wife sat next to him with her son on her lap. I was at the back in the open jeep, panning the searchlight, and Hasan was straining his eyes to locate some 'game'. After about an hour we got on Kund Road. Till then, we had had a total drought.

Suddenly, I sighted a big leopard about twenty metres to the left. Hasan and I shouted in unison and asked Mr DFO Sahib to stop. Shouting was necessary because the 3913 had the diesel engine of an international tractor which made a big racket. Our jeep stopped, and the couple must have been watching the animal for about fifteen seconds when I located another leopard perched on top of a pencil-straight teak tree about a metre away from the madam and the baby. Before I could ask the boss to move the jeep, the leopard lost its grip and came down crashing near the front left tyre and instantly scurried into the forest. Nobody had seen what I had seen, and they all wondered what had made the thudding sound. Later at the FRH, I told them what I had seen, and we all thanked our stars for being in one piece.

This was a one-time exception when the magic of DD Road had failed. Barring this exception, this haunt had been my full entertainer, indeed a happening place. After the passage of more than twenty years, I remember the incidents that took place at each nook, corner, and turning of my all-time favourite haunt – DD Road.

THE FOREST REST HOUSES (FRHS)

FRH Chikhaldara

FRH Tarubanda

FRH Dhakna

FRH Koktoo

B

THE WILY LEOPARD

Among the large cats, the leopard is the most adaptable. It can thrive in various agroclimatic zones. Unlike a tiger, it is an excellent tree climber and can survive very well in a scrub forest. Even a sugar cane field can be a good permanent home. An unofficial conservative estimate puts their population in the sugar cane fields of Western Maharashtra at five hundred plus. It is eclectic in food habits and has an extraordinarily long list of items on its menu card, right from small wild herbivores like wild boars, langurs, deer, and antelopes to the domestic ones such as calves, dogs, pigs, and poultry. It can as well consume frogs, crabs, and carcasses as well as leftover food at *dhaba*s, the wayside restaurants. This versatile large cat also deserves separate space.

The following seven stories would be exclusively on leopards. The first one deals with various practical issues associated with the release of a leopard in the wild. The next one is about its coexistence with its bigger brother, the tiger. It also narrates a personal experience where a leopard makes its kill just about a couple of strides away from the author. The next two stories are about the author's thrilling encounters with a leopard. These stories again show how a leopard avoids conflict with human beings in spite of being in very close proximity to them and having an upper hand in the likely event of man-versus-wildlife combat. The fifth story talks about how a courageous person reacts in an emergency situation and saves himself from the attack of a wild animal. The sixth story is about the author's face-to-face encounter with a leopard while walking at night-time in the core area of the MTR. The last story is about the general relationship of the mother and the young one in the wild. The focus of this story is on the union of two leopard cubs with their mother after a substantial gap.

All these seven gripping stories are educative too. Unknowingly, the stories provoke you to draw your own conclusions and make you wonder how you would have reacted to the situation if you were there.

5

RELEASING A LEOPARD IN THE WILD

Generally, when a leopard is seen at such places where it is not supposed to be seen, panic spreads. Matters become more serious when it attacks human beings, either accidentally or out of extreme hunger. They approach the Forest Department, and the department sets up cages to trap such animals. These trapped animals are generally sent back to the forest. So are the ones that have tripped into unwalled wells, very likely while chasing dogs. As human safety is of supreme importance, naturally, the leopard gets a raw deal. A rough estimate indicates that 90 per cent of the trapped leopards are innocent. Tempted by bait, a famished leopard just walks into the trap.

During the first decade of this century, I was party to 104 leopard trappings in the sugar cane fields of the Junnar division of the Pune district for a good three years. The Sanjay Gandhi National Park in Borivali, Mumbai, has a similar problem. The national park is an island of beautiful forest abounding in wild animals but is surrounded by a sea of humanity. When a leopard chases a dog at night – say, along a *naala* (channel) – and at dawn finds itself in a concrete jungle, it gets totally disoriented. People complain, traps are laid, and the poor chap is doomed.

The Forest Department does not have the facility to house them all. Initially, the strategy was to release these trapped individuals in the dense forests of Eastern Maharashtra, i.e. Vidarbha. It was conveniently thought that such an individual would adjust itself in the dense forests of, say, Melghat or Pench or Tadoba. But that's not how these animals are hard-wired. A strong homing instinct kicks in; they start their homeward journey and trigger off accidents. Radio-collaring permission was not easily forthcoming during my days. Therefore, we injected a rice-sized device called a transponder chip into the animal and tracked it quite competently.

During my tenure in Melghat as FD of the MTR, one such guest came to Melghat from somewhere. I still remember the leopard being put in the trolley of a tractor and driven to Koktoo. I happened to be travelling along the same route, and I noticed an interesting thing: the herbivores of the wild welcomed the guest behind bars with their alarm calls with as much enthusiasm as they would have done to a free one. It was the first time that I had gauged the speed at which these calls are relayed.

When our guest reached Melghat, there was no provision or permission for any transponder chip or a radio collar to monitor its post-release movements. But releasing a carnivore at a new place does put a lot of stress on the animal, and it needs monitoring. A number of questions need to be answered, like how long the animal was in captivity, what the status of the resident leopard is, whether it is male or female, why it was captured, and so on. Therefore, we did what we thought was the next best thing to do – we sprayed the fellow with a fluorescent colour and managed to monitor it for about two months.

At the time of release, a lot of precaution has to be taken. Many a time, suspecting foul play, the leopard does not leave the cage, and you cannot force it to go out. An animal in captivity develops an understandable hatred towards human beings, and hence, in some cases, on being let out, it goes straight at the nearest human being. There have been cases where some drivers who had not taken sufficient precaution were mauled. All the probable directions in which the animal may go after release should be anticipated and kept clear of human beings.

I have seen two of our staff members miraculously escape a certain mishap just because the leopard was alert. It so happened that these two persons had foolishly gone for a walk in the forest along the path that the leopard was most likely to use. The head-on 'crossing' was on a turning, just about a hundred seconds after release. The alert leopard sighted the two bipeds first, dodged them by hiding in a bush by the roadside without their knowledge, let the two men pass, and then continued on the road.

An animal which has remained in captivity for a long time or one born and brought up in captivity generally does not possess the skill to make a kill. As far as possible, such an animal should not be released in the wild, or a 'soft release' methodology has to be tried. In such cases, we have a large enclosure in the area of release in which the animal has to be kept and artificially fed. One day the gates of the enclosure are kept open, leaving the option to the animal to stay on inside or to step out. Slowly, this animal gets adjusted to the new environment, acquires hunting skills, and leaves the enclosure forever. The presence of domestic cattle of all ages makes things easier for such a leopard.

Ideally, the leopard should be released as early as possible after it is trapped, lest it loses its killer instincts. It's desirable, however, to do its medical examination and embed a transponder chip before release. Second, the location of release has to be close to the spot from where it had been captured. But the local people oppose such an idea of release for fear of the leopard attacking them or their property, especially their sheep, goats, poultry, cattle, and dogs.

Unfortunately, in his anxiety to get rid of the 'burden' permanently, a local forester's tendency is to release the animal far away from his jurisdiction. This tendency has resulted in the discovery of some neutral, non-controversial venues. I knew of one such secret venue where more than fifty leopards were released. But the homing instinct tends to pull them from the place of release to the place of capture. In the wild, they travel for several kilometres, conquering all adversities to reach their destination. It is precisely during this journey that accidents take place.

Once, we had a whole crowd of leopards to be released, and some temporary arrangement for their stay was made. At night, one of them who had been with us for a long time broke open the cage and went towards human habitation. It stayed missing from the cage for the entire day, making us feel very jittery. We had launched a massive leopard search and were praying hard. Immediately after dusk, our prayers were answered. Realising the harsh realities of 'freedom', the runaway leopard had come back to its chamber on its own.

Sometimes releasing a leopard that has been in captivity for a long time can be rather tricky. One such leopard was being released, and we had taken all the possible precautions. The animal sped away towards the forest in the direction we had manoeuvred by blocking the undesirable outlets. As we were winding up, we also heard alarm calls from the forest, which really was an 'All is well' call for us. That was when I saw a slight movement in the far corner of the open patch where the animal had been released about ten minutes back. It was our leopard, rolling in the dust there. It then just sat and looked at us, as if urging us to take it back home. We left with a heavy heart. Our feedback told us that for one full week, this leopard did not know how to behave in the forest and was often found sitting opposite the RFO office, creating a traffic jam. One day, however, it disappeared in the wilderness forever.

In 2003, a film titled *Leopards of Bollywood* was being shot for the National Geographic Channel. I was the anchor and presenter in this forty-three-minute film, which was later telecast fifty-eight times on National Geographic Channel. The shooting had been going on for about four or five months during weekends, and the last shot, a leopard being released, was being filmed. The enthusiastic director wanted to use three cameras for covering this shot. Accordingly, I, along with the main camera person, was standing on the ground about fifty metres in front of the cage mounted on a truck. A remote-controlled camera was placed on the ground, below the cage, to cover the 'jump to freedom'.

The director wanted to sit on top of the cage with a third camera so that he would definitely cover the leopard, irrespective of the direction the animal took. I tried to dissuade him, but he was very keen. The gate of the cage opened. Suspecting that the man above his cage would indulge in foul play, the leopard stuck its neck out of the cage, looked up, growled, and went back in. As it repeated the growl a second time, our man on top started trembling and sweating. Satisfied that there was no adverse action from above, the leopard finally jumped out, came straight towards the main camera, took a U-turn, and went into the jungle. The director couldn't have asked for a better story to tell his grandchildren.

An interesting anecdote – and let's make it the last one. There was one area where a leopard had created terror by attacking, killing, and eating a good number of humans. The foresters were installing traps everywhere to capture all leopards, irrespective of whether they were the culprit or innocents. Any complaint about *bibtyacha vavar* (the presence of a leopard), and a trap cage would be instantly set up. That was when a delegation of ladies went and met the CM of Maharashtra and gave him a written representation. The topic for their representation was, amazingly, to discontinue setting up these trap cages. The CM was indeed flummoxed. On enquiry, it was learnt that their wild men folk had suddenly turned tame and had begun to return home much before dark, and the women saw in it the collaborating hand (or snarl?) of the leopard, and they just loved it.

6

PEACEFUL COEXISTENCE

It was September 1979, and I had settled down well in the doctor's quarter at Tarubanda. Mr B (name changed), who was trained in my senior batch, had recently joined as assistant conservator of forests (ACF) in the DFO's office at Chikhaldara. I knew B very well because we were together for one full year in 1977. He had very few friends, and I was one of them. What had brought us together was our fascination with birds. He was my guru in birdwatching and often took me along for long walks through the beautiful Forest Research Institute (FRI) campus in Dehradun. B was a man of few words, with very strong idiosyncrasies. He was also notoriously unpunctual. I would often address him as 'Dada', which, in Marathi (as well as in Bengali), means elder brother. It also means a bully in Marathi. All these relations aside, the fact remained that he was ACF (my boss) and I was a trainee ACF, holding charge of a range (the subordinate).

One morning I got a wireless message from Chikhaldara that he would be reaching FRH Tarubanda and, post lunch, would be inspecting my 'marking' work in Coupe Number 4 Rangrao. Marking is an important activity in which the matured trees due for harvesting are given a red band at a height of four and a half feet above the ground. Coupe Number 4 Rangrao was located on the Tarubanda–Kund road, about three to four kilometres from Tarubanda. (The villagers of Kund have now been relocated for providing undisturbed habitat for wildlife.) As the rainy season was still not over, this road had not been repaired, so it was not jeep worthy. The inspection would have to be done on foot.

B reached Tarubanda late for no apparent reason. Then post lunch, he kept chatting with the villagers till about 6:00 p.m. (an activity which he could so easily have performed after returning from the field inspection) and then finally expressed his desire to visit the field. It was too late now to walk down to the site, so I immediately summoned a tractor. It was an old (really old) Massey Ferguson tractor. Excessive usage over jungle tracks had reduced it to a barely functional assemblage of tractor parts. Every single part loudly declared its presence except, of course, the horn. The self-starter and the clutch plates had given up their ghosts long ago; the headlights were a just a pair of empty, cavernous pits. B, RFO Ingle, Forest Guard Patorkar, and I took our perches on the tractor, totally mobbing the driver. The tractor lurched off for the site, negotiating problem areas like the patches of black cotton soil where the tyres would dig themselves deep into the monsoon slush. At one turning, I remember, it skidded and performed an uninstructed 180-degree turn, ready to take us back to Tarubanda.

By the time we reached Coupe Number 4 Rangrao, it was almost dark. We disembarked, and the driver reversed the machine and parked it facing Tarubanda. He did not switch off the ignition; the starter was not functioning, remember? He did not leave his seat either and appeared very tense, urging us to make it snappy. 'This is animal time in the jungle,' he muttered, 'not human time!' Marking register in one hand and a measuring tape and an electric torch delicately balanced in the other, B moved in. He reached the teak tree nearest the road and tried to read the tree number in torchlight.

As he flashed the light, the blood-curdling roar of a tiger broke out from very close quarters. (The locals later confirmed that there was a dangerous beast in the area – a tigress with three cubs; nothing can be more dangerous.) We all leaped towards the tractor, where the now trembling driver sat. The driver had the tractor moving even before we could settle down. Jerking, bouncing, skidding, clinging to anything that didn't come off, we somehow reached FRH Tarubanda. The poor driver was still sweating and nursing his goose pimples. So traumatised was he that even years later, he would break into a shiver whenever I reminded him of the tigress's roar at Coupe Number 4 Rangrao. So much for B's first field inspection.

By dinner time at the FRH, my boss had regained some of his composure, and over meals, he assured me that he would come again for checking the marking in Coupe Number 4 Rangrao. His professional pride, however, had taken a denting; he was generally in a bad mood and began contradicting most of my statements. When I told him that I had been regularly seeing the pugmarks of a leopard near where we had heard the tiger roar, he snorted in disbelief. He was of the firm opinion that tigers and leopards do not coexist in the same patch of forest; if they ever do come close, the leopard is killed by the tiger. My view was that they lived in 'peaceful coexistence' except when it came to stealing one animal's kill by the other, and in such circumstances, both tiger and leopard could engage in serious fights. B was very adamant about his point of view and was keen on a wager. So after laying a bet with me against peaceful coexistence, my guest proceeded late in the night to Chikhaldara. (In my mind, I was wondering how I was going to peacefully coexist with Dada.)

A month had elapsed after Mr B's tour. It was mid-October, and we were reeling under the October heatwave. To beat the heat, the villagers of Tarubanda slept outside their homes for about a fortnight. The Tarubanda–Kund road begins as a narrow dusty track at the doctor's bungalow, where I was resident. It moves between rows of houses, the last of which is Somji Patel's. Half a kilometre farther down, it crosses the FRH before setting off towards Kund. From Somji's house to the doctor's bungalow, it would be a difficult, cramped walk after sundown.

One evening a couple of strangers came to Tarubanda. They were in the business of buying cheap cattle from needy tribals and selling them for a profit in the bigger markets. They had a pair of bullocks with them. As it was getting dark, they took my permission to spend the night at Tarubanda. They tethered their animals to a *palash* tree just outside my gate (the tree is still there), gave them fodder and water, and retired for the night to the veranda of the health centre.

The stuffiness of the night had driven me outdoors too. A nice string bed with a well-tucked mosquito net fixed to bamboo poles was soon organised for me under the moonlit sky. My olive-green mosquito net which my forester father had so affectionately packed in my holdall really came very handy. It protected me not only from the menacing mosquitoes and other insects but also from rats and reptiles. It also provided me psychological security from wild animals, including tigers, leopards, bears, and hyenas. As I lay on the string bed, I had the pleasure of listening to the crickets' chorus and the calls of a variety of owls and nightjars, some cuckoos, sometimes peacocks. Of course, the main attraction was a variety of alarm calls from the herbivores warning their jungle brethren about a carnivore on the move – a tiger or a leopard or a pack of wild dogs on the prowl.

I was very tired and soon went off to sleep and slept like a log. I am an early riser, and as usual, I got up to the chorus of the *jungli murgis* (grey jungle fowls). The light was just sufficient to see the surrounds. What I saw in that dim light really shocked me. One of the two bullocks which were tied about ten metres from me had been killed and partly eaten .The other one was in a state of shock and was neither eating nor drinking. I checked the pugmarks around the kill and concluded that the kill was made by a leopard. On following the leopard trail, I learnt that the leopard had come along the Kund–Tarubanda road (where the tigress with the three cubs lived) to the FRH, walked past the sleeping men, women, and children, reached the last house, and then made the kill. Just about ten metres from the kill was I, blissfully sleeping in the vicinity of a hungry leopard.

They tethered their animals to the Palash tree.....

Important lessons learnt – given the choice, a hungry leopard prefers non-human herbivora, and tigers and leopards do coexist. Of course, B would never concede defeat, but I knew that I had won the bet about the peaceful coexistence of tigers and leopards. The evidence here would be incontrovertible. But have I said anywhere that B was known to be reasonable?

7

LEOPARD CROSSING

After completing my range charge, I did the sub-DFO's charge at Dharni and Amravati and went in January 1982 as DFO (*bade sahib*) to Alibag, followed by postings at the Mantralaya, Mumbai, DFO of Akola, and director of Forest Guards Training School at Pal. Pal was a tiny remote village with no education facility for my children; hence, I had to keep my family at Jalgaon, a district. In August 1991, I got my promotion order and was posted as CF and FD of Project Tiger, with headquarters at a tehsil place – Paratwada. This was the only post of CF in the entire state with headquarters not at a district. Also, as compared to the much-sought-after executive territorial postings, wildlife posting was supposed to be a side posting those days. Hence, when my promotion order came, I received condolence messages instead of congratulatory ones.

I went to formally call on Mr Indurkar, the then chief CF (wildlife), the top boss in the field of wildlife in the entire state of Maharashtra. I told him that I was not formally trained in wildlife and wondered how I would manage. He reassured me that he had full confidence that I would manage the MTR well and that I was going to enjoy this charge too. In a lighter vein, he said that he would soon administer to me a 'capsule' so that I could understand and speak 'wildlife jargon'. He was serious, and soon, he sent me for a three-week capsule course in wildlife management at Hrishikesh organised by the WII in Dehradun. This course was immensely useful for me for understanding the basic concepts of wildlife management. Mr Indurkar was absolutely right. Not only did I enjoy this charge for more than four years, but also, this was my most enjoyable responsibility in my entire service career.

Quality education was not available at Paratwada for my daughter, aged 9, and my son, aged 4. In fact, when we went to the best English medium school for my children's admission, it was recess time in the school, and the scene was shocking. Some children were sitting in class on the floor on dirty gunny bags, some others were urinating in the open, some were sharpening their catapult skills by trying to kill birds, some were trying to catch frogs, and some others were trying to consume lantana fruits, basically cherished by sloth bears in the wild. My daughter, Deepika, was in a state of shock. I recollect returning home after securing her admission in the 'best school' in Paratwada. She looked quite dispirited.

'Baba, are you bad in your work?' she asked me.

'No, child. I am quite sure I am not,' said I.

'How is it then that other uncles go to big places and we land up here after Pal?' she wondered.

I had no answer. Deepika's innocent question left me pondering. I thought that the headquarters at the *taluka* was such a big minus point and resolved to get the headquarters moved to Amravati, a district, so that good officers would not hesitate in joining as FD of the MTR in the future.

My predecessor FD was Mr Gogate – my guru, my mentor, and a hard taskmaster. He was ten years my senior, and he made no secret of this fact. He affectionately insisted that I stay at his residence before I took over the charge. He literally held my hand and showed me the important initiatives in the field which he had taken and which were required to be carried forward. One such initiative was the soil and moisture conservation technique he had adopted for ensuring a supply of drinking water to wild animals during the difficult summer months.

Before I could formally take over the charge, he took me to a spot called Pipalpadao to show how it worked. *Pipal* means the *Ficus religiosa* tree, and *padao* is a dumping place for timber in the forest before it is carted away to the depot. With a ban on the harvesting of forest produce in the MTR, most of the *padao*s had become redundant. However, these old names were useful in describing locations in the MTR.

It was August, and the rainy season was in full swing. Melghat started just ten minutes after we had left the FD's office at Paratwada. I have always felt that the beauty of Melghat is in its changing seasonal looks. With a green cover spread all over, the MTR was flaunting its best look. We started with the gradually sloping hills which slowly transformed into steep and later precipitous slopes to reach a high point at Ghatang and then descended to Semadoh. Mr Gogate showed me the tourist complex there on the bank of the Sipna where the huts have been constructed without felling any trees. This was followed by a visit to the Nature Education and Interpretation Centre. He also told me about a nice trek from Semadoh to Makhala via Bhoot-khora (valley of ghosts). The story goes that there were mass hangings of the freedom fighters by the British here, hence the name. Semadoh is in a valley, and Makhala is a plateau. I vaguely remember having done the trek, which involved a tough climb through a *naala* bed with boulders and lots of banyan trees where, my guide told me, the hangings had taken place.

The sun was setting as we reached Pipalpadao. The FD's Ambassador car could not have traversed the slushy jungle track. So it had to be left behind at Pipalpadao with our driver Hasan. Mr Gogate led me on foot through the tall grass along the jungle track. He showed me big fresh tiger pugmarks on the track, travelling in the same direction as us. With the setting sun, I got a strange feeling of having entered a *chakravyuh* (a trap with one-way entry and no return). The light was fading when we reached our destination, and I saw what Mr Gogate had been very keen on my seeing. Very soon, it got totally dark, and here we were, two lonesome persons in the middle of a forest abounding in wildlife. I did not panic because my companion was cool and composed and seemed to know what he was doing.

The evening sky, fortunately, was clear, and for our return walk, we had a full moon for company. In the interest of organisational benefit, the gesture of taking me around by him was praiseworthy. At Pipalpadao, Hasan was anxiously waiting for us. How he wished we had carried a walkie-talkie with us so that he could have communicated with us! He was indeed visibly relieved at seeing us in one piece. It seems that about half an hour after we had entered the forest, a big leopard had come near the car, paused for a moment, and taken the same track that we had taken.

The leopard was roaming free whereas Hasan was in a cage

This was Hasan's first sighting of a leopard, he later told me, from a car parked in a forest. The scene had reversed for Hasan; the leopard was roaming free, whereas Hasan was in a cage. He feared some mishap if the leopard were suddenly to encounter us on our journey back. Luckily, we were talking loudly, which would have warned the leopard of our presence and made it duck away. I am sure with its eyes adapted to night viewing, it must have seen us from very close quarters.

The leopard incident had given me a fair idea of things in store for me in the days to come. As compared to my responsibilities as sub-DFO in Dharni, being the FD of Project Tiger would be a complete change of role. From being a timber harvester, I would now become a wildlife manager. I would have to stop talking about cubic metres of timber and revenue earned and start propagating a ban on the felling of trees in these habitats. Earlier, I would look at a tree for 'girth at breast height' (gbh); now I would look for 'snags', 'den trees', and 'down logs' as niches for birds and wildlife. In short, I would shift from production forestry to wildlife management. It was another matter that even as a timber harvester, I was indulging in my true love – wildlife management – on the sly. Now I would be doing it in the open as my 'duty' – and that too in the patch of wilderness to which I had long ago sold my soul, Melghat. It was indeed with great excitement that I looked forward to taking charge and enjoying myself to the hilt for the next four or five years.

I must say I was fortunate to get seniors like Mr Gogate and Mr Indurkar, who played an important role in moulding me. Mr Indurkar retired when I was halfway through my charge as FD of the MTR. By sheer coincidence, I chased Mr Gogate's chair in four postings during my service career, and every time I benefitted by his aggressive briefing to me about the new chair.

8

LEOPARD'S DINNER

One of the important jobs assigned to me during my range charge was to establish a four-hectare central nursery at Tarubanda. This nursery was to produce about a million teak (*Tectona grandis*) root shoots. This seedling stock would suffice not only for me but for the neighbouring ranges too. Nearness for close supervision, road connectivity, power supply, and plentiful water for irrigating the seedlings are the essential factors for selecting a new nursery site. These requirements were met by the forest land abutting the water reservoir behind my residence, and the site was finalised by the DFO of Chikhaldara. However, the continuous barbed-wire fencing of the nursery would create a barrier for wild animals approaching the water body, especially at night. Hence, I had purposely left open a couple of 'water approaches' along small rivulets passing through the nursery. These were fenced lanes about twenty feet wide through which wild animals could approach the lake without any impediment. Unfortunately, these lanes did not gain much popularity with their users: the wild animals.

Wild animals approaching a water source are very sensitive to any new activity in the neighbourhood and approach it with extreme caution. Herbivores expect carnivores lurking around a waterhole to kill them, and carnivores, in turn, suspect lethal human presence. They know only too well that the slightest lapse in concentration can cost them their lives. One evening, along with Neemkar, my driver, I sat behind a bush just about five metres from a waterhole by the name of Chacharda. I was very hopeful of a 'big' sighting at this quiet old waterhole where, just the previous evening, I had seen a beautiful dark-brown sloth bear. Around five in the evening, a barking deer very cautiously approached the waterhole but failed to register our presence till it had had a couple of gulps. Perhaps the animal was relying more on its olfactory sense than the optic one. As the wind direction changed, the animal simultaneously smelt and sighted us from very close quarters. It got startled, gave a loud alarm call, and ran. For a long time, we could hear its footfalls deep down the valley as also its alarm calls. It must have traversed about three to four kilometres before it ceased giving the alarm calls. We found the overreaction of the barking deer rather funny and burst out laughing.

When we recovered from our bout of laughter, Neemkar looked at my khaki T-shirt with black stripes and seriously commented, 'Sir, the barking deer mistook you for a tiger and pushed all the panic buttons.'

Coming back to Tarubanda, I was feeling guilty that my nursery had blocked the approach of wild animals to the Tarubanda tank. The situation had not improved much despite ten years passing before I was back to Melghat as FD of the MTR. Only a few animals were taking a detour and using the lake water for quenching their thirst. Many were still feeling insecure to use my artificial approach lanes. Hence, to suit their convenience, I thought of developing a small alternative water point at a place by the name of Hathkua. Long back, the community well of Tarubanda village was at Hathkua, two kilometres away inside the jungle. With the passage of time, a new community well had come up alongside Tarubanda near the lake, and the well at Hathkua had fallen into disuse. In Hindi, *hath* means 'hand', and *kua* means 'well'. So Hathkua means a well which has a water level so high that one can draw water by hand without the help of any rope.

When I visited Hathkua, I found that the well had silted up and that the approach had been jammed by a heavy covering of lantana thickets, making it almost impossible for wild animals to reach it. So we got it de-silted and uprooted the lantana bushes. We also took care to provide a gradual slope so that the wildlife could have a smooth approach to the well without fear of drowning. After about a week, I started getting feedback that wild animals had begun using the Hathkua waterhole. I also personally verified from the pugmarks and hoof marks that the 'new' old waterhole was being accepted by the denizens. It was definitely a preferred destination for drinking water to the Tarubanda Lake. In due course, most of the lake-going wild animals got diverted to Hathkua, and that was quite satisfying.

One day I thought I would hide myself and observe the 'visitors' first-hand. So I got a machan constructed on a tree near Hathkua. Care was taken to ensure that the machan was properly camouflaged with twigs and my olive-green mosquito net. The use of a searchlight for observing wild animals was not a taboo then. So I planned to use it after dusk. The jeep battery would be our power source, which, because of its heaviness, could not be carried up the machan and was kept at the base of the tree. As the length of the searchlight wire was just about six feet, a very low machan was constructed on the tree. So effectively, I was sitting just about five and a half feet above the ground. 'Two is company and three is a crowd' is the basic rule we apply in such situations. So I had a young forest guard for company, and the third – Rafiq, the driver – was sent away around 4:00 p.m. with instructions to wait in hiding nearby in the direction of the village. The vehicle was parked in the direction opposite to the one from which the wild animals were expected to approach the waterhole. As I did not have a walkie-talkie that evening, the driver was to come and pick us up only when I flashed the searchlight in his direction.

Nothing happened for about an hour. Then a very suspicious peacock approached the waterhole and took its first sip after about fifteen minutes of waiting. The peacock was followed by a sounder of seven wild boars. (Interestingly, there was a waterhole called Sukli-bhura nearby. An old Korkoo had told me that *sukli* means 'wild boar' and *bhura* means 'to drown'. He said that a long time back, a thirsty wild boar had drowned there.) It was turning dark when five sambars arrived at the scene.

When five Sambars arrived at the scene.

The sambar stag leading the herd stopped suddenly, looked in my direction, cocked its ears, lifted its tail, bent its foreleg, banged on the ground to create a thudding sound, and gave a loud alarm call. The breeze was blowing from the machan towards the sambars. So when I queried my companion with a signal as to the cause of the alarm call, he gestured back, indicating that perhaps we could be the cause. I wasn't convinced. Time ticked by, and it had now become totally dark. I switched on the searchlight. The sambars stayed generally motionless and very alert but silent. Their silence, however, was punctuated by their ominous alarm calls. They were neither drinking water nor going away. They appeared mesmerised. This went on for about half an hour. I could not hold down my feeling of discomfort any longer and decided to verify that there were no other animals in our vicinity. I carefully started sweeping the area around our machan with the searchlight – nothing within the arc of visibility.

I don't know why I turned the beam down directly below the machan, but when I did that, my heart leapt into my mouth, and my blood froze. A pair of sharp bright eyes were staring back at me. It took me a fraction of a second to see that a full-grown leopard was sitting directly under me. I could have stretched my leg and stroked its whiskers. We had not the slightest idea when the leopard had tiptoed its way and parked itself under us to stalk the sambars. To add to the drama, Rafiq had seen the beam. He had taken it as a signal to approach, and approach, he did, bouncing merrily on his steed. It was the commotion of the jeep's arrival that broke up the gathering: the leopard went away in one direction, and the sambars smartly headed in the other. I felt guilty for messing up the leopard's meal.

On our way back to Tarubanda, the forest guard asked me, 'Sir, the leopard is such a good tree climber. What would have happened if the jeep had not arrived at the nick of the moment?' hinting, of course, that the leopard would have attacked us.

My answer to him was 'We are not the leopard's food, and it would not have harmed us.' Subsequently I came across a good number of such 'harmless' leopards during my service.

9

COURAGE PAYS

Long back, we had a very courageous Sikh officer whom we may call here only as Mr Singh, posted as DFO at Chikhaldara. He had a Willys left-hand-drive petrol jeep, registration number 1201. After about ten years of service, this vehicle came to me. About it, more anon. Mr Singh was a man of huge appetite; rumour has it that he required a dozen and a half eggs for breakfast. He was so strong that for changing the flat tyre of his jeep, he never used a jack. He would just lift the jeep and hold it up while Gulab, the driver, changed the tyre. Gulab had lots of stories of the DFO, the *bade sahib*. Mr Singh, it seems, had a distinct dislike for sloth bears. When Mr Singh came across a bear on the road, he would make the driver chase the bear and, if possible, run the jeep over it. Once, I asked Gulab the reason for this intense and exclusive hatred of the DFO for just one wild animal. In reply, Gulab had the following story to narrate.

Some guests had come visiting Mr Singh from Punjab, and he, along with his guests, was on an evening walk near his official residence at Chikhaldara. As they neared the forest garden, about a hundred metres from his residence, suddenly, a sloth bear came charging towards them from behind a lantana bush. As the six-footer waddled menacingly on its hind legs towards Mr Singh, he let his hair loose, emitted a war cry, and counter-attacked the bear. The bear perhaps did not expect such a courageous reaction and beat a hasty retreat.

As mentioned earlier, bears charge without provocation. Within seconds, the victim is maimed for life. It requires immense courage to face a bear. 'Fight or flight' is the rule for survival. I remember meeting a very short Korkoo from the now rehabilitated village Kund who, armed with one small axe, had single-handedly fought five (one male, one female, three grown-up young ones) sloth bears. I had seen the injuries on his person and had developed high regard for him during my Tarubanda days. This was a typical case of standing your ground and fighting it out. On the other hand, there are cases of successful flight, as we saw in the case of Aziz in FRH Chikhaldara. But a combination of flight and fight is the rarest of rare, as happened once during my days in Dharni.

The summer of 1980 was on its last legs, and monsoon was about to begin. It was the ideal time for tapping edible gum from forest trees such as *kulu/kadhai* (*Sterculia urens*) or *dhavda* (*Anogeissus latifolia*). The method was to cut a nick with an axe on the tree and revisit the tree later to collect the gum that would ooze out of the nick. Sometimes excessive tapping would eventually kill the tree. To minimise this 'tapping to death', we had some areas declared as 'closed' for gum tapping. The best time to collect gum would be the early hours of the morning. 'The earlier you go, the better you harvest' was the unwritten rule.

One greedy young man once entered the 'closed area' around four in the morning for collecting gum. He was not only doing an illegal act but was also entering the forest at a time meant for our nocturnal brethren. The result was that in the darkness, what he thought was a rock suddenly stood on its hind limbs and charged. Looking at the size of the attacker, the short-statured Korkoo took to flight. He ran fast through the trees and under the lantana bushes and managed to dodge the devil. But he ran out of luck and tripped on a leopard taking its after-dinner rest under a tree. Naturally the leopard resented this intrusion and made it known in no uncertain terms. Our tired 'gum thief' had no option but to stand up and fight.

'......gum thief' had no option but to stand up and fight.

In the first round of combat, the man received claw injuries on his head and chest. However, he soon recovered, stuffed his left arm in the leopard's mouth, ripped open the animal's belly with the axe in his right hand, and spilled out its internal organs along with the poor thing's dinner. After a brief fight, both the combatants collapsed because of injuries and bleeding. When the man, who was expected to reach home by late morning, did not reach home by late afternoon, his wife, his old father-in-law, and some villagers started search operations. It was late evening by the time they had reached the spot. The leopard, unfortunately, was dead, but the man was still alive.

The villagers put the injured man and the leopard in the same bullock cart, came to their village for a bite, and set off for Dharni. By the time the bunch had reached my residence, it was Sunday morning. Sunday being a bazaar day, a big crowd had gathered to see the leopard. We immediately rushed the injured man to hospital. Later, after he had gained consciousness, we contributed money and sent him by bus to the district hospital at Amravati for better treatment. The man, who used both flight and fight strategies in one incident, survived. As an officer, I certainly frowned at his offence, but as a human being, I could not help appreciating the man's courage.

Another man who earned my appreciation in the above leopard case was Namdeo, the inspection hut *chaukidar*. After the injured man was dispatched to Amravati, we focused our attention on the leopard. I quickly summoned the veterinary officer to my residence, who performed a brief autopsy of the leopard under the pre-monsoon showers. The leopard had now to be skinned and its carcass buried. But nobody was prepared to go near the carcass as it had started putrefying in that hot and very humid weather. By evening, I could see maggots attacking the carcass. The stink made me feel giddy, and I vomited. My advisors suggested the name of Namdeo for the skinning and burying operations. After near interminable slogging, stretching up to midnight in the torrential rains, the skinned carcass was finally rolled over in a pit dug adjacent to my residence. I can never forget Namdeo's efforts, though some gave credit to the bottle of rum provided to him by somebody on the sly.

When the above incident took place, I had no jeep. But looking at my workload and for attending to emergencies, jeep 1201 was provided to me in just a couple of days. Yes, this was the same jeep that was with Mr Singh about ten years ago. A left-hand drive petrol, the Willys jeep still had a good pick-up, but the battery had left its youth way behind. It, therefore, had to be push-started, the horn just about cleared its throat, and the headlights could only be sensed in pitch darkness. Long and loyal service on the rough Melghat roads had really taken a heavy toll on the health of this jeep. Our maiden trip in the field told us we needed to respect the old lady's age.

The monsoon had still not started. My companions that evening were Mr Purohit, the RFO of Dharni, and Jumma Chhotu, the driver.

Purohit was a thin enthusiastic young man who was keen on learning jeep driving, and Jumma was an old stalwart but extremely timid; perhaps experience had beaten all the bluster out of him. I had been driving light motor vehicles for the last ten years and was pretty good at it. I drove down from Dharni to Dhakna and inspected a teak plantation on the Dhakna–Dolar road. As it was getting dark, I suggested that we go back to the Dhakna FRH. But Purohit was in a mood to drive and, if possible, try to spot some wild animals that had totally eluded us that evening. So he moved into the driver's seat, I sat next to him, and Jumma continued sitting behind. From the Dhakna–Dolar road, we planned to take a slight detour, a left turn, about two kilometres of drive on plain ground and back.

We must have travelled about a kilometre inside, with Purohit acquitting himself decently on the wheels. The light was fading fast, and it had almost become dark. Hence, Purohit bent a little bit to grope for the headlights switch. In the process, he totally missed registering a black hillock on the road. It was a gaur, the Indian bison. It was a loner, measuring about six feet at the shoulder and weighing about six to seven hundred kilogrammes. Jumma and I yelled in unison for Purohit to stop. Purohit, the learner, did just that. His foot jammed hard on the brakes without engaging the clutch pedal. The engine went dead, and the jeep juddered to a stop about a foot from the gaur. The normal instinct of any wild animal in such a situation is flight, but this one was not normal – either in instinct or in size.

The jeep, remember, wouldn't start without a push. Grass in mouth, the gaur stopped chomping as it measured us up. Beginning with mild astonishment, the look turned so contemptuous that it withers me still. Purohit was fiddling with the ignition keys, Jumma was stuttering helpful stories in my ears about loaded tractors overturned by loner gaurs, and our own loner gaur was dispensing scorn enough to last me decades. The pantomime lasted for two full minutes before the animal decided to break the spell. It resumed grazing as if nothing had happened. For a long time, the gaur did not clear the road; in fact, it did not budge an inch. The *chomp-chomp* continued unabated, punctuated by an occasional raising of the massive head to keep us in our place.

We did not realise when moonlight had quietly crept in. Finally, slowly, grudgingly, the mountain moved from the front to my side of the jeep. Jumma started his second round of commentary. In that open jeep, there was no barrier between me and the huge hulk just about two feet away.

I remembered, in my childhood, with my father, I had passed through a herd of one hundred plus gaurs near Deolapar in the Nagpur district but had never felt so tense. Absolutely unbidden arrived the trivia of music composer Naushad's brother killed by a solitary gaur. Also arrived the not-so-funny now memory of another gaur attacking my friend's Land Rover and accidentally running away with the door on its head. However, we kept our cool and did not do anything stupid. The majestic animal took its own time grazing as it slowly moved behind and eventually disappeared into the darkness. After about half an hour, from the rustling sound, we could guess that the danger was about a hundred metres away. Two intrepid men quietly slid out, pushed the vehicle back to life, and hopped in. I drove down in the moonlight to the safety of FRH Dhakna. Courage and a huge dollop of luck had paid off.

10

IN AND AROUND BITKILPAATI

Bitkil in the local (Korkoo) dialect means 'buffaloes', and *paati* means 'water body'. True to its name, Bitkilpaati provided an ideal all-weather water-sports spot for the domestic buffaloes in the pre–Tiger Project days. The beneficiary buffaloes were basically from the nearby Korkoo village Dolar, named after Dolar Baba, a tribal saint. Then came Project Tiger in 1973, and Bitkilpaati came to be included in the core zone of Project Tiger. This 361-square-kilometre core zone has now become a compact block of total wilderness area without any village. The core zone was soon christened Gugamal National Park. A national park entails severe restrictions on grazing and fishing. Hence, the buffaloes' presence in Bitkilpaati was slowly reduced, and soon, Bitkilpaati became just another *paati* without *bitkil*. As the biotic interference at this waterhole located in the Dolar River diminished, wildlife started converging there, and soon, it became their hub of activity. It was (and still is) a waterhole located on the Dolar–Gurgipaati (*gurgi* means 'horse') fair-weather road, and we used to pause there to look out for wildlife. Bitkilpaati was of special significance to me because a lot of interesting incidents took place near it during my tenure as FD.

The first time I heard about this unusual name, Bitkilpaati, was in the summer of 1992. The then director of the WII had come down with his trainees, and they were all witness to a very unusual scenario. In a dry *naala* bed of the Dolar River near Bitkilpaati, a tigress was seen sitting under the harsh sun. Closer observation had revealed that she was guarding the dead body of her grown-up cub. The dead cub was later loaded on top of a minibus and brought to FRH Koktoo for a post-mortem examination. Under these unfortunate circumstances, I, as the FD of Project Tiger, had my first and last dead tiger sighting in Melghat.

The second time I passed by Bitkilpaati, I was a witness to another unusual sight. In Melghat, particularly in the core zone, when one sights wild animals, they shy away into the forest, away from our vehicle. But on this occasion, at Bitkilpaati, I witnessed sambars and nilgais coming perilously close to my jeep. I could almost touch them. The reason for this unusual behaviour, I realised later, was that the entire valley was terrorised by a large pack of wild dogs, and the herbivores felt safer in our company. They definitely knew that wild dogs are wary of human presence.

On a third occasion, I sighted a rare bird named the black-capped kingfisher near Bitkilpaati. It was Prachi Mehta, an ornithologist and a junior research fellow (JRF) from the WII in Dehradun who had discovered the black-capped kingfisher in Melghat. This bird, till then, was thought to be restricted to the coastal areas of Mumbai and migrated only a few kilometres along the creeks. I remember how my enthusiastic driver Neemkar manufactured a makeshift tripod out of the branches of a vitex tree to facilitate my photographing the rare bird. I still remember following the bird all over and Neemkar chasing me with his 'tripod' till I got a good shot.

Another memorable incident that took place near Bitkilpaati was when I went walking there for an important inspection, walking because it was still September and the fair-weather roads were yet to be repaired for a jeep ride. I got so engrossed in the inspection that it became almost dark at Bitkilpaati. We were a team of three to four persons walking along a jungle track to Dolar, which was about six to seven kilometres away. Our departmental elephant had walked on this route about a fortnight ago, and there were patches of black cotton soil where the elephant's feet had sunk a good six inches deep inside the soil. After drying, these footprints had become mini wells.

By the time we came to the first black cotton patch, it had become totally dark, and I couldn't see a thing. I was worried that a careless landing of my foot in one of these holes could so easily twist my ankle. My rechargeable torch's 'charge' had got exhausted. In such a situation, my men would generally use a dried bamboo stick and set it alight. But there were no bamboos in that patch of forest. It was a moonless night, and since I was not used to such a situation, I felt totally disoriented. Luckily, a very enthusiastic and courageous forester by the name of Giri was with us. He was used to such situations and could see better in the dark than I could. He told me to just follow him blindly. But I first needed to see him before I could follow him, and I couldn't. So he hung out a white hanky from his hip pocket, and I followed that hazy-looking spot. This obviously slowed our progress to a snail's pace. I remember my worried staff waiting for me at Dolar had pushed all the panic buttons and dispatched a well-equipped search party, whom we met just about a kilometre before Dolar.

The fifth and final incident, I have to describe in some detail, was when I landed in a tight spot because of an overenthusiastic forest guard. Summer indeed is very harsh in Melghat. In May, the afternoon temperature in the shade soars up to forty-six degrees Celsius. Teak, the predominant tree species, sheds all its leaves, and the jungle becomes a monstrous landscape of huge pencils scattered everywhere. Water is restricted to small pools in rivers and rivulets, and most wild animals in the vicinity converge at these waterholes to quench their thirst. In the MTR in the early 1990s, we shortlisted numerous such waterholes and kept strict vigil over poachers there. Along with the vigil, we undertook a waterhole census around the full moon in May. We would construct a machan near the waterhole and carefully note the number of animals, the number of species, the time of visit, and other details about the wild animals visiting the waterhole. The local tribals would make amazing machans on a strategically located tree using locally available poles, bamboo, and grass. The tribals and guards who did good work of machan construction were always fulsomely praised. This had initiated an informal healthy competition among the field staff of MTR who loved to show off their machans.

It was May 1993, and one such enthusiastic forest guard named Kasdekar (name changed) was waiting on the Dolar–Koktoo (core area) road near Bitkilpaati to invite me to watch wildlife in his beat from his 'luxury machan' over the waterhole. He was of the opinion that it was a now-or-never situation as the monsoons would soon come and I might never be back on this less frequented path. I knew that I was alone and entering the forest at the most sensitive time of the year, when all thirsty wildlife would converge towards waterholes during summer evenings. I also knew that we would be disturbing wildlife and also risking our lives. Equipped with my torch, I reluctantly accepted Kasdekar's invitation.

Our 'five-minute' walk was a fairly steep climb through a dry *naala* bed. After some time, it became totally dark, and we could sense the presence of thirsty wild animals converging towards the waterhole. After thirty minutes of brisk climbing, we saw no sign of the machan, but my host was sure the machan was 'just a minute away'. Another five minutes elapsed. The brisk climb in the summer made me feel thirsty, and I was completely drenched in sweat. With every passing moment, I was losing my patience. Kasdekar also realised that rather than a 'pat on his back', it was likely to be a 'brickbat' evening for him. To pacify me, he promptly hastened his pace and tactfully increased the distance between us.

At last, he shouted, 'Here it is, sir!'

I flashed my torch in the direction he was pointing and saw a faint image of his machan. But what attracted my attention was just behind him – a pair of bright shining eyes. Immediately, I shouted at Kasdekar, who, in his hurry, was about to stumble on a leopard. Shocked, he stopped and came running back towards me at top speed. The thirsty leopard was a potential threat to us, and it also stood as an impediment between us and our destination – the machan.

After a brief whispered 'conference' about our next step, we decided not to retrace our steps. So we waited patiently for the leopard to slowly go ahead. We finally reached the machan, which was just about thirty metres away. We promptly climbed to the safety of the machan top. The thirsty leopard continued his journey to the waterhole, drank water in our presence, came back under our machan after about twenty minutes, and finally disappeared into the forest. I patted Kasdekar's back for giving me an 'experience of a lifetime' at his excellent waterhole and a comfortable machan at a strategic place where wildlife could be observed without their knowledge. It was well past ten when we slowly descended and reached my car, where a worried Hasan was anxiously waiting for me.

I had learnt three important lessons from this excursion:

1. Night in the jungle is meant for nocturnal animals, and we should not unnecessarily encroach on their timings.
2. A leopard attacks human beings only under grave provocation.
3. In a rural set-up, an enthusiastic person's 'five minutes' can mean any length of time.

SOME LARGE MAMMALS

Barking deer (Muntiacus)

PC: Anant Zanjale

Spotted deer(Axis axis)

PC: Prakash Thosre

Sambar (Rusa unicolor)

PC: Anant Zanjale

Gaur (Bos gaurus)

PC: Anant Zanjale

SOME LARGE MAMMALS (CONTINUED)

Sloth bear (Melursus ursinus)

PC: Anant Zanjale

Leopard (Panthera pardus)

PC: Prakash Thosre

Tiger (Panthera tigris)

PC: Prakash Thosre

Wild dog (Cuon alpinus)

PC: Prakash Thosre

11

MOTHER'S INSTINCTS

Whether in the wild or among humans, the bond between a mother and her young one is strong. In the wild, whether among birds or mammals, it is almost always the mother who brings up the young. She looks after their safety and provides them with food and grooms and trains them till they are independent. She drills them into remaining quiet and still when she goes out looking for food or for a quick gulp of water or creates distractions when she sees some animal approaching her brood. Interestingly, nature seems to have taught the young ones to obey the mother's instructions unquestioningly right from birth. They instinctively know that disobedience can cost them their lives – not surprising at all because young ones without these genes for obedience to their mother would have got eliminated in the ruthless battle for survival millions of years ago.

One summer afternoon I was in the grassland inspecting the water facility we had created for wildlife. While observing the habitat through my binoculars, I caught sight of a *mal titavi* (yellow-wattled lapwing). At the mother bird's feet was a recently hatched chick that just couldn't keep pace with her. As I approached closer, the mother nudged the chick to hide in the grass and flew away, giving loud alarms calls to divert my attention. I knew exactly where the chick was. So I went very close and took some pictures of the chick. The mother hovered frantically in the sky while the chick lay flat, pretending to be dead. Some performance it was! Hats off to the chick and to the mother too. It was only after I had gone some distance that the mother's alarm call subsided and I saw them walk away happily.

You must have seen how at the slightest suspicion, the mother langur calls her infants in, and they quickly get back into the safety of their mother's arms. It's fun watching a row of wild boar piglets blindly following their mother wherever she takes them out for a walk. I have also seen a mother blackbuck keeping its obedient day-old fawn motionless in the shadow of a two-foot *palash* bush till she finished grazing nearby. I was witness to an incident in which a mother sambar staked her life and combated a large pack of wild dogs to save her fawn. Unfortunately, she lost the fight.

In the case of herbivores staying in herds, mothers do not battle alone. Often the other members come to the rescue of the young one. I saw a tiger trying to attack a gaur calf. Immediately, all the females in the herd encircled the calf, facing outwards, their horns ready for attack. The tiger knew it was beaten and slunk away. In jungles, we generally avoid sloth bears as they charge without provocation. Attack is almost certain if you suddenly encounter a female bear with young ones. But the same mother is so playful with the cubs who hang by her chest, ears, or tail. Often they go piggyback riding on the mom.

Being too inquisitive about wild mothers and their cubs can almost always be asking for trouble. I once invited this trouble. There was a hole dug in the side of a hill with a good number of trails converging towards it. I was told by the forest guard accompanying me that it was a striped hyena's den and that four cubs stayed in it. Keen to see them, we approached the den quietly, thinking that the mother hyena had gone to feed. Initially, we heard some very weird noises. Later, we heard some sounds as if human beings were talking. This was followed by a sudden mock charge from the den by the mother. It had us running for our lives through the spiny Ziziphus bushes. The bruises, I carried for a fortnight. The lesson of not taking chances with wild mothers, I carried for a lifetime.

a sudden mock-charge from the den by the mother

In 1960, I used to stay in bungalow 41/1, Ramgiri Road, Civil Lines, Nagpur, now the Officers' Club. We were half a dozen brothers and sisters who had a great childhood playing in the five-odd-acre campus. One evening my father, a forest officer, came back from the jungle with an interesting gift for us wrapped up nicely in a basket. It was a tiger cub! Seating it by the rear windscreen of our Hillman car, we took it for a ride through Itwari, Dharampeth, Sitabuldi, and other busy parts of Nagpur. I was 8 or 9 years old then and still remember the looks we drew from passers-by who suddenly realised that it was a real tiger cub. It stayed with us for about a week before it was sent to the Maharajbag Zoo. I often wondered what could have happened to the cub's mother. Did she desert it, or was she killed? Or was there another explanation?

It was more than thirty years later in August 1993 that I got an inkling of what might have happened. I was then the FD of Project Tiger. Through newspaper reports, I learnt about two 'abandoned' leopard cubs which were found in the forest near Semadoh. There was also a photograph in the newspaper showing a local leader feeding the cubs with a milk bottle. Immediately, I rushed to Semadoh. Preliminary enquiry revealed that the cubs were found three days back by a villager about ten kilometres away from Semadoh on the Chikhaldara road. One cub appeared sick and was not drinking milk, whereas the other seemed to be in good shape. I was not prepared to believe that the mother could 'desert' her cubs and wanted to give a serious try at reuniting mother and cubs.

I visited the site where they had been found. The spot was about five metres from the main tar road. Closer inspection showed a hollow 'down log'. My surmise was that the hungry mother would have gone in search of food, leaving the cubs in the safety of the hollow down log. The very young cubs were struggling to walk a couple of paces. Their stepping out must have coincided with an enthusiastic passer-by sighting and picking them up. So ignoring the advice of cynics who felt it was too late, I decided to attempt the reunion.

At that very spot, around five that evening, the cubs were put in a transport cage to ensure their safety. A rope was tied to the gate of the cage, which reached a machan on a neighbouring tree. On the machan sat our man Jajoo, holding the rope in his hand with instructions to open the gate when the mother arrived. It was very brave of Jajoo to volunteer to sit alone in the darkness on a rainy jungle night where an angry mother leopard, an expert tree climber, was suspected to be lurking. By 7:00 p.m., we completed these arrangements and bade goodbye to Jajoo.

Around 11:00 p.m., I reached the spot. Jajoo came down from the machan with this story. About half an hour after we had left, the cubs began cheeping at their loudest. In the quiet of the jungle, the call reached the mother, who was about four kilometres away in a deep valley, and she called back. In about half an hour, she was at the cage. He promptly opened the door. She met the cubs and licked them but left without accepting them. We found the cubs loitering hesitantly nearby and took them to Semadoh. My guess was that over-handling of the cubs had made the mother suspicious. Hence, as advised by my colleague Ajay, we rubbed mud, urine, and excreta of the cubs onto them and repeated the experiment the next evening. This time, the mother came and carried her healthy cub away. The rejected sick cub died in captivity at the Wadali Rescue Centre in Amravati after a couple of days. We had created history in Melghat in reuniting the leopard cub successfully with its mother after a gap of about four days.

Like other animals, a tigress too is extra sensitive when with cubs. When threatened, she attacks and can kill, as in the case of the Memna tigress. Of course, the first attempt by her is to avoid confrontation, as personally experienced by me in the case of a tigress near Harisaal. I have narrated this interesting encounter in my article 'The Elusive Melghat Tiger'. The tigress alone bears the burden of bringing up the cubs. The motherly instincts function for about two years towards making the cubs fit to live on their own, and then they take off. Those cubs of a carnivore that lose their mother at a very tender age cannot procure their food as they miss out on the most important training sessions on how to make a kill. Such cubs become unfit to live in the wild. They either die of starvation or get captured and spend the rest of their lives in captivity. In very rare cases, they may turn into man-eaters. The lesson for us humans is very clear. Think twice before picking up such orphan cubs.

C

THE ROYAL TIGER

The tiger is the most charismatic species found in Indian wilderness. It is a symbol of vitality and an indicator of the health of a forest. It is said that in 1900, the estimated tiger population in our country was 40,000, which came down to 1,827 by 1972. Though the massacre was basically by poisoning, it is true that the *maharaja*s and their friends, especially from abroad, also had a major role to play in lowering the tiger numbers in India. Figures available indicate that highest toll of tigers was taken by a single *maharaja* from the present-day Chhattisgad. He alone (friends not included) accounted for killing 1,710 tigers. Next in the list is a *maharaja* from Madhya Pradesh who killed nine hundred plus tigers. Looking at the situation, the then prime minister of India, Mrs Indira Gandhi, thought that unless some immediate steps are taken, this beautiful animal would vanish from India's wilderness forever. Hence came the initial nine Project Tigers in India in different agroclimatic zones. Cynics who were supposed to be experts had predicted in 1993 that the tiger would vanish from the Indian wilderness by the turn of the century – and had to eat their words. Indeed, Project Tiger is a big success story of conservation. The hero of the story, the tiger, finds a special place here in my book.

My personal interaction with the Melghat tiger has been described on the following pages through six stories. A tiger in Melghat killing and eating a human being was unheard of till we experienced it at Memna near Chikhaldara. This experience is shared with the readers in my first story. An abortive visit to the tiger's den, my frustration on not seeing it in Melghat for one and a half years, how the mighty tiger is mortally afraid of the whistling hunters, my happiness at the first tiger sighting, and clicking the first photograph of the elusive Melghat tiger are the following real-life stories.

12

TRAGEDY STRIKES
BEFORE VIP VISIT

P eople generally visit the MTR for sighting a tiger. Very few come to experience the wilderness. Unfortunately for the visitors, in spite of the seventy-two-strong population during my time, tiger sighting in Melghat was – and remains – very difficult. The reasons are discussed in my article 'The Elusive Melghat Tiger'. Even as FD of the MTR, I took a very long time to sight my first tiger. The tiger, of course, would be sighting me at will. Those who came to Melghat with tiger-obsessed eyes almost always went back disappointed. Sighting a herd of gaurs or sambars or blue bulls or spotted deer never amounted to a patch on the ultimate thrill they came looking for. Though we had carved out a separate tourism zone for seeing large mammalian wildlife, it really did not help the cause much. The situation became tenser when the visitor happened to be a VIP.

Normally, while preparing for a VIP visit, we used to put our heads together to decide the route along which we would take the VIP. Besides the condition of the road, factors such as nearness to a water body or a salt lick, visibility through ground flora, the locations of partially eaten carcasses, and pug/hoof marks were kept in mind. Sprinkling *mahua* flowers to attract herbivores – which, in turn, might lure a carnivore – was also considered. Generally, an alert, experienced person with all senses functioning well was deputed to accompany the VIP. I remember having blacklisted one officer who had lost the way in the jungle while accompanying the Honourable Governor. To a long list of qualities was added courtesy, patience, and cool-headedness.

Here is a horror story that one of my colleague FDs had to narrate. The Honourable Governor and his wife were being taken around on elephant-back for seeing wildlife. The chief wildlife warden and his wife were accompanying the esteemed guests. Their best *mahavat* was in the seat, manoeuvring the elephant. As there was no sighting for a long time, the ladies got busy talking shop, much to the annoyance of the *mahavat*, who urged them to keep quiet. They kept mum for some time and again started. While Madam Governor was in the midst of narrating the recipe for making *aonla* pickle, the *mahavat* suddenly stopped and made the elephant sit down in the middle of jungle and asked the lady to dismount. Everyone was aghast. It indeed required a lot of coaxing to restart the journey.

In another incident, the principal chief CF had come on a tour of my area. After the inspections during the day, he expressed a desire to go tiger sighting at night. Equipped with two searchlights, we left for our outing in an open jeep. We drove for about half an hour without any luck. The boss was getting impatient, and we were busy praying and straining our eyes when I saw a single red eye shining down the road. I knew it was a nightjar, and I said that to the boss. The problem with this bird is that it is overconfident of its camouflage and does not take off till the intruder is very close to it. Here, I did not slow down, and as the jeep drew very close, the bird took off like a helicopter and landed like a helicopter too on the lap of my boss. It was an open jeep, remember? The unexpected landing, of course, made the boss take off from his seat. We came across another three or four nightjars who behaved well, but the boss couldn't be persuaded of their good manners. He kept ducking and jumping in his seat. Looking at his nervous state, I suggested that we head home, and we wound up not seeing either a tiger or any other wild animal, for that matter.

The famous cartoonist R. K. Laxman came visiting too, and my officers took him around. He had some decent sightings, and towards the fag end of his tour, the great man came over to our Nature Interpretation Centre at Semadoh. Here, he was requested to give his remarks in our 'remark book'. He preferred drawing a cartoon. It depicted a Project Tiger officer desperately trying to climb a tree to save himself from a chasing tiger.

One day I got a wireless message that the then CM of Maharashtra, Mr Sudhakarrao Naik, was coming to Melghat. He and his family were to spend three days exclusively in the MTR. 'The bigger the VIP, the more the tension' is universal rule number one, to which I add rule number two: 'The bigger the VIP, the poorer the sighting.' Luckily for us, Mr Naik had been an old-time *shikari*. He knew the jungle creed only too well: if it is a dry run today, tomorrow you may hit jackpot. Unfortunately, the sightings remained dismal three days running. On the last outing, the CM became so desperate that he took to panning the searchlight everywhere. As we were approaching FRH Kolkaz in the moonlight, my colleague Ajay Pillarisett sighted a barking deer and called desperately for us to stop. The CM's searchlight, however, had totally missed out on the deer. To his credit, Mr Naik was a sport and took the poor sighting in his stride. He unveiled the statue of his uncle Mr Vasantrao Naik, the former CM of Maharashtra, at old FRH Kolkaz. He also hosted an excellent meal for my entire staff. The next day, he even accepted my request for more staff and also released substantial funds from the CM's relief fund for equipment for the staff.

We, in turn, had organised a high tea for the CM and his family at the Sadhukundi patrolling hut. They were very happy with the ambience, so happy indeed that the next day, on his way to the helipad, the CM suddenly decided to visit the hut all over again with his friends Jabbar Patel and Arun Sadhu. This sudden veering of the CM towards the core area messed up the VIP security net, which upset the DIG police hugely. He was sore, and I was worried too. Luckily, people were in their places, and things were in decent order.

While we were preparing for the CM's Melghat visit, a rather tragic event unfolded. I got news that a tiger had killed a man and eaten a part of the body near Chikhaldara, where the CM was due to land the next day. During my service and my earlier childhood days in Melghat, human–wildlife conflict was limited to crop raiding by herbivores and cattle kills by the carnivores. I had never ever heard about human kills by any Melghat tiger, let alone a tiger turning into a man-eater. So this news quite surprised me.

At one edge of Chikhaldara's upper plateau is a tiny village called Mariampur. In the early nineties, a Christian priest at Mariampur had worked very hard at dissuading the villagers from the terrible habit of drinking. His sermons had had a positive impact, and strict prohibition was observed in the village. However, there were always a few who would sneak away to a small tribal village called Memna, about three or four kilometres down the Chikhaldara–Semadoh road. One had to pass through a Christian graveyard before entering the village. This graveyard is still on the main Chikhaldara–Semadoh road, with the village a few hundred metres inside to the right. Since the area had a lot of wildlife, the topers returned to Mariampur before dusk.

Around that time, everyone in and around Memna knew about the presence of a tigress with three cubs. She avoided human presence, and if humans came her way, she growled. Ominous indeed! It was the last day of April 1992. I was busy preparing for the CM's visit to Chikhaldara and to my area in the MTR when I got news of this human kill near Memna. I rushed to the spot, located the dead body, and identified it as a tiger kill. The tigress seemed to have killed the victim near the graveyard and dragged the body to a *naala* nearby, where the cubs had nibbled at it. I met the members of the victim's family and consoled them.

......but the alcohol fumes were too thick to be penetrated.

I spoke to my staff at Memna and Mariampur villagers, walked around the neighbouring forests, and reconstructed the sequence of events on the day. The victim had gone with a couple of friends to Memna from Mariampur in the evening. After a few drinks, as they set off on their return journey, this man refused to accompany them. He was drunk enough to tell his companions that he would shoo away the tigress by stoning her. Reluctantly, his companions left him behind. The sun had set in Memna when the forest guard heard a commotion in the village that a long-haired drunk man was creating. He coaxed the man to set off homewards. The drunk lurched out of Memna and reached the Chikhaldara–Semadoh road, but instead of turning left, he turned right and reached the graveyard. He lowered himself on some gravel that was heaped there for road repairs and, in his drunkenness, started throwing stones all around.

The last person to see him busy thus was a 'fire watcher' named Babulal. (A fire watcher, as the name suggests, is employed to keep an eye on any sign of conflagration during the summer months.) Babulal tried to persuade the man to move, but the alcohol fumes were too thick to be penetrated. The rest can only be conjectured. Some of the missiles would have gone the tigress's way, and retribution would have been swift and merciless. The body was dragged to a nearby *naala*, and there were nibble marks on the victim's thighs.

I kept a close vigil in the area for almost a year after the incident. There was no further 'misbehaviour' on the tigress's part. The misadventure was soon forgotten. One individual from the bereaved family was given employment with the Forest Department, and the family was given a cheque at the hands of the CM to compensate for the victim's death. What was most satisfying was that the CM knew where the fault lay and did not grill any of us. Not all VIPs are as understanding as Mr Sudhakarrao Naik was.

I recently (2015) visited Memna and met Babulal, who is still in good shape. We sat in the graveyard where the victim was buried and relived the sequence of events leading to the tragedy which took place twenty-five years ago.

13

A KNOCK AT THE
TIGER'S DEN

There was something unique about my relationship with Mr Madhav Gogate, my immediate predecessor at the MTR. I happened to successfully chase him in as many as five chairs during my career. Every time he would brief me so well about the charge that I found it easy to settle down in the new chair. At the MTR too, while he was briefing me into the seat, he minced no words while criticising a senior IFS officer who had said that he couldn't work at the MTR because the wildlife there put his own life in grave danger. At the same time, he praised the work of a fairly junior person in the organisation by the name of Giri, who happened to be just a forester.

Those days, the biggest threat to MTR was from illegal grazing in the core area by Kathiawadi cattle. As per law, the grazing of cattle is banned in a national park. These cattle had come in multiples of thousands and had the potential to permanently ruin the good fodder areas of Melghat, thus depriving the wild animals of their food. Also, there was a fear of wild animals catching infection, especially where both shared a common waterhole. Emboldened by the support of their political well-wishers, the Kathiawadi graziers had bulldozed their way illegally from the Pirkheda towards the Chiladari side of the core. They had even attacked Giri with slingshots (*gofan*). Giri moved around on elephant-back and gave them a fitting reply. In fact, he was required to fire sixteen rounds of ammunition. Had Giri not done that, the floodgates would have opened, and irreparable damage would have been caused to the core of the MTR.

The day I joined as FD, I received a wireless message from Giri saying that the '*makhar* of gaurs has started'. I could not understand the term, and hence, I called for the details. It seems on a particular day in the month of Shravan, there is an annual get-together of gaurs in which a good hundred-odd assemble. The duration of *makhar* was for two to three days. In 1991, the event took place at two spots: one under a banyan tree near Gobiaani cut and the other near the Gugamal plateau under a *haldu* tree. That was my first interaction with Giri.

Giri was the forester in charge of the most interior rounds in the MTR, namely, Dhargad, Koktoo, and Dhakna. For a visitor, Koktoo was a beautiful site, but for a forester posted there, it could be the loneliest and most depressing spot on the earth. You do not see any human being for days together, let alone your family. In such a situation, the two popular options were to abscond from duty or succumb to the loneliness and get addicted to drinks. Giri was different. He walked through his area every day, made critical observations, and documented them. A map of his rounds showed permanent water bodies, nests of crested serpent eagles, porcupine burrows, trees bearing tiger/bear claw marks (tigers mark their territories, while bears climb for honeycombs), locations of endangered plants, tiger dens, and so on. A full-day field excursion with Giri was a learning exercise.

Melghat then had about 650 floral species, out of which 350 were of medicinal importance in Ayurveda. Giri could identify most of these plants along with their technical names and their uses. In fact, he authored a book in which he gave the local names and body parts of plants useful in Ayurveda and the locations where they are found in Melghat. During field excursions, I was a beneficiary of his running commentary on medicinal plants and the interpretation of nature. Giri was a sociable person. To have easy interaction with local tribals, he had picked up their language. He could sing some of their songs too. He was a decent cook who specialised in soups. During field visits in the rainy season, he would cook and serve local wild leafy vegetables along with the regular meal on a wild banana leaf.

To get first-hand information about the porcupine burrow, he had crawled into the porcupine burrow at the Makadi ('spider') *naala*. He vividly described what he saw inside the burrow. He said that there was a big central hall to accommodate three to four animals comfortably, a master bedroom, a children's room, and a storeroom stocked with bones and antlers. What Giri did by crawling into the burrow was obviously dangerous. There have been cases when persons who entered the burrow could neither turn back nor crawl back and died of suffocation.

On the Bori–Koktoo road, Giri had located the nest of a crested hawk eagle on a very tall *ain* (*Terminalia tomentosa*) tree. He observed the eggs getting hatched. After the chicks became big enough to eat meat, the mother would kill a small bird, remove its feathers on a specific stump of tree, and bring only the lump of meat in the nest for the chicks to feed on.

Those were the days when I was desperately looking out for a photograph of the Melghat tiger, and most of my field staff knew about it. Giri had located a tiger near Hazarivad in a den. He once took me for a sixteen-kilometre trek to show a tiger in its den. I remember throughout our trek, we were travelling in a *naala* bed which had some flowing water. There were patches of *Saccharum munja* grass on the riverbed. We saw plenty of tiger scats containing this grass. So the myth that a tiger would rather die of starvation than eat grass was exploded. Giri was taking us to show a tiger that he had been observing in a den for the previous four days.

We stopped about a hundred metres away from the cave to plan our move. We could vaguely make out that it was a huge natural cave on the bank of the *naala*. Giri felt that he should go towards the rear entrance of the cave and create some noise so that the tiger would be flushed out and step out of the main front opening. Ravi Wankhade and I thought that this was a good chance for us to photograph a Melghat tiger. The lenses we had were quite ordinary; hence, proximity to the subject was essential. Ravi selected a rock about ten feet away from the mouth of the den where we would sit with our cameras ready. I told Giri and Ravi that when the tiger did come out, it could finish us off in one jump because we would be sitting in its way. But Giri assured me that I should not worry; his last four days' observation showed that when the tiger came out, it immediately took an acute right turn. Ravi appeared to be convinced.

So we took our position and waited with thumping hearts and trembling hands, holding our cameras. Giri went to the back entrance of the den to flush the tiger out. He created a racket in the tiger's backyard, which made us, sitting as the tiger's two morsels, feel more nervous. There was no expected action from inside. After waiting for some time, Giri tiptoed inside the cave from the rear entrance. I was losing all patience when I found Giri emerging from the entrance in place of the tiger. The tiger had perhaps gone for a kill. I think of this episode with a mixed feeling of frustration and relief. As I write this about twenty-five years later, I think what I and Ravi and Giri did was foolhardy.

Later, Giri took us on a conducted tour of an 'in use' tiger den. It was a palatial structure in the rocks that appeared to have been in use for many generations. It had five or six chambers; the best one was on first floor, with one window just sufficient for a tiger's head from where it could survey the vast area and decide on its menu. The presence of tiger hair, the odour, and the ambience provided me with the experience of a lifetime. This experience was the first and the last of its kind. Giri has retired from service and obtained the required formal qualifications in Ayurvedic medicines and runs a roaring practice as a doctor in Paratwada.

14

THE ELUSIVE
MELGHAT TIGER

He wouldn't let me see him for a year and a half after I took charge. I missed him by seconds. I was always told that he had just visited. I saw his spoor. I even saw the food he had eaten. My only consolation was the knowledge that he was keeping a close watch on me. I wandered through the wilds, strained my eyes, stretched my ears day and night, patrolled the trails, and kept vigil by the kills but never caught a glimpse. I was the CF, for heaven's sake, and FD of Project Tiger. The tiger, however, was letting me know in clear terms that I was merely that. There was no question who the boss was. I had been posted to Melghat in 1991, and as the months went by without any sighting, I was turning a little frantic. Of course, I had often encountered his clan from the late 1950s onwards, but now, considering that I was in charge of his territory, my need to spot him was getting to be a matter of honour.

The laws of the jungle, however, don't care a hoot (let alone a roar) for the laws of bureaucracy, and as one learns through experience, His Majesty will make his appearance in the fullness of time. There is no hustling him. Meanwhile, there is so much else to absorb and admire all around the jungle that the tiger may well be just a metaphor for the grandeur and beauty of the untamed lands – crested serpent eagles, wild boars, sloth bears, foxes, snakes, sambars, flying squirrels, a porcupine burrow, colourful insects, gorgeous plants, flowers, and age-old trees. The heart, nevertheless, pines for the elusive striped wild cat.

The tiger, I assure you, is a thorough gentleman – and the Melghat tiger a gentleman among gentlemen. I say this after meandering over 150,000 kilometres in the Melghat forests alone. Given the terrain, it's easy to miss the magnificent cat, and I was missing him like a champion, as on All Fools' Day of 1992. The then director of the WII in Dehradun, H. S. Panwar, had come to Melghat with a batch of wildlife trainees. Though I was expected to accompany them, I opted to go into the forest alone. The reward was immediate. I saw a sambar stag with two females, a mother bear carrying its young one on its back, and a crested serpent eagle taking off over my left shoulder. I felt sorry the group had missed these wonderful sights. Back at the FRH, I rushed to them with my tales. But when I saw the wide-eyed looks of the party, I knew I had eaten crow. They had seen a tigress sitting on the dry riverbed under the bright eleven-o'clock sun.

...a tense Barkhade standing about half a km...

A few days later, I had arranged to meet Barkhade, my forester, at Kuwapati at 6:00 p.m. I reached fifteen minutes late to find a tense Barkhade standing about half a kilometre from our rendezvous. The reason? Exactly at six, instead of encountering the FD, he had run into the real thing, the super boss himself, and had discreetly removed himself and his bike. Serves me right for being late, wouldn't you say?

On another winter evening, I got a wireless message that a tiger had killed a six-hundred-kilogramme gaur the previous night. Promptly, I instructed that a properly camouflaged machan be constructed near the kill. We sat patiently till midnight, our tiger-obsessed minds not open to appreciating some rare sights – a ruddy mongoose nibbling at the carcass, a pair of tree pies trying to steal a morsel – when we heard the telltale sound: a panicky barking deer dashing from a waterhole. Tensely, we waited . . . and waited . . . and finally, we gave up. An inspection of the nearby tracks showed that the tiger had come to the kill, seen us, and backed off. We learnt later that after we had left, the tiger came back and polished off a shoulder.

I was disappointed, naturally, but I was not going to give up. Now imagine this. I was on my regular walk through the forest at nine in the morning down a fair-weather road in the company of Surajpal, a knowledgeable local. At a distance of about two hundred metres runs a river screened by a thick patch of forest. We suddenly noticed pugmarks that sparked off an animated discussion. And then all at once, the langurs gave the alarm call, and a tiger roared from the riverside. In a flash, Surajpal shimmied up a tall tree and scampered down with the news of a big tiger on the riverbed. We were across the vegetation and onto the riverbank in a shot, but we were not fast enough. The tiger had vanished, just vanished, stripes and whiskers and all.

Determined to break the jinx this time, I occupied the seat in the minibus that offered the best view on this November journey from Khatkali to Dhargad. A sounder of about twenty wild boars trotted across, and peacocks stared at us from the middle of the road and called raucously. We would soon be crossing the Sulai *naala*, where there had been frequent tiger sightings. My polo-neck pullover was getting to be too warm for comfort, and I decided to get rid of it. As I was removing it, the driver whispered that a tiger was on the road. Frantic, I almost tore it up my nape and chin and nose, but by the time I emerged from the tunnel, they had all seen the tiger, while I was left fuming. I had to be satisfied with pugmarks again.

And there was the time when a tigress came to check me out. This miss was at Harisaal, where a gaur was killed by a tigress with cubs. The arrangement was a little different this time. A dilapidated cage, adequately camouflaged with twigs, was kept about twenty metres away from the kill. My friend Anant and I ambled through very tall grass and sat in the cage over the kill that moonless night, while our better halves parked themselves in my car a fair distance off. In the pitch dark and absolute quiet, we could hear ourselves breathe. Then came the alarm call of a sambar, and we knew that the tigress had arrived. Within minutes, we heard the crushing of bones, a feast out there in the open. Soon, there was a rustle near us, heavy breathing, and the strong smell of the carnivore at nose-punching distance. The curious tigress was probably inspecting the bipeds in the cage. Anant had frozen, and I was melting into a puddle of sweat. Eyeball to eyeball with a tigress – and I couldn't see the blessed creature! A rustle (and a suffocating odour) receded, and we let ten, fifteen, twenty minutes go by. Clearing our throats loudly, we lunged into the safety of Anant's jeep and headed dejectedly towards Harisaal. Five minutes later, my car followed, with the ladies shrieking in delight. They had seen a tigress with three cubs right on the road in the full glare of the headlights.

Anyway, my bad luck, like all bad things, ultimately ran out, and I did sight the tiger as many as fourteen times over the years. The fact remains that the Melghat tiger is a very shy and elusive animal.

In my interactions with visitors, I have always insisted that they should enjoy the whole experience while they wait for the lord to appear. Disappointing though it may be to visit a reserve and return without a sighting – especially today, when the animal is threatened – a jungle excursion always leaves you a richer, deeper, recalibrated person. This is the difference, really, between a visit to a zoo or a safari park and total wilderness. Melghat is a vast patch of wilderness, with well-spread prey biomass, waterholes, and undulating terrain thick with undergrowth. There are many fascinating creatures and features in nature to enthral an appreciative audience. Revel in them till you hear the rustling leaves and espy the pink tongue and bright eyes staring at you from the waterhole, a cave, or behind that bush on your right.

15

THE WHISTLING
HUNTERS

The incident of a tiger getting into the Tapi River to get away from the whistling hunters and then following the girls who had rescued it to their village had set me thinking. I started reading about wild dogs, searching through my childhood experiences, quizzing my forester colleagues, and visiting areas terrorised by them. These wild dogs, the whistling hunters, are known as *dhole* in Hindi and *kulsund* in Marathi, particularly in Western Maharashtra. Easily identified by their elegant dog-like looks, tawny coat, ears rounded at the tips, and a black bushy tail, they are social animals who live and hunt in packs. A pack is generally a family or a union of two or more families.

In the normal course, deer or wild pig is their preferred food. However, large packs can hunt down bigger animals like gaurs, wild buffaloes, bears, leopards, and even tigers. They generally hunt during the day by tracking their prey, initially by scent, and then pursuing it by sight and outrunning it. If they get scattered in the chase or if they come across humans suddenly, they signal to one another by whistling; hence, they are popularly called the whistling hunters. Intriguingly, they do not generally attack cattle and, like other wild animals, are scared of humans. They have a rather cruel way of hunting – they begin feeding on their prey even before the animal is dead. I have seen many unannounced curfews in valleys terrorised by large packs of wild dogs. When hounded by these predators, members of the deer family come within arm's reach of humans. The boldness of these dogs is legendary. Stories about their attacks on powerful animals abound. I witnessed one such incident before I joined the Forest Department.

This was in the late 1960s, and I was sitting in an *aaraam-kursi* in the veranda of the Koktoo FRH. This FRH is now in the core area of the MTR. I was taken to this beautiful hundred-year-old FRH by a DFO 'uncle' who was then my father's colleague and who later became my colleague too. As was the custom those days, this gentleman was carrying his personal gun with him. It was a very hot summer afternoon, and as most of the trees had shed their leaves, visibility was excellent. At a distance of about three hundred metres, we could see a huge tree at the base of which there was something like a mound that seemed to be pulsating. I picked up my binoculars and was amazed to see that the mound was a large pack of wild dogs. Naturally, I wanted to know what they were up to. Closer observation revealed that these dogs had chased a tiger up the tree. Normally, a tiger is a poor climber. But since it was a question of life and death, it had managed to scamper up, and there it was on its perch, so scared that I could actually see it trembling.

Intending to help the tiger, the DFO fired a shot in the air in the hope of scaring away the dogs, but quite the reverse happened. The terrified tiger lost its grip and fell and was torn to pieces and polished off by the hungry beasts. In the melee, a couple of dogs were also grievously injured. The tiger perhaps could have survived had Uncle not fired. Wild dogs are scared of humans and often abandon their chase when they sense their presence. In such grave situations, tigers too come closer to human beings to save themselves. Only if the tiger had sprinted a bit farther and come up to the FRH Koktoo, it might have lived. On the other hand, the dogs would have gone hungry. But that's life.

FRH Koktoo reminds me of my personal experience with wild dogs from very close quarters. I loved this FRH and frequently camped there after I took over as FD of the MTR in 1991. My visit to Koktoo was a welcome change for the staff too, who felt a bit lonely there. To draw courage, the staff had installed an idol of the god of courage – Bajrangbali Hanuman – on a masonry platform under an *amla* (*Phyllanthus emblica*) tree just in front of the kitchen. We had a watchman at Koktoo who once met me and requested me for a transfer to Paratwada, a big town. Reason? In broad daylight, he had seen a tiger sitting on the platform adjacent to the god's idol when his colleagues had gone out patrolling. Trembling behind the door of his quarters, he had watched the monster through a crevice for a good half hour, and that had indeed demoralised him. I transferred him to Paratwada to guard our campus during night.. But he continued getting nightmares of being attacked by tigers and bears and screamed and ran in the middle of night. As a consequence, he started giving me sleepless nights too, so finally, I transferred him to office duty.

Just within a kilometre from FRH Koktoo is a spot called Amrai (mango grove) Number 1. This spot has lots of old mango trees and has a perennial pool of water in the Koktoo River. It was here that I had my first proper sighting of the whistling hunters. One summer afternoon I was passing by Amrai Number 1 when I noticed something unusual. There was a female sambar standing alone in a pool of water, with the hair on its body standing erect like needles. It was mortally scared of something. I asked Hasan to stop the car and went closer. To my surprise, it did not move away, and I soon saw why. In an adjacent smaller and shallower pool, her grown-up fawn had just been killed by a pack of fourteen wild dogs who were feeding on it. They dispersed when they saw me approaching. I quickly climbed a tree which luckily had a machan and waited for them to return to the kill. In half an hour, they returned and wolfed down the entire fawn in about twenty minutes. Then they cooled off in the pool of water for some time and went away whistling. I was fortunate enough to photograph this from the treetop.

Herbivores getting terrorised by wild dogs is quite a routine feature in the forest. In search of security, these herbivores occasionally come perilously close to human beings. I have come across persons who have patted sambars on their backs from my jeep when wild dogs have been in our vicinity. The unfortunate animals often pay with their lives for this misplaced trust. The villager tells himself, 'God has sent me food at my doorstep. Why should I refuse?' and hacks the animal to death. However, carnivores getting chased by wild dogs is a relatively infrequent phenomenon. Only once have I seen a leopard getting chased in the tourism zone area near Pipalpadao. The leopard, excellent climber that it is, niftily climbed a big tree in my presence when the wild dogs persuaded it to.

An old forester had this unique experience to relate about a tiger chased down by a pack. It was February; winter was still not over, but the forest-fire season had just started. Lots of teak timber was lying in the forest. To safeguard this precious timber from fire, this forester was camping at the *padao* with some labourers. After dinner, the labourers lit small fires to keep themselves warm. They organised a bed for the forester at the centre, lit a fire for him too, and, forming a circle around him, went off to sleep. Around midnight, our hero woke up with a start because he realised that somebody was lying very close to him, brushing against his back. When he turned around, his eyes jumped out of their sockets when he saw that his bed mate under the romantic moonlight was a tiger. Oh yes, he panicked but soon recovered enough to realise that they were surrounded by a large pack of wild dogs. He woke up the labourers, who shooed away the wild dogs. After ensuring that the pack had gone off some distance, the tiger cautiously walked away in the opposite direction. After listening to this story, I was keen on getting a first-hand experience of a tiger coming very close to human being when chased by a pack of wild dogs. My wish was fulfilled surprisingly soon but not altogether first-hand.

In earlier days, we had the post of a 'dak-runner'. The person's job was to travel on feet from office to office delivering *tapal* (government letters) in remote forest areas, much the same way as a postman does. One such dak-runner was travelling alone along a jungle path. Suddenly, he noticed a tiger sitting right across the path some distance away. Following standard practice, he climbed up the nearest tree and waited for the tiger to move. Time ticked by, but the Lord of the Jungle was in no mood to oblige a mere dak-runner. Suddenly, a large pack of wild dogs arrived on the scene.

but the lord this time barked up the same tree in a flash.

Tigers do not normally climb trees, but the lord this time barked up the same tree in a flash. The wild dogs surrounded that tree but, when they noticed a human presence, soon scampered away. After ascertaining that they had disappeared, the tiger descended from its perch. After ensuring that the tiger had travelled a sufficient distance, our dak-runner too climbed down and continued his journey. When I heard of the dak-runner's adventure, I summoned him, and together, we visited the spot the next day to examine the evidence. It was a big *mahua* tree, and it bore the tiger's claw marks and body hair on its bole up to about six metres, marking the distance up to the first branch where the tiger had found its perch. The dak-runner climbed up to show where he had sat. The ground, of course, showed the footmarks of the tiger as well as the wild dogs.

The above incidents clearly show that a tiger gets terrorised by a big enough group of whistling hunters. But that does not make the tiger any less majestic. The secret of its majesty rests on many factors, courage being just one, which, in any case, it has in abundant measure. It is the sheer numbers that tilt the scales in the dogs' favour. The entire pack of *dhole*s would be nowhere when confronted with a million red ants.

16

THE MOONLIGHT TRYST

I t was the first week of January 1993, and an exercise to estimate the herbivore population was in progress in Melghat. This exercise was popularly called 'herbivore census'. The methodology adopted was of block count. The procedure required laying down sample plots and the actual counting of wild animals seen. Note was also to be taken of their droppings and footmarks as one walked up and down along the grid line. For this purpose, we had divided ourselves into fifty-odd teams, each headed by a uniformed representative of Project Tiger. Each team had six to eight members comprising mostly forest labourers and some wildlife lovers. As the movement of wild animals is conspicuous during dawn and dusk, I was insistent on the teams being in their respective plots by six in the morning. Reaching their plots on time was a tough task because the teams had to leave their respective camps around 4:30 a.m. The team had to withstand biting cold as the temperature in Melghat around that time hovered between zero and five degrees Celsius. I was personally monitoring this task through my wireless set and paying surprise visits to ensure that the exercise was carried out punctually and in right earnest.

On 6 January 1993, I left Paratwada after lunch for patrolling in our newly purchased Maruti Gypsy. As the Madhya Pradesh border was sensitive to illicit cutting and poaching, I took a rather circuitous route. From

Paratwada, I entered Madhya Pradesh and travelled through Bhaisdehi to Raipur and back to Paratwada via Semadoh. I had never travelled on this route. It was around eight at night that I was on the Raipur–Chunkhedi road when I saw a Project Tiger jeep left unattended in a dense forest. The vehicle belonged to one of our outstanding officers, Mr Ravi Wankhade, who then worked as the research officer. The driver on the jeep was Jumma Chhotu. Ravi then was a very fit person, a champion short-distance runner. Looking at the circumstances, Hasan and I were convinced that the vehicle had broken down and that Ravi and Jumma needed our help. So we both got down and together called out loudly to Ravi Wankhade. To our shock, in response, we heard the deafening roar of a tiger from about two hundred metres away. We gathered courage and kept calling. Slowly, our eyes got used to the darkness, and at a distance of about half a kilometre inside the jungle, we saw a faint light. With the aid of a powerful torch, we walked in that direction and called again. This time, we got a human response. We walked farther and were soon joined by a couple of labourers who took us to where their boss was resting.

Ravi was stretched out into his sleeping bag.

The scenario was interesting. Ravi was stretched out in his sleeping bag in a dry *naala* bed, glued to his mini transistor, listening to the news. At a distance of about ten metres, a *chulha* was lit, on which one labourer was cooking dinner, assisted by two others. Two fellows had gone for fetching water, and another two were sent to check on us, the intruders. Ravi was more in shock than I was. He wondered what had brought the FD to his beat absolutely unannounced. In fact, nobody knew my programme; nor did I know Ravi's. Ravi was not personally expected to implement but rather supervise the activity. We had accidentally bumped into one another.

I told Ravi that I was passing by, had seen his jeep deserted, and had come over to investigate. I asked him why he was camping in the open in a *naala* bed in a dense forest, particularly when there was a tiger in the vicinity. In one breath, I also insisted on taking all seven of them to the Raipur FRH. Ravi politely refused. He reminded me of my instructions to start the fieldwork at 6:00 a.m. and that if they were to stay in an FRH, they could not start the work on time. I was visibly moved to see the level of dedication of this class-one officer towards his duty. He was aware of the presence of a pair of tigers at close quarters but had preferred to stay with his team in the field. Incidentally, Ravi later got to spend a record number of years in Melghat.

A hot and tasty dinner was almost ready when I was preparing to leave for Paratwada. Ravi invited me for dinner with him, and I gleefully accepted. The menu was simple: *besan*, (ground gram), *bhakri* (thick local bread made from powdered sorghum), and some wild leafy vegetables. As there was no hot plate (*tawa*) available, the *bhakri* was roasted in the big leaves of *mahul vel*. The dinner I had that night was absolutely delicious. I often relished such simple and tasty vegetarian food in the field. While we were having our dinner, I mentioned to Ravi that I had heard the call of a tiger. Ravi told us that there were two. On being asked as to how he knew that there were two tigers, Ravi had the following story to narrate.

He said that he had seen a pair of tigers that evening in broad sunlight. His other six companions were also witness to this 'sighting'. He added that a big loner gaur had recently been killed by the pair about a kilometre away, just beside the road. I was very shocked when he told me of the utterly stupid thing he and his team had done. After seeing the tigers to their heart's content, they had all got down from the jeep, formed a human chain, and decided to walk towards the tigers to have a closer look. There was also a tacit understanding that nobody would leave the hands and break the chain and run away. The team leader was Ravi, who was wearing his running shoes. The rest of the team members were Korkoo tribal boys who were sporting *dhotis* and were barefoot.

The chain slowly and carefully moved towards the feeding tigers. When the chain reached about fifteen metres from the tigers, the male tiger put down its morsel, twitched its tail for some time, roared, and gave a mock charge towards the idiots. All rules of the game were forgotten, and the chain disintegrated into seven pieces! They turned tail and ran as fast as their legs could carry them. Interestingly, Ravi, our champion state-level sprinter, was the last one in the race. The local boys had beaten our champion sprinter hollow in flight. As expected, Ravi got a good lashing from me for what he had done. He assured me that the foolish act would not recur.

In the privacy of my mind, though, I really envied Ravi's good luck and prayed that I were as lucky. I did not want to be bunched with the two previous FDs before Mr Gogate, whose score of tiger sightings was zero during their entire tenure of four years plus. I was dying for a sighting and knew that this was my best chance. So after our dinner, we planned a visit towards the pair of tigers having their dinner.

It was Nawami (the ninth night) in the Shukla Paksha (the first fortnight), and the time was around 9:00 p.m. The moon was right above us. The situation was ideal for a moonlight sighting. I did not want to take any chances this time. Hence, I carefully selected a dark shadow on a slope just about thirty metres before the spot where we expected to see the tiger. I switched off the ignition and let the jeep roll in neutral gear for about ten metres, selected another tree, and stopped under it. While stopping, the new vehicle made a creaking sound. Then everything became absolutely quiet. Soon, we could see very clearly in the dark. It was now a battle of patience between us and the tiger. The tiger lost it by being too inquisitive. Five pairs of eyes desperately looking at the road soon saw a shadow on the road moving towards the jeep. We were all motionless and signalled to one another about the royal presence.

The boss was coming to investigate. The shadow had come as close as five metres from the jeep when I switched on the headlights. It was a huge male. Dazzled, it kept walking till it was barely five feet away from the jeep when one of us, thinking that the animal might charge at the vehicle, flashed the searchlight on the animal, which suddenly realised that it was walking into some sort of trap. In a flash, the tiger leapt into the bushes by the roadside and disappeared. The sighting must have lasted for about a minute, but it gave me happiness for a lifetime. I was saved from the ignominy of being branded as a FD who had not seen a Melghat tiger.

17

THE CAMOUFLAGED CAT

In the early nineties, the then CM of Maharashtra, Shri Sudhakarrao Naik, had come for a three-day tour of Melghat. He was keen to promote wildlife tourism in Melghat. Accordingly, the Maharashtra Tourism Development Corporation had spruced up their tourist facilities at Chikhaldara and also increased their publicity drive. I still remember their prominent ad for attracting tourists, which said, 'Come to Project Tiger Melghat to see seventy-two ferocious tigers in their natural habitat.' The result was that some tourists from Western Maharashtra started trickling into Chikhaldara and a few at Semadoh, hoping to see at least one of the promised seventy-two.

The intrinsic limitations in Melghat for poor wildlife sightings are the low tiger density basically because of limited water resources and frequent fires, the hilly, undulating terrain, lots of undergrowth, and the absence of meadows and therefore the low count of gregarious prey species like chital (except for the sporadic released population). Because of these limitations in Melghat, spotting even a hare would be cause for excitement. No wonder then that frustrated tourists bitterly criticised Project Tiger. Our minibus drivers received the brunt of tourist wrath on behalf of the department.

So we thought of carving out a separate tourism zone for Melghat. Accordingly, a flat terrain near Semadoh was selected where rigid fire protection measures were adopted, grazing banned, the movement of vehicles restricted through the construction of manned gates at strategic points, the pollarding of edible pasture species done, and a water facility, salt licks, wallows, and viewing lines created. And sure enough, one started seeing the large mammalian wildlife in this tourism zone from November onwards. The drivers of minibuses felt relieved at finally getting compliments from the tourists.

My predecessor had constructed a beautiful Nature Interpretation Centre and huts on the banks of the Sipna at Semadoh. We also provided two minibuses for tourists to move around in the tourism zone area. With this basic facility now available, even my frequency of visits to Semadoh increased. I also started holding meetings of the field staff there. It was June 1994, and I had come to Semadoh with my family. The monsoons had still not arrived in Melghat. I got busy in a meeting with the field officers. That evening, my family members, who had gone for a round of the tourism zone, had come back very excited at sighting a tiger, a rare event in Melghat, especially in broad daylight. With sightings being so difficult, photographing a tiger was then considered an impossibility. Those were the days when photography with the camera-trap technique had still not come. Though there were more than seventy tigers in the MTR, there was no photographic evidence of even one. As FD of the MTR, I would feel sad about this shortcoming. So when I got the news from my family members about a tiger sighting in the flat tourism zone area, I thought if I planned properly, I too had a chance of sighting the tiger and, with some luck, of photographing it too.

Tracking the Tiger

If one has to observe wildlife, then 'two is company, and three is a crowd'. Hence, I left for the tourism zone around five in the morning along with our driver Hasan. By the time we reached the spot, there was just sufficient light to observe around. At a place near Dunda-aam, I saw fresh tiger pugmarks on the forest dust tract. Leaving Hasan in the Ambassador car, I quickly got down and followed the trail. The air was filled with the aroma emanating from the parched soil after a light pre-monsoon shower had hit it during the night. After walking for about two hundred metres, I came across a dry *naala* on a turning.

About twenty-five metres to my right, I saw a herd of about twenty gaurs standing in a circular formation, with each one of them facing out. They seemed to be guarding a couple of calves in the middle. The gaurs had seen me; as usual, I expected them to turn tail and run away. But today they hardly took cognisance of my presence at close quarters. All this was indicative of the presence of a carnivore in the vicinity. I now began to search for an herbivore, preferably a monkey, to support me with its alarm call for locating the tiger. Suddenly, from the top of a tall tree a little ahead, abutting the road on the left, a lone langur started giving alarm calls. I looked at the langur through my binocs and realised that the langur was looking in the direction of the gaur herd, suggesting to me that the tiger was hiding in a bush near the herd; the langur could see it, and the gaurs could smell it.

Realising that I was standing alone about twenty metres from a tiger, I quickly retraced my steps and reached the safety of my car. Hasan quickly took the car where I had seen the gaur herd. Suddenly, pandemonium broke loose, and the gaurs were seen running helter-skelter in the *naala* bed. The langur had become extremely nervous, as one could make out from its body language. It had given up giving alarm calls and had got busy in reaching higher and higher on the tree, with its eyes glued in the direction of the tiger. In fact, it had reached a point where one thought that the thin branch would break and it would come crashing down. Obviously, the tiger, which was crouching so far, had come out in the open and sprung at the gaur herd. I continued in the car for some distance and encountered the panic-stricken herd rushing past the car across the road from my right to my left. After seeing the Kuvapati gaur terrorising two tigers, I was surprised to see a single tiger chasing a herd.

On the Lens

The herd had crossed the car, but the car had blocked the tiger's chase. We suddenly had to apply emergency brakes and had unintentionally deprived the tiger of its legitimate food. In the dim light, I managed to take a few photographs of the tiger at handshaking distance, saliva oozing out of its mouth, perhaps in anticipation of the mouth-watering food that it was just about to capture. I was not satisfied with the photograph as the early morning light was not sufficient for a good picture and was very keen on revisiting the spot for clicking some more.

So we went ahead up to the tourism zone gate, where Hasan and I celebrated our sighting over a piping hot cup of tea. We then picked up an old tribal watchman, Gannu Buddha (appeared to be in his seventies), for company's sake, without expecting any concrete contribution from him, and came to the spot where we had seen the tiger. It was about eight, and the sun had come up. Hasan drove; I sat by his side, the side where the tiger was expected to be seen. Gannu was sitting on the rear seat of the Ambassador car. We stopped at exactly the same spot where I had taken photographs.

Gannu suddenly stiffened and said, 'Ye dekho (Look here),' but we could not see a thing.

The motionless tiger was actually far closer to the car than we had expected. It was near my door and so well camouflaged that we could not sight it. I took some nice pictures in good sunlight with a normal lens from a distance of about two metres. It was frothing at the mouth. Gannu had earned his trip in spades. This tiger picture was later made into a poster for the wildlife week and distributed all over the state.

The 'gentleman' tiger looked at us, retreated
farther and sat near a bamboo clump

After I had taken photographs to my heart's content, we took the car
a little ahead and got down just to see how the tiger was taking it. The
'gentleman' tiger looked at us, retreated farther, and sat near a bamboo
clump, so well camouflaged that we could not spot him for quite some
time. He was a real 'cool cat', neither growling nor giving any indication
of charging. Emboldened by his behaviour, the three of us held our
hands together and ran towards him. He swiftly moved ahead and hid
himself so well that we shot past him and landed in front of a dry *naala*
bed. The tiger had tricked us in typical '*chor*–police' fashion (*chor* means

'thief'). It is because of such tricks and the excellent camouflage that this magnificent cat still survives in the Indian wilderness.

Here, I must put on record that what we tried was foolhardiness of a high order. In fact, I had taken my officer Ravi Wankhade to task for a similar foolishness in January 1993, the day of my first tiger sighting as FD of the MTR. Playing around with a tiger can misfire. We were fortunate to get away scratch free and survive to tell the story. Incidentally, I am told that Gannu is in his late nineties and narrates this story to his great grandchildren with considerable lung power.

MAGIC OF CAMOUFLAGE

A tiger sees you numerous times before you see it once!

PC: Prakash Thosre

Lost in bamboo forest?

PC: Prakash Thosre

Lurking in the grassland!

PC: Prakash Thosre

Try to locate body parts of this head

Prakash Thosre

D

THE LESSER MORTALS

So far, we have covered certain general topics that have given us idea about various locations through the map of Melghat. Locations frequented by me during my tenure in Melghat are covered in my articles under the heading 'Habitat'. Later, we covered stories related to leopards and finally about tigers. Now it is time I speak about other wild animals such as wild boars, gaurs, and sloth bears and general topics about maiden experiences in the wild, how courage helps in overcoming a difficult situation, and the special instincts of wild mothers.

18

THE DIRTY DOZEN

It was September 1994. The monsoons had still not receded. Most of our temporary earthen roads, especially in the core area of the MTR, were closed down. They were shredded by numerous rivulets running across them, and in sloped areas, they had themselves turned into temporary rivulets. The black cotton soil patches (a rare occurrence in Melghat) had become soggy, making even walking difficult. Forest roads had temporarily lost their identity, and the treeless grassy patch blended beautifully with the neighbouring forest to lose itself there.

Of course, the grass diversity on these roads was phenomenal, with grass heights varying from below the ankle to above elephant height. Given this scenario, patrolling by jeep in the core area of the MTR during this period was humanly impossible. Poachers assisted by their domestic dogs become a major threat in Melghat in the monsoons. There is no alternative to foot patrolling here in this season. As FD of the MTR, I was expected to lead from the front and would often be a part of a patrolling party, especially in such areas and in such season.

On that rainy September morning, I reached the Vairat village to start my day-long patrolling-cum-trekking expedition. This village was located at the westernmost edge of the Chikhaldara plateau, and the hill adjacent to Vairat is the highest point in Melghat (a little below four thousand feet above mean sea level). It is twenty-four kilometres from Chikhaldara. Just before one reaches Vairat, there is a saddle point with a narrow strip of road with deep, vertigo-inducing, precipitous slopes on either side. Most of the time in the monsoon, the saddle point is engulfed in thick fog, and in early winter, it is fragrant with the blooming of the abundant clematis climbers, locally called *raanjai* (*Clematis* species) or *raanmogra*.

Vairat was a village of *gaoli*s, a community who rear cattle and sell milk and milk products. The boundary of the core area then touched Vairat. Grazing in the core was banned. The *gaoli*s of Vairat found the lush green grass in the core just too tempting to stay out of. This created tension between the Project Tiger staff and the villagers of Vairat. I remember in February 1991, two tigers were poisoned to death by two offenders from Vairat. It seems that a buffalo from Vairat had gone grazing deep in a ravine in the core area and was killed by a pair of tigers. These tigers, after polishing off a part of the buffalo, had gone for drinking water when the offenders approached and poisoned the carcass by injecting a powerful insecticide in it. When the Project Tiger staff went to Vairat to arrest the offenders, the entire village had turned hostile and attacked them. Now Vairat has been relocated to make way for wildlife.

On that rainy, foggy morning, I was dropped at Vairat by a vehicle. My idea was to walk cross-country about thirty kilometres to Koha (another village which has now been relocated to make place for wildlife). Two is company, they say, and three is a crowd. It most certainly is for a walk in the forest. The fewer the people, the less the disturbance to wildlife, consequently the better the chances of sightings. So I had picked just two colleagues to give me company: Ravi Wankhade, the ACF, and Ajay Pillarisett, the RFO. Both were genuine wildlife enthusiasts. Besides, the former had an acute sense of sound, while the latter complemented him with excellent vision. I couldn't have asked for better audiovisual aid!

From the Vairat core area gate, we started walking through a thick cloud cover accompanied by a light drizzle. As we went down, the cloud cover thinned out, and we got a beautiful panoramic view of the vast area of the Melghat forests dotted with many tiny habitations, the nearest one being Kund village. This village too has been shifted now, and the entire village area has turned into a beautiful meadow. We were soon greeted by the loud melodious calls of the grey jungle-fowl. Then we cautiously crossed Bana Kapar. In the local dialect, it means 'steep slopes abounding in sloth bears'. On numerous occasions, I had seen sloth bears in this area. A couple of kilometres from the main road, there is a waterhole called Chacharda, where, the previous summer, I had been greeted by an inquisitive sloth bear standing on its hind limbs and surveying the intruder. I remember having considered dashing to the safety of my jeep a little distance away. On another occasion, I had parked my car on the main road and walked down the slope to check the water level at the Chacharda waterhole. As I was heading back, my driver Hasan, sitting at higher elevation, had alerted me on the walkie-talkie of a bear obstructing my access to the car and helped me take a detour.

Chacharda is on the right side, whereas a little ahead on the left is Kati-da, a spot where an anicut is constructed for storing water for wildlife. Both these spots are a little away from the main road and involve walking down. After Kati-da, the downward slope is divided in two prominent patches of gradual slopes over two plateaus. Once the fair-weather road is repaired, a smooth drive on these patches is indeed an enjoyable experience and is better than most of the tar roads in the rural areas. Before we reached Rangrao, the dilapidated FRH, on our left, we could observe the remnants of the last *heti* where the graziers had illegally stayed along with their cattle. By the way, FRH Rangrao was known for the ghost stories associated with it, especially that of the 'headless horseman'. Some years ago, this thatch-roofed FRH had been gutted by fire. We surveyed the plinth, the door space, and the half-fallen walls of the FRH.

Just near Rangrao, there was a waterhole called Sukalibhura, where I was told a thirsty *sukali* (wild boar) had got drowned while drinking water. A little ahead of the FRH, we came across an open space on the right where Rangrao was located. I was told that it was shifted because an epidemic had broken out. There was an old village well in the vicinity where a windmill had been installed in the past by the Project Tiger authorities to draw water for the wild animals. Near the well, I had seen an unusually luxuriant growth of *tarota* (*Cassia tora*) and *gokhru* (*Xanthium* species) in deep black cotton soil. Both these weeds are indicators of human habitation. Normally, they grow about a foot or a maximum of two feet in height, but here I was, walking through a tunnel of about ten-feet-tall *tarota* and almost-as-tall *gokhru*. I have neither seen nor heard of *tarota* growing so tall. It was the first and the last 'sighting of a lifetime' for me.

After a relaxed lunch on a wild banana leaf at Sipna-khandi ('saddle abounding in teak trees' in the local dialect), we proceeded to Gangaram-nala, where we witnessed an unusual scene: water gushing out with great force and without pumping the hand pump fitted to our bore well. Around a turning after Gangaram-nala, we passed by a huge *kadhai* gum tree, popularly called the 'fair maiden of the forest'. Its leafless looks on a moonlit night prompted some people to call it the 'ghost of the forest'. Incidentally, this tree yields excellent edible gum. Owing to excessive tapping for gum, most of the trees in the buffer area are dying, and hence, seeing such a healthy tree was a rare treat to our eyes.

As we walked through the dense forest, Ravi alerted us to a faint rustle, and soon, Ajay saw a black boulder-like structure come rolling down the hill to our right. We instinctively froze like statues in the knee-high grass on the road, closely watching through the screen of grass at the boulder's next move. It turned out to be a huge wild boar tusker that landed just about five metres ahead of us on the road. It smelt something fishy (or whatever term they have for human smell) and raised its nostrils and sniffed hard.

We instinctively froze....

We, of course, had no choice but to sit frozen. Then suddenly more rustling and rolling . . . and another . . . and yet another. We counted a dozen, each one weighing upwards of about sixty kilogrammes. Interestingly, every one of them sniffed the air, and none were able to locate us. Imagine the drama: three defenceless humans sitting within direct eye contact of a dozen beasts at very close quarters, each one capable of killing all three of them. This pantomime must have lasted for about thirty seconds. Then whether it was a whisper from one of us or a slight movement or change in wind direction, the 'boss' noted our presence. It instantly gave out a loud snort, and the whole sounder dashed away.

We waited till the sound of their departure dissolved in the jungle air and then got up and opened our thermos and ran over our singular experience. I, of course, had learnt two important lessons: one, wild animals instinctively avoid human presence, and two, playing a 'statue' in wildlife habitats can be rewarding.

19

GAURS: EXTREME MOOD SWINGS

The gaurs have short curved horns. Male gaurs grow up to six feet at shoulder height and weigh up to nine hundred kilogrammes. They have unique white stockings below the knee on all four legs. They ordinarily live in small herds of eight to twelve animals. Such a herd is essentially a family party. In quest of pasturage or because of other causes, several families may unite to form larger assemblages. I remember one such assemblage in my childhood near Mogarkasa in the Nagpur district, where I had seen a hundred-plus herd one night when I was accompanying my forester father. More than a hundred pairs of eyes glittering on a turning in the headlights of our jeep is one of my abiding childhood memories. Bulls, when mature, are given to wandering, usually in quest of grazing, generally alone. They feed on grass, leaves, and bark. They have a keen sense of smell but poor hearing and eyesight. Their huge heads, massive bodies, and sturdy limbs make gaurs an embodiment of vigour and strength. Ironically, they are very shy and avoid man. Generally found in herds, an injured or loner male can be a dangerous customer as he often charges without provocation.

Some of my personal observations about gaurs are that their calls are extremely varied. In fact, there appears to be a special call even while calling the young one lost in the forest while grazing. Second, gaurs, when encountered in a herd, tend to shy away. They disperse on a signal (snort) from the leader of the herd, who happens to be the most powerful male. In case of a solitary male, his reaction is generally to stay put. If the encounter with a human being is too sudden, then the loner may also flee, as it happened with the Banaam gaur which suddenly came to know of our presence. Third, the security of young calves is not only the individual responsibility of the mother but also the community responsibility of the herd, especially of females.

This incident was narrated by a very famous music director of Bollywood who passed away a couple of years ago. It took place in the 1960s, not in Melghat but near FRH Kolsa in the Tadoba-Andhari Tiger Reserve. The music director had shot a loner gaur and, presuming that it was dead, had instructed his younger brother to do the skinning, and he himself proceeded to the FRH to attend to the cooking. When the brother approached the gaur, he realised that the gaur was not dead but was only injured. But it was too late. The gaur attacked and killed the man so brutally that small bits and pieces of his body were required to be plucked out from the trunk of a *mahua* tree where the gaur had rammed the body. From that day, the music director gave up hunting and, on every anniversary of the tragic event, would visit Kolsa to commemorate the day when the tragic incident took place.

At another time, long back, a loner attacked a friend's old Land Rover without provocation. Those days, the imported Land Rovers had aluminum bodies. When the loner gaur dashed his head on the jeep, unfortunately, his horns penetrated the aluminum door, which came off. He carried the 'burden' on his head for about half a kilometre till he got rid of it with some difficult acrobatics. Readers would recollect how fortunate I was when, on two occasions, I narrowly escaped from a loner gaur which was at handshaking distance from me: once in a conked-off old Willys jeep and on another occasion at Banaam, while I was sleeping out in front of the protection hut, where I was about to be crushed under the hooves of a huge loner gaur.

This incident occurred in 1989, before I became the FD of the MTR, when I was posted as the DFO of Akola. I had come to Melghat to witness the experiment of modern firefighting with the help of helicopters. Taking advantage of this visit, I wanted to visit the core area of the MTR. I was on the Kund–Rangrao road when, about two kilometres from Kund, I sighted a loner male. There appeared to be something wrong with the animal because it stood absolutely motionless. I got down from my vehicle alone and walked towards the animal. It still did not move. When I reached very close, the gaur tried to run away from me but crashed. The animal must have been very unwell. It could have contracted foot-and-mouth disease, which spreads among gaurs when the habitat and the water body is shared with domestic cattle. The animal just could not get up. I immediately informed Mr Gogate, the then FD, on the wireless from Kund. He tried his best through veterinarians to save it but could not. As soon as the animal died, it was skinned. That specimen was later stuffed and made into a nice trophy. It is kept at the Semadoh Nature Interpretation Centre. It stands there even now.

I have lots of interesting stories about gaurs. But the one I narrate last is unique in the sense that the gaur either moves with a family or is a solitary male. In this case, for about a month, two old male gaurs were sighted on a regular basis at Kuvapati (*pati* meaning 'a place with water'). This area was then part of the tourism zone. It was indeed a rare partnership. At least I had not heard anything of that sort during my career. One summer day I got a message that one of these two had been killed by a tiger. Immediately, I decided to visit the site.

By the time I had reached the spot, it was already past 5:00 p.m. The kill was just adjoining Kuvapati–Chaddupati road. The tiger had eaten a portion of the gaur and was likely to return to the kill in a short time for more. Normally, I would have got a temporary machan constructed on a nearby tree to observe the tiger returning to the kill. However, there were only huge pencil-straight teak trees (each worth a couple of lakhs) and some bushes in the vicinity; hence, building a machan was impossible. In those days, I had a new open Maruti Gypsy painted in camouflage colours. I converted it into a machan. A searchlight was put in place. It was parked about ten metres away from the kill and was covered up in such a way that it looked like just another bush thanks to my ever-enthusiastic driver Neemkar. I sat motionlessly in the 'bush' and then waited for the tiger.

A ruddy mongoose was the first to visit. It nibbled at the gaur carcass and went away. Then came the gaur's friend – the other big male gaur. He stood quietly near the body of his friend as if to pay homage to the departed soul. Then suddenly, he moved to the nearby bushes and destroyed them with his hooves and horns. For a moment, I felt worried that he might uproot the 'bush' in which we were sitting. However, in a few minutes, his anger subsided. He returned to the friend's body, stood quietly as if to say his prayers, took a round of the body, and slowly walked away. The gaur must have moved just about eighty metres when a male tiger came to the carcass and started feeding.

a male tiger came to carcass and started feeding.

It was followed by a female. They were obviously too frightened of the gaur's fury to come closer to the kill while it was around. I observed the feast for more than an hour from the safety of my 'bush', amazed at the lone gaur's extraordinary courage that had kept at bay two full-grown, hungry tigers that had killed his friend.

The courage and the human sentiments shown by the gaur are etched in my mind forever. This was my longest sighting of a tiger in Melghat. I saluted the lone bison for the guts it displayed. The two tigers seemed very tiny and helpless indeed in the presence of the mighty loner. They dared not step out in the open for as long as the gaur was there. I had learnt a lesson that even wild animals have sentiments. They care for their friends too.

20

A WAKE-UP CALL

I t was the summer of 1995. I would soon be completing four years as FD of the MTR. The thought that I would soon be saying goodbye to my beloved Melghat was making me restless. I wanted to spend as much time in my patch before the monsoons arrived. Once it began to rain, the road network would be in shambles at least for the next five months. As of now, the temperature was increasing and the level of water in waterholes decreasing. Waterholes, which had become hubs of activity of wildlife, required round-the-clock vigil to guard against poachers and poisoners. The entire forest floor, with its carpet of dry leaf litter, had become as flammable as a can of petrol. With each passing month, my graph of touring days was showing a steep climb. In May, I had recorded twenty-five touring days, during which I had managed to sight two different tigers in the MTR within a span of five days. For the first time in fourteen years of my married life, I was spending my wedding anniversary visiting waterholes with weird names like Gurgipati, Bhatibonga, Talaam, Dokra-aam, and so on.

It was a sizzling-hot day on 11 June 1995. The afternoon temperature in the shade was about forty-six degrees Celsius. The previous two nights had seen me sleep in my car and on a machan top. Today I had decided to sleep more comfortably in a bamboo protection hut at Banaam. Located in the midst of thick forest, this spot has a couple of old mango trees abutting a waterhole in the rocky bed of the Gadga. To ensure that wild animals coming to quench their thirst did not get disturbed, an elegant bamboo hut was constructed – with local material as well as talent – a little distance away from the perennial water source. The nearest village was Koha, which has been relocated to provide an undisturbed habitat for the tiger. It was just a twenty-odd-minute drive between Koha and Banaam, but I was treated to a feast in the form of 'sightings', including a nuclear bear family with just one cub accompanying parents and no less than five gaur herds, something unusual for Melghat. The last time I had visited this spot in the evening, there had been no gaur sightings. It had just been a variety of owls on the roadside trees, enough to make it look like an owl safari. Just about two hundred metres before the Banaam hut, I saw a huge loner gaur grazing just about twenty metres away from the dust track on which I was driving and wondered, *This six-hundred-kilogramme beast could be more dangerous than the sum total of all the five herds put together!*

It had become totally dark by the time I reached Banaam. I got down from my jeep and took a deep breath, soaked up the ambience, listened to the sound of silence, and looked up to admire a clear star-filled sky. *Wow! So much happiness – all free of cost!* The bamboo protection hut, with a lantern lit inside it, was a perfectly artistic creation made out of local material: poles, bamboos, and grass. Transversely cut pieces of teak logs were partially buried and fixed in front of the hut to make a sitting arrangement for the field staff. The local craftsman had also made two roughly finished relaxing chairs out of bamboo and fixed them to the ground lest they got stolen.

The local forester arrived within minutes and saluted. He was a tall well-built man by the name of Khan. On my insistence, he sat on the stool, and we started talking. Khan was from the plains of the Amravati district. He had completed three years in the present posting and was longing to go back to the plains as he had to marry off his daughters. His immediate concern, however, was for my safety. He had heard the call of a *shaitan* (devil) from the nearby *amrai* a little while ago. He was sure it was a bad omen and that I should reconsider my plans of staying in at Banaam. I cross-checked to confirm that Khan was serious and meant every word that he had uttered. So I suggested we remain silent and try to hear the fellow. After about five minutes of pin-drop silence, we heard the call. It was a deep *boom-o-boom*, a call unique to the brown fish owl (*amrai ka ghuggu*). It took a fair bit of time to make Khan change his opinion, and I thought I had convinced him.

After a long day in the field, I was feeling a little tired and very hungry, and in such a situation, the food always tastes very delicious. I tucked it in ravenously and went for a fifteen-minute post-dinner walk towards the Banaam waterhole. The brown fish owl had ceased calling, and crickets had intensified their chorus. The terrain was flat and rocky. Wherever the soil was available, grassy patches had come up. These grassy patches in rocks had been intentionally burnt in the winter, because of which an early green flush had appeared.

The rock wouldn't let the temperature really come down; it must have been around forty-three degrees Celsius at ten at night. So I decided to sleep out in the open. Accordingly, the rocky bed was swept clean of ants, centipedes, scorpions, and so on. To sight bigger creatures like, say, snakes, a dimly lit lantern was kept beside my repositioned sleeping bag. Neemkar fixed his bed a few metres away from mine. Before bidding me good night, Khan had fetched my walking stick with a spear at one end and kept it near my bed. The *shaitan* was still bothering him, I thought. I passed it on to Neemkar and fell asleep gazing at the sky.

It was well past midnight when both of us woke up to a slight rustle somewhere. Lying down, we tried to locate the source that had woken us up. By the moonlight, both of us simultaneously located the source: it was a shining black wall which stood about three metres away from us. It was the six-hundred-kilogramme gaur. Here, we lay helplessly on the ground, and the huge wild bull, unaware of our presence, was munching happily and, in the process, inching towards us.

...was munching happily...

Even an accidental tap on our body would have resulted in crushing us to a paste. I whispered to Neemkar to pass me the spear. Neemkar only smiled, thinking it was a joke. Our weapon couldn't have given the fellow anything more than a scratch. The bull, which was too focussed on feasting on the green fodder in the summer, totally missed out on our whispers. So far, the breeze was blowing from the gaur towards us. In about three minutes, the bull had grazed to within a few feet of us. Suddenly, the wind changed direction, and it got a whiff of our bodies. It raised its head, paused for a fraction of a second, gave a loud snort, and dashed away from us. The impact of the hooves over the rocky surface made a sound ominous enough to prompt Khan and our cook to rush out towards us, suspecting that something terrible had happened. They were relieved to see us in one piece. It was already thirty minutes past four, and I had a long day ahead, so we got busy preparing to move out.

As my Gypsy was about to move, Khan sidled up to me and whispered in my ears, 'Sir, dekha aapney, shaitaan kya kar sakta hai? (See what the devil is capable of?)' I did not know where to look.

21

UNPROVOKED ATTACK

I had three tenures in Melghat spanning a little more than six years, during which I have travelled more than 150,000 kilometres in Melghat alone. Many a time, the travel was on foot, cross-country, and through dense forests abounding in wildlife. We never carried any weapons. Hence, I was frequently asked questions like 'Aren't these wild animals dangerous?' 'Why don't you carry guns with you in areas infested with wild animals?' 'Don't you feel scared?' My simple answer was 'The streets of any large city in our country are more dangerous than these wildlife areas'. It is a fact that most creatures of the wild are scared of human beings and avoid human presence. Confrontation with human beings is their last option, resorted to only in grave crises, basically arising out of security for the young ones or their own selves or when a carnivore is so disabled that it can't procure its natural prey. Of course, if you are stupid enough to disturb a feeding tiger or a tigress with cubs, then you are asking for trouble. Also, due care has to be taken if you are dealing with a loner herbivore – a gaur or a wild boar.

As a rule, there is no unprovoked attack in the wild. The sloth bear is an exception to the rule as it attacks without any apparent provocation.

The Korkoos of Melghat are scared of only one wild animal, and that is the sloth bear. In the local dialect, they call it *bana*. There is a line in their morning prayer which says, 'God, don't let me come across a bear today.' During my tenure as FD of the MTR, we used to have five or six serious bear mauling cases annually in my area. Most of the victims were disfigured beyond recognition, the injuries being basically on the head, face, and chest. Some of the attacks result in the death of the victim, as it happened once at Hurricane Point at Chikhaldara, where a woman tourist died on the spot in a ferocious bear attack. One of my senior colleagues, Mr Singh, had a distinct dislike for bears. His driver Gulab told me that once, while Sahib was driving, he ran over a bear just out of dislike.

It is said that bears are short-sighted. A hazy human figure is taken for the enemy, and the rule they follow is 'attack is the best defence'. Unlike other wild animals, bears are quite unpredictable. They often begin a charge and abort the idea for no apparent reason. I have known of a case on the Chikhaldara–Vairat road where a pair of bears had attacked a bunch of about a dozen persons returning from the weekly market and injured each one of them. In stark contrast was the bear my driver Neemkar and I had encountered, drinking water at the Chacharda waterhole a little ahead of Vairat. It stood on its hind legs as if to attack, but before we could run to the safety of our Gypsy, it suddenly changed its mind, got back to its four-legged stance, and ran away from us. It is also said that the bear is a noisy walker, and if you are walking quietly, you can hear it before it sights you.

I had a first-hand experience of the unpredictable behaviour of bears. It was a December morning in 1994, and I was at the Koktoo FRH. I had particularly enjoyed walking in all directions from this FRH, travelling each valley and footpath. It was time for a repeat of my favourite excursions. The pleasure of observing wildlife while on a walk is much greater than doing so from the safety of a jeep/car. It was one of those bracing mornings, and I had arranged to walk along with my team on the Koktoo–Bori road. My open Gypsy would follow about a kilometre behind, close enough to reach me in less than three minutes at a message from the walkie-talkie.

I had for company our trusted tracker Surajpal, Prachi Mehta, a senior research fellow from the WII in Dehradun, and Forester Jamunkar (the name is changed). Surajpal had a small axe in his hand and a thermos round his shoulder. Bespectacled Prachi had a bird book in one hand and a pair of binoculars in the other. Jamunkar was a well-built person in uniform, and he carried a walkie-talkie in his hand. It was a beautiful morning with a little chill in the invigorating, unpolluted air. Our excursion began in total silence. Initially, we had for company only the sound of big sporadic dew drops coming down from the leaves of tall trees and hitting the soil. Later, this sound was drowned by the shrill calls of spotted owlets followed by that of the grey jungle fowl. As our team crossed Hatti-kund, we had a couple of good sightings of flying squirrels. It was fun watching them feed on the young leaves of miscellaneous tree species. They would travel towards the summit of the tree and then glide about eighty to a hundred metres and alight softly on a bough or the trunk of a tree. They would feed at the summit and glide again to reach the base of the next desirable tree species. One wondered how this utterly tree-dependent animal survived devastating forest fires.

Then we crossed the Dendra-khora. In Korkoo language, *dendra* means 'crabs', and *khora* means 'valley'. Indeed, true to its name, this valley abounded in king-sized crabs. The sun was about to rise, and slowly, a variety of other birds had started joining in with their specific calls, making the orchestra unique. The golden rays of the winter sunlight had just entered the Koktoo valley. A little ahead after the next turn was a natural salt lick which we had supplemented with coarse salt and mixed up with the soil. This is the place where I was anticipating some herbivore sighting, and right enough, as we approached the turning, we sighted a huge male sambar with majestic antlers licking salt at the salt lick.

I was enjoying the scene through my mini-binocs, particularly the clouds of breath puffing out of the sambar on that wintry sunny morning, when suddenly, the view was blocked by a mountain of black hair. It was a bear doing the blocking. It was on its hind limbs and was charging towards us. The beast had long nails and was making funny sounds and frothing as it grunted. Within no time, it had closed in on us from fifteen metres to about five.

Aage aaya to saale ko fod dalunga.

Now watch the positioning of our team. Surajpal had quickly come in front of me and was reassuring me that I need not worry and that he would split the beast into pieces with his toy axe. Jamunkar had ducked behind me and was breathing heavily, sweating profusely, tugging at my hand, and urging me to run before it was too late.

The most chilled-out person was also the closest to the bear, still looking at it through the pair of binoculars and delightfully finding the charging beast 'a beautiful animal!' In that frozen moment, lot of things ran through my mind. If the charge was to be translated into a mauling, Prachi would have been the first one to get hit. As her local guardian, how best to ensure Prachi's safety was the thought in my mind during that fraction of a second.

Perhaps looking at our body language, the bear came down on all its four limbs and just disappeared into the forest. We were hugely relieved, and Jamunkar instantly got busy informing our driver Nimkar, urging him to come soon. We had not moved a single step – nor had we spoken a word – when suddenly, the bear reappeared, back on its two hind limbs, and charged. Fortunately, it again turned out to be a bluff, and then it again disappeared, this time for good. That was the first and the last time a wild animal had ever charged at me, however mockingly. In hindsight, I thought it was a wise decision not to listen to Jamunkar and try to run. The bear would most likely have been provoked into chasing us and mauling us. Did our standing firm do the trick? I would think so.

Now let us imagine a situation where the bear had not only charged but also attacked us. Had it done that, it would have invited huge trouble upon itself. I say so because more than two decades after the incident, I still remember Surajpal's confident body language. Flourishing his tiny axe, he had whispered in my ears, 'Sahib, ghabraneka nahi! Aage aaya to saale ko fod dalunga,' meaning, 'Sir, don't be afraid! If the bloody fellow comes forward, I will split it open.' It was not an empty threat. He was in a murderous mood and would have implemented what he was saying. His words still ring in my ears. Such raw courage and loyalty are difficult to come by today.

E

THE BRAVEHEARTS

T hanks go to my predecessors, Mr Ghanekar in particular, who did the recruitment of the frontline staff of Project Tiger. Each hand-picked member of the Project Tiger team was a gem. This bunch of hundred was equal to about five hundred elsewhere. These dedicated gems made my work easy. It is impossible to pick and choose the outstanding ones. Here, I present the glimpse of extraordinary work done by some field officers for the readers to get an idea of their dedication to duty.

22

CHILD OF THE WILD

C handar Khadke is his real name, but for most of us, he is just Chau. He worked as watchman in the FRH Koktoo and would cook for me when I stayed there. He used to stay in Bori (a village now shifted) and was a professional grazier who would graze his cattle around Koktoo during the pre–Project Tiger days. For this reason, he knew the Koktoo valley inside out. He is the same person who had searched out my predecessor, Mr Ghanekar, and his team (including the elephant) who had gone missing in the Koktoo forests. Today, after thirty-five years, Chau still believes firmly that they lost their sense of direction as they had crossed Bhulanvel. Chau sometimes accompanied me during my excursions from FRH Koktoo. During such outings, Chau would open up and reveal his treasure of interesting jungle experiences. However, on one occasion, I became a part of an interesting story which he must be narrating to the guests staying in Shahanoor FRH, where he works now.

I had heard much about the porcupine burrow from my forester Giri, who claimed to have crawled into it and was fortunate to return alive. For the less fortunate ones – mainly the poachers, who do not know how to crawl back – the burrow turns into a grave. Giri used to vividly describe the various chambers inside the burrow and had strongly recommended that I see at least the storeroom, which can be safely viewed as it is near the mouth of the burrow. Chau had been telling me that there was a nearby spot where he could show me a burrow in occupancy. (I had earlier seen deserted burrows.) During one of my stays at FRH Koktoo, I decided to visit the porcupine burrow at Chatubanda. I decided to take Chau along with me. Two of my DFO colleagues, Ashraf and Krishna Mohan, also decided to join me for the excursion.

Chatubanda's unique feature is that there is a big *naala* with a dead end at a spot where, in the rainy season, water falls from a great height, resulting in a picturesque waterfall. The location of the nest was typical of a porcupine. It was located on a precipitous slope abutting the *naala* at a height of about thirty-five to forty feet from the *naala* bed. Animals prefer such a situation to dissuade predators and poachers from coming too close. It was February, and the *naala* bed was dry and had lots of boulders. The slope by the sides of the *naala* bed had a cushioning of dry grass, which made the surface deceptively slippery. One look at our destination made it look like a hole drilled into the side wall of the *naala*. There were three to four prominent trails, converging towards the hole, indicative of the routes followed by the hosts for commuting to and from the nest. The trampling of grass in the grassy patch had highlighted the trails. As I prepared myself for climbing up towards the porcupine nest, my colleagues preferred to take a stroll along the dry *naala* bed through the boulders. I climbed up the steep slope with the help of my multipurpose stick inherited from my forester father. It had a sharp spear at one end. The last five metres of the climb were rather steep and slippery. I climbed carefully without looking back. Soon, I reached the mouth of the porcupine burrow.

The burrow was roughly circular, about one and a half feet in diameter at its mouth, from where I could see about three feet inside. The inspection of its mouth showed that the nest was in use because it had no cobwebs. I could also see at the entrance the tiny foot marks of the hosts and could collect a couple of shed quills as souvenirs. About half a foot inside on the right, there was a shallow pit. This is what Giri had called the storeroom. There were a couple of gnawed bones in a fashion typical of a member of the rodent family and small pieces of shed antlers of deer. My long-cherished desire was fulfilled. I looked down, where I could see both my colleagues looking up at me and signalling me to be cautious while descending.

I looked up and was surprised to see one of our fittest foresters, Dongre, hovering there. He had obviously come to pay his respect to me and had taken a different route to reach about fifteen to twenty feet above the porcupine burrow. As he tried to salute me from a precariously cramped position, he slipped on the dry grass, and before I could even suck my breath, he zipped past me towards the dry *naala* bed with boulders. Neither I nor Chau had any chance of catching him. We both were sure that he was going down to go 'up', or if he was frightfully lucky, then we would see him in hospital with life-threatening injuries. With a lot of effort, I looked down. To my relieved surprise, I saw Dongre hanging on to dear life by a tiny but deep-rooted shrub. The scene appeared to be straight from Bollywood. Some help was organised for rescuing Dongre, who reached the *naala* bed with some minor bruises but was quite shaken up. I do not recollect who rescued Dongre and how he was rescued because I was in a tight corner myself.

...I saw Dongre hanging on to dear life by a tiny but deep-rooted shrub.

Seeing an excellent jungle walker and an expert in jungle craft skidding past me had really made me feel nervous, and I sat down at the mouth of the burrow. Having lost my confidence, I started trembling and refused to go down on that slippery slope. Efforts from all my colleagues, including the injured Dongre, just failed to boost up my morale. As I sat at the mouth of the porcupine's burrow, a stray thought also entered my mind: what if, after hearing the commotion at its door steps, the head of the family comes out to investigate and thinks about admonishing the intruders? In the later part of my service, it actually happened with me when an annoyed hyena mother gave me a mock charge at the mouth of its burrow. Only those who have undergone a similar experience can imagine my state of mind.

Chau, who was a mute witness so far, sprang into action and took my spear-headed walking stick. With the help of that spear, he dug into the difficult steep patch and constructed some ten to fifteen steps for me. He made me reverse my stance (facing towards the earth), went down a few feet, held my foot, and placed it on the step. He did that for each step till I had descended the steep slope. All the while, Chau was as exposed to the danger of slipping as I was. I am grateful to him. I am still in touch with Chau, who is working as a *khansama* in FRH Shahanoor.

Incidentally, on two other occasions later in service, I had opportunities – one each in the Nashik district (Anjaneri-western *ghat*s) and in the Pune district (Tamhini-western *ghat*s) – to catch hold of my field team members who were uncontrollably going down past me. In the former case, it was my colleague in his early forties, Mr Vispute, who was walking parallel to me at a higher level. As he was temporarily unsighted, I paused and made a casual enquiry about him to somebody who was overenthusiastic. He immediately overreacted and yelled at Vispute, saying that I had called him immediately. In his effort to reach me quickly, he moved towards me rather swiftly across the contour. Soon, Vispute gathered momentum and lost control over his speed and was about to go down the valley when I caught him by literally embracing him and swirling around.

In the second case, the person who landed in trouble was a very young wiry forester named Dorge. That day, we had been trekking for almost ten hours and reached a high point in the western *ghat* from where I got an excellent shot of the sunset. Our plan was to descend two thousand feet into Konkan, where we had called the car. It was then that my local staff lost the way. To ensure that the boss was not inconvenienced, everybody was running about, searching for a footpath going down. It was during this rush that the forester had slipped from about thirty feet above me. This time, out of reflex, I caught him by his collar as he was going down. Unfortunately, when he slipped, he hit a rock, which uprooted a pair of his incisors in the upper jaw. He was so stunned that he was not aware of leaving little bits of himself up there. He was bleeding profusely from the wound, and we had to rush him for medical help, keeping a hanky pressed between his jaws to stop the blood flow. He later got excellent artificial teeth fitted, and most of his colleagues do not even know about the mishap. He is now promoted and is working as RFO of Saswad near Pune.

23

SURAJPAL

I love chatting up with young foresters and always share with them a piece of wisdom I have gained in the jungle: make friends with the local person, no matter if he is totally illiterate. Snubbing a local is suicidal; boasting that, as a trained forester, you know everything is worse because cockiness in the jungle can give you experiences worse than death. You switch the local off forever, and you deprive yourself of all the knowledge that virtually runs in his blood. On the contrary, if you encourage him, he lays out for you the entire wealth of knowledge that his tribe has been gathering for generations. You must give scope to the local person to open up as he is a reservoir of information. I can claim with all humility – and pride too – that my best teacher in the field of practical issues encountered by a wildlife manager was an illiterate person whose debt I acknowledge even as I write. Without him, I may not have known a teak from a tamarind or a crow from a cockerel. Recognising the call of a grey jungle fowl or of a peacock or partridge or reading the pugmarks of various carnivores or their scats would have taken me several lives.

Meet Surajpal, who was recruited as a wildlife tracker but doubled up as the watchman of the FRH. He was a gifted cook too. Originally a man of few words, he would really open up and share his practical knowledge with me. While accompanying me in the field, he would display multiple facets of his personality: guide, bodyguard, botanist, naturalist, and extraordinary interpreter of various signs and symbols in nature.

For an occasional visitor, Koktoo is quite a paradise, but a longish stay there makes the attractions turn pale. Spending a three-year tenure there has been nothing short of a punishment for many forest guards. Living away from their families, with nobody to talk to in the remoteness of a jungle abounding in wild animals, turns some into manic depressives. So many have come, and all those many have gone, but Surajpal stays on. I have seen him work there in 1991, and he is still working there today in 2019.

Running a double establishment is a bane in Melghat. Many foresters stay alone in that remote place and keep the family where an education facility for their children is available. They generally go back to visit their family once in a month or two, often immediately after collecting their monthly salary. Once, I was walking in the jungle, and Surajpal gathered courage to talk to me on the delicate issue of salary. He said that for some reason, he had not received his monthly salary for the last six months. Entering home without his salary was asking for trouble, so he hadn't gone home for a long time, he confided in me with the innocence of a child. Of course, his salary was soon released, and he patched up the bruised relationship with his wife. This childlike, shy, sub-five-foot personality would morph into a maestro once out on a day-long trek.

It used to be a long day for Surajpal when I took him on a field visit to the Banapoi ('water point for bear') or Dokra-aam waterhole near the Chipi anicut or a tough climb to Chiladari or Gugamal and back. He would get up very early, serve me tea, bring hot water to my bathroom, prepare and pack breakfast and lunch for me, and be ready with his backpack in front of the rest house at daybreak. Proudly wearing his camouflaged dress, sporting a tiny axe in his hand and a determined expression on his face, Surajpal would be a totally transformed personality. His innocent looks would be replaced by the looks and body language of a soldier leaving for the battlefield.

The typical excursion would often begin with the sighting of a flying squirrel in the wee hours. Then with the first sunrays, the activities of various birds would start. Then we would check for fresh nail marks of bears trying to reach for the beehive on the *arjun* (*Terminalia arjuna*) trees beside the river Koktoo. How to differentiate the pugmarks of a big leopard from those of a tiger cub, the hooves of a gaur from those of cattle, the scats of a leopard from those of wild dogs, how to make out from the pugmarks whether a tigress is pregnant – all practical aspects in the field would be discussed. Seeing us hang around a bit too long towards the beginning of our long trek would prompt Surajpal to gently remind me that it would be dark by the time we climbed down in the evening. He knew that one wrong step in dark in the undulating terrain could give us broken bones. He often had a stopover spot ready in his mind even before the excursion began – a scenic spot, often by the side of a waterfall where all of us could quench our thirst. During breakfast, in his own modest way, he would tell us to listen carefully to the whistle of a wild dog or a leopard's grinding call or the bark of a deer.

Sitting with him on a machan and observing wild dogs on their kill was an unforgettable treat for me. Because of my presence, the wild dogs had left a fresh kill and dispersed in the forest. I summoned my man who sat with me and, like a fortune teller, went on predicting the course of events. The pack would return in half an hour. It did. The alpha male would start the party. You bet the fellow did. They would then sit down in the water to cool themselves. He foretold their departure time to the minute and even predicted the sequence in which they would jog out. And finally, Surajpal said, 'Let there be some whistling,' and by god, that was some whistling! An utterly masterly, mesmerising performance! Both by the pack and by our man!

On one such walking excursion, we were examining a tiger trail. We all agreed it was a fresh trail. Surajpal was very certain that it was a very fresh trail and the tiger had just passed from where we were standing. Ten minutes back, the motorcyclist carrying fresh milk for us to FRH Koktoo had passed the spot, and the pugmarks, Watson, were on the bike tyre marks. The tiger had to be nearby, said Surajpal, and pretty much cocked his ears. Immediately, a loud roar came from very close quarters. With the agility of a monkey, Surajpal shimmied up a nearby tree and started surveying the neighbourhood for the tiger. Soon, he located the animal in the dry bed of Koktoo River and urged me to come up. Realising that I was not as well made for the ramrod-straight tree as he was, he came down in a flash and guided us towards tiger. Greedily, we rushed for the tiger, but the animal was in no mood to entertain us. Disgusted with the racket that we had created while stamping on the dry leaf litter, it just disappeared among the leaves. It is this vanishing trick that has helped this magnificent cat survive in the wilderness.

Walking in the forest is always an enjoyable experience, except for certain seasonal problems. Once, I had gone walking in the rains wearing shorts, thinking that crossing flooded *naala*s would be easier. But the bloodsucking flies had literally bled me by attacking my exposed legs. It was Surajpal again who had applied the juice of an herb, calling it his tincture of iodine. I remember in the same tour, I had expressed my desire to photograph the enigmatic *bhulanwel* in fruiting. After a lot of effort, he had searched out a fruiting specimen hidden deep under some vegetation and earned my gratitude along with a little tip for himself. Another seasonal hazard was in November in the form of the spiny dried seeds of *kusal* grass. This grass grew gregariously in pockets. The dried seeds would poke into the socks and get embedded into the skin, making walking difficult. Surajpal would remove the *kusal* from my socks from time to time. Once, while he was sitting on the steps of the Koktoo rest house, removing *kusal*s from my socks, he was replying to the queries of Dr Dhore, the famous taxonomist who specialised on the flora of Melghat. Surajpal supplied the eminent Dr Dhore with a month-wise timetable of the plant species from which honeybees collected nectar. The scholar had got himself an entire annual chart from my illiterate friend even before all the *kusal*s had been plucked out from my socks.

It was Surajpal who had told me that a tiger may kill a leopard and eat it too, but killing a bear and eating it too is a difficult task. I was, of course, deeply sceptical and probably showed it. One day he came up triumphantly and dragged me to two tiger scats to prove his point. Once, near Dhondriaam, Surajpal also showed me very fresh tiger scat with very prominent long bear hair. But it isn't always that the tiger wins. A close friend observed an interesting drama in the Panna National Park in Madhya Pradesh. Through his binoculars, he was looking at a tiger cave in which a tiger had just entered. After a while, a bear entered the same cave. The place reverberated with the sounds they made during the intense battle. After about fifteen minutes, my friend saw a battered and bloodied tiger leave the cave in defeat!

Surajpal, who once saved my life from a bear attack by putting his life in danger, still continues at the same post where I had bid him goodbye some twenty-four years ago. For his excellent work and for showing him the elusive tiger in Melghat, the secretary to the governor honoured him with a coat on behalf of the Honorable Governor of Maharashtra. Surajpals exist everywhere. It is just a matter of identifying them, keeping egos strictly at bay, and making them talk. There's no better way of knowing the forest. Or does this principle apply to everywhere else in the world too?

24

PRACHI,
A COURAGEOUS GIRL

It was almost one year since I had taken over as FD of the MTR, and now I had really settled down in my chair. One day I got a phone call from my dear friend Vishwas Sawarkar of the WII in Dehradun. He informed me that he proposed to send three lady researchers to Melghat to work for their PhD study. He said that he preferred Melghat because I was there and that the young ladies would get all support from the Forest Department, be it accommodation, security, or various permissions. I consented, and soon, they landed up in my office, with their equipment in tow.

The lady JRFs were Azra Musavi, Prachi Mehta, and Sonali Pandit. Azra was a sociologist, Prachi an ornithologist, and Sonali a botanist. It was arranged to lodge them in our tourist complex at Semadoh. I delivered a brief sermon to the girls. Basically, I told them not to venture out alone in the forest, especially at night, not to go out with strangers nor accept lifts, and so on. All the time, Prachi was nodding extra sincerely, trying to conceal a mischievous smile. I organised a government transport for them and sent them to Semadoh.

In the bureaucracy, it is said that a person's reputation reaches before the person lands up. Prachi was no exception. She had earlier worked in the remote areas of the Bori wildlife sanctuary across the border in Madhya Pradesh. This area then boasted of the highest density of ungulates in India. The sanctuary also abounded in a sizeable number of tigers and other carnivores. Riding a mo-bike on muddy paths of the dense forest, either alone or with an assistant on the pillion, was supposed to be Prachi's forte. Very dedicated, sincere, and hard-working, she loved her work. Good. But what worried me as her local guardian was her bold and carefree attitude, bordering on daredevilry.

The Semadoh tourist complex had twelve self-contained huts located on the bank of the river Sipna. Amazingly, these huts were constructed in dense forests without felling a single tree. The three of them were allotted a self-contained hut. Being in the forest, these huts harboured a variety of rats, which were followed by the rat snake. Word soon got round that Prachi had domesticated and kept a large snake as a pet and to shoo away any prospective intruder. Other visitors to the hut would be a variety of mosquitoes, some centipedes, and, very rarely, scorpions.

The three researchers first moved together, but later, their fields of interest often made them proceed in different directions. Each was provided a local assistant by the WII. A Gypsy jeep had arrived too from Dehradun. Among the three, Prachi was the most enthusiastic. Soon, she made friends with local staff members: the officers, the forest guards, the watchmen, the trackers, and the drivers. Taking help and support from these friends, Prachi would venture out in the field irrespective of whether the Gypsy was available to her or not. These friends kept me in the loop. They enjoyed narrating in great detail the adventures of Prachi. One feedback I got was that she would alone venture to take a lift in unknown trucks. This upset me, and that's perhaps the only time when I gave Prachi a piece of my mind. Otherwise, she got along splendidly. All of us were hugely impressed with this city girl moving fearlessly among wild animals and gelling so well in the remote tribal areas of Melghat.

Prachi and her husband, Jayant Kulkarni, who is a former IFS officer, have established an NGO in Pune to continue their work on wildlife research and conservation. She is an eternal Melghat lover – *Melghati*, a term fondly used for those who continue their association with Melghat even after their formal association ceases. Though about twenty years have elapsed since she finished her fieldwork on ornithological studies for her PhD, she has constantly remained in touch with Melghat. She and Jayant continue to do a lot of research projects there. I am a *Melghati* too. During the last two decades, I have kept visiting Melghat on one pretext or the other, and every visit has been a refreshing experience. Chatting with the old field staff and reliving the Melghat days is what I look forward to when I visit Melghat. Prachi too does that, I suppose. Prachi and I have independently made special efforts to sight the elusive Melghat tiger. When we met up, we would often compare our tiger-sighting scores.

I remember one occasion when her mission misfired. I had come over to Semadoh for camp with my family. The next morning, my ten-year-old daughter, Deepika – who, by then, had become Prachi's fan – decided to go for a field excursion with Prachi. Thanks to the new 'guide' (a young tribal boy), they lost their way in the forest, and the two-hour walking excursion towards 'Halduballa' stretched into a ten-hour ordeal, during which they had a bear sighting too. A search party was about to start for them when both these girls touched the Semadoh–Chikhaldara road that evening, thirsty, hungry, and tired. I saw Prachi on the back foot for the first time. She must have been wondering how I would react to the ordeal my daughter had undergone. Incidentally, after about twenty-five years, when I asked Deepika about the incident yesterday, the entire incident appeared to be permanently etched in her memory. For the first time, Deepika admitted that they were perilously close to a bear.

Prachi was extremely courageous and seemed to love living life on the edge. Once, while she was driving through the tourism zone area, her Gypsy conked off, and she spent the whole night alone in the vehicle. She has recorded in an article the ambience, the moonrise, and a curious bear trying to peep inside the jeep through the glass window shield. On another occasion, she sat alone on a tiger kill in a hammock right through the night, waiting for the tiger to return to the kill. On numerous occasions, I was a witness to Prachi's daredevilry. Once, we were having breakfast at FRH Koktoo when suddenly, we heard the alarm call of a sambar. Not caring for my cold response, Prachi almost ran into the forest along with a watchman. After about half an hour, she was back with a beaming face. Hiding behind a lantana bush, she had seen a mother leopard along with two cubs – a very dangerous proposition indeed!

On another occasion, a sloth bear rushed out of a bush, stood on its hind limbs, and charged twice on the four of us: Prachi, a forester, Surajpal, the watchman, and me. Prachi was in the forefront. We were excited but a bit tense. I was furiously doing emergency plans in my head. We all stood our ground, and Prachi remained cool as a cucumber. The bear decided to resume its walk after putting us on notice. Prachi is an excellent professional. Among other achievements, she reported the sighting of the black-capped kingfisher in Melghat, a bird which, till then, was reported only from coastal areas and is known to migrate only a few kilometres inland along the creeks. She is an outstanding person too. She has left an indelible mark on the minds of many. All her acquaintances in Melghat still talk about her qualities as a person and a professional.

....Deepika....decided to go for field excursion with Prachi.

25

UNSUNG HEROES

I am a *Melghati* who enjoyed three very successful tenures in Melghat. Much of my success may be attributed to my outstanding colleagues and the frontline field staff that included drivers, illiterate trackers and watchmen, and the local tribals besides the usual retinue of rangers, foresters, and forest guards. They sweated it out, and I got the credit. They voluntarily risked their lives to give me an 'out of this world' experience. They groomed me and made me walk in the field fearlessly. They taught me to read and interpret the jungle, something which neither any training academy nor any of my bosses had taught me. Most of them worked very dedicatedly, separated from their families, in remote forest areas with just trees and animals as their companions. Though some were illiterate, they were my teachers in the field craft. We patrolled together, stayed together in huts, and ate our meals together in the field. I respected their word and encouraged them to talk. They are my unsung heroes. The list is long, but here, I offer a representative sample.

Somji, the Master Night-walker

Somji Babya Kasdekar was his full name. But everyone knew him as Somji Patel. He was the Patel of the Tarubanda village. Clad in a white *dhoti*, *kurta*, and turban, Somji was simplicity personified. He was dark and had white protruding teeth and conspicuous wrinkles on the forehead. He was always barefoot and wore an endearing (and substantial) smile. Though we had some differences, I appreciated the positive side of Somji's personality. He knew the Melghat forest very well. He was a barefoot botanist who had excellent traditional knowledge of the flora. He was a *bhumka*, and his word was respected not only in Tarubanda but in the neighbouring villages too. During my early days (1979), he provided me with guidance as well as labourers for my fieldwork: nursery, plantation, timber extraction, patrolling, and firefighting or wildlife management. He would be summoned when a VIP visited my range. During the time when hunting was permitted, he would organise trips for the *shikaris*.

What amazed me about this magician was his capacity to walk alone in the forest at night. I have seen him leaving Tarubanda after dinner, barefoot, alone, for attending meetings at Chikhaldara, where he would reach by morning. After finishing work in Chikhaldara, he would leave after dinner and be back at Tarubanda the next morning. This means he used to traverse unshod about ninety kilometres, two nights running, across extremely dense forest abounding in deadly denizens such as tigers, leopards, and bears. Nobody knew his age, but the stories he recounted of the *gora sahib*s (white masters) made me estimate his age at seventy. He taught me jungle craft.

Ironically, this hero of mine died in a road accident on the streets of Delhi, where he had gone to attend a political rally. His *lamjana/ ghar-jamai* (son-in-law), who stays in his house now, had come to FRH Tarubanda to meet me during my last visit there in 2015.

Courageous Jaju

Readers would recollect Jaju as the tribal boy from Semadoh (*simba* in Korkoo means 'jungle fowl', and *doh* means 'deep water in a riverbed'), who, on a rainy night, sat perched on a tree alone in the jungle where a leopard mother, an expert tree climber, separated from her cubs was at large. He was our wildlife tracker. I did not spend much time with Jaju in the field but would have interaction with him whenever I camped at Semadoh. He was a simple, courageous person who knew how to read the jungle. He had a uniquely innocent way of describing an event in the field.

One day, at the FRH, I asked him if he had seen any unusual fight in the field, say, between a tiger and a leopard or a tiger and a bear. He told me that he had not but that he had seen a 'battle' between a tiger and a huge lone wild boar from behind a lantana bush. He said that the combat went on for more than three hours and that the jungle reverberated with their roars and grunts. The modus operandi adopted by the wily boar was unique. It had taken its position at the base of a big *mahua* tree and was always facing the tiger. When the tiger ferociously charged at the boar, the latter would swiftly move out of way at the last fraction of a second, resulting in the tiger bumping hard into the tree trunk. It was quite like a scene from a Charlie Chaplin movie. It was the tiger that retreated with a bloody nose. Jaju was very keen that I visit the 'battlefield', but that was not to be.

Neemkar, the All-rounder

In the MTR, I was blessed with excellent, ever-willing-to-work drivers. Neemkar was one such driver to whom I had entrusted Project Tiger's new open camouflaged Gypsy. He would convert this Gypsy into a mobile hideout by covering it up with branches of trees. From this ground-level hideout, I saw plenty of wildlife, including tigers, from very close quarters. While driving, he would locate the tiger pugmarks on the dusty path, trace their outlines, and prepare plaster casts of tiger pugmarks during tiger census. He was a good cook and often helped in the kitchen. Once, in Rangubeli, he missed out on seeing a pair of tigers because he couldn't accompany me for a short excursion in the nearby forest because he was busy cooking. I am sure even today, he regrets having volunteered to cook while I got to watch the romantic pair of tigers. He is my lone witness to the rare sighting of the caracal, and I am sure the memory of that sighting excites him even today.

I cannot forget the tripod he rigged up from branches of the vitex tree for my camera as I shot the rare black-capped kingfisher. He was an excellent swimmer, a quality that I particularly admired during our visit to a huge waterfall when he swam, held me by my hand, and took me to the desired spot. He had excellent eyesight, which is so essential for life in the wild. He showed me the shining eyes of a snake swimming in a river about three hundred metres away from our jeep. Once, while travelling alone, he saw a ferocious tiger. He would get goose pimples whenever he narrated the tiger story, and to conceal his goose pimples, he would rub his hands vigorously on his body. We often ribbed him on this.

Neemkar retired a couple of years ago and settled down in Paratwada. On my next visit to Melghat, I propose to meet Neemkar at Paratwada and recreate for him the tiger moment. I bet the goose pimples would recur (quarter-century gap, no bar).

Ajay, the Trust Builder

Ajay Pillarisett is his full name. He spent his entire service in the wildlife wing of the Forest Department. He dealt very courageously with man-eating tigers and did extensive research on the most dreaded wild animal – the sloth bear. Once, his motorbike conked off near Banakapar (*bana* means 'bear') in the core area, and he had to walk back to Chikhaldara. Soon, he came across a bear which charged at him. With just a briefcase as his weapon, he kept the bear at bay. Such combats require extreme courage. I remember having spent one night with him on a machan in the farm of a local from a remote village for studying the destruction that wildlife causes to the agricultural crops. Ajay was an excellent birder, and I learnt to recognise many birds in his company.

I remember once, we had left very early in the morning for work. Unfortunately, we could not get time for either breakfast or lunch, and it was nearing 4:00 p.m. The whole day was spent on tea and biscuits. We were planning a stopover at FRH Churni (the FRH with the last hand-pulled *punkha* in Melghat). I was extremely hungry, totally exhausted, and totally, unrecognisably covered with dust. I was longing to reach FRH Churni when Ajay tapped the driver's back and asked him to stop the jeep, jumped out, and told me that he would be back shortly. Ignoring my protests, he went running down a cattle track towards a very interior village named Navalgaon. A uniformed person daring to defy the FD's orders was unheard of in those days. When he returned, I was fuming and asked him what had been so urgent. Ajay had a short story to narrate in reply to my query.

It was about five to six years ago that Ajay was the RFO at Semadoh when a young boy of ten to twelve years from this village was accidentally picked up and dragged by a leopard. His scalp was ripped open, and he had lost his hair. Ajay had taken him personally to Amravati for treatment. During the treatment at Amravati, the boy's mother had kept all her silver ornaments with Ajay because she was afraid that they could be stolen in a big city like Amravati. I was indeed quite delighted to see the tribal's trust in an RFO. It was towards this boy's hut that Ajay had gone scampering down just to find out about the health of the boy. As a professional and as a human being, his behaviour was par excellence. Ajay has settled down after his retirement in Mumbai (Badlapur), where he has an ancestral house.

I repeat that this is not an exhaustive list of my unsung heroes. In MTR, I came across numerous Patels, Jajus, Neemkars, and Ajays who made each day in Melghat a memorable one for me. I salute them for everything that they have done for me and for the MTR.

F

THE *SAHIBS*

This chapter offers the readers an interesting bunch of eight stories. A couple of them would take the readers to the thrilling days experienced by a generation of old-time foresters going back to the middle of the last century. It also includes topics dealing with the life of foresters when I joined the service in the late 1970s in the Melghat forests and when I came back to the same area a decade later at a higher position. During my first posting in Melghat, my designation was *chhote sahib*. Though held by a fresh recruit like me, this post wielded lot of power and gave me plenty of first-time experiences which are written as a story captioned 'Maiden Experiences'. This chapter also contains a story about an enjoyable trek in the core area of the MTR during which, for four days, I walked from dawn to dusk and stayed in the specially constructed patrolling 'bamboo huts'. There is a story in which I dream that I am the DFO in the 1960s in Melghat and that there is a very strong bond of trust between me and the forest dwellers. How cracks develop in our relationship and what efforts were made to restore the situation is given in another story.

26

MAA SAID SO

My father was a forester too. It thus happened that I had first learnt about forests literally on my mother's knees. Both my parents belonged to the Central Provinces (CP); my *maa* (mother) came from Jabalpur, a big district, and my father hailed from Berdi, a small village in the Chhindwada district. CP then held a major chunk of the forest and accounted for a substantial tiger population in India. My father joined the forest service in CP in 1943. When Maa spoke of those days, she would often refer to places like Jagdalpur, Baloda Bazaar, Bilaspur, and Sarguja (Ambikapur). All these beautiful places are now in the newly formed state of Chattisgarh and are notorious for Naxalite activities.

Whenever the topic of those days in the 1940s and 1950s came up, Maa would get totally engrossed and would narrate incidents as if they had occurred just yesterday. She would tell me that male buffalos were used for pulling carts (*bhaisa-gadi*) in Jagdalpur, similar to how bullocks are used to pull the bullock cart (*bail-gadi*). These buffalos were the descendants of the wild buffalos then found in good numbers in our country, especially in Assam, Coastal Orissa, and CP. It is so sad that this powerful, brave animal, which has the capacity to shoo away a tiger, is on the brink of extinction in Maharashtra, being reduced to barely a herd, breathing its last in the Gadchiroli district, across the Chhattisgarh border.

Talking about Sarguja reminds one of tigers. It is said that in the year 1900, the estimated tiger population in our country was 40,000, which came down to 1,827 by the year 1972. Though the massacre was basically by poisoning, it is true that the *maharajas* and their friends, especially from abroad, also had a major role to play. Figures available indicate that the highest toll of tigers was taken by the *maharaja* of Sarguja (Ambikapur). He alone (friends not included) accounted for killing 1,710 tigers. Next in the list is Maharaja Scindia of Gwalior, who killed nine hundred plus tigers and with whom my uncle, Major Gaikwad, worked.

My father, who was a vegetarian, never indulged in hunting (*shikar*), but relatives like Major Gaikwad were rather keen *shikaris*. During holidays, Uncle Gaikwad would come up with the idea of hunting something 'big'. But my father would dodge him by delaying tactics or taking him to the wrong places. He would ultimately land up shooting a partridge and a couple of quails in our residential campus, peanuts for somebody who wanted to be out hunting tigers. To strengthen his team, Major Gaikwad would instigate my *mama* (maternal uncle) to join him. To evade his hunter relatives, my father once purposely organised camping in a dilapidated building which was already occupied by a barn owl. My *mama*, a city-dwelling teacher, was compelled to flee from the jungle after listening at night to the discordant screams and the weird snoring and hissing notes produced by the owl. That was the last time Mama joined Major Gaikwad for his *shikar* (hunting) trips.

Maa recollected that Mr Havetson, a British forester, was my father's first DFO. He was a very hard-working person. He would leave for the field in the morning with a hurricane lantern every day so as to reach the work site at daybreak and would leave the site after dusk using the same lantern. For his extreme devotion to duty, he was affectionately called Jungli (a forest dweller) by his colleagues. I had the privilege of meeting Uncle Jungli and his wife when the grand old couple in their

80s had come all the way from England to Chikhaldara (Melghat, India) for their journey down memory lane.

Mr G. G. Takle, who went on to become the first inspector general of forests in India, was my father's first Indian boss. There is a road named after Mr Takle in the FRI campus at Dehradun. He was a brave man and an excellent shot. My father was once walking with him in the jungle when, on a turning in a dry *naala* bed, a hungry, injured tiger leapt at them. Mr Takle, who had a loaded gun in his hand, had fired at the injured beast while it was airborne and killed it. I had the privilege of meeting him too.

In 1952, my father was sub-DFO in Allapalli, where he held a heavy charge which included the far-flung Bhamragad and Sironcha too. Practically single-handedly, he ran a charge big enough to require six or seven DFOs today. Maa vividly recollected our Allapalli days, particularly the night when I was born. Electricity had still not reached Allapalli. It was a moonless night, raining cats and dogs, and my father was out on tour. It was at Allapalli, the mecca of forestry in India, that I was born, which pretty much marked me out for life as a forester. The midwife, Maa recollects, was a dark ugly crone, so dark that only her teeth showed in the dim light of the sooty lantern. My two siblings, sister aged 5 and brother aged 2, had been woken up by my yells, and they added to the chaos. Difficulties came in a heap. The flour had run out, and when Maa sent someone to grind flour on the *haath-chakki* (the household hand mill), fitted in Maa's room, she found a full-grown cobra wound round the stone wheel. By the time Bhaiyyalal, our local help, was summoned, the cobra had vanished, adding to the uneasiness of the night. With the first rays of the sun, the rain stopped. Soon, my father appeared on the scene. The enthusiastic staff, Maa tells me, welcomed my arrival with a twelve-gun salute.

Life in Allapalli was rather monotonous for Maa, who was born and brought up in a big city. There was virtually no social life or sources of entertainment, and doing nothing but minding the babies had really begun getting on her nerves. So it was decided that we too should join my father on his tour. On the day of our family outing, Father got up very early and left. A separate bullock cart was organised for the family.

Bhaiyyalal walked alongside the bullock cart. Our first stop was at the Glory of Allapalli, a patch of the forest where the teak trees were pencil straight and unusually huge in height and girth. Each tree that size would fetch about a million rupees in today's market. Maa thought of stopping there because she was convinced that this beautiful patch was discovered by my father, although the credit had gone to a senior British officer.

Beyond this patch, we were to cross a stream. The cart man got down from the cart, and he, along with Bhaiyyalal, held the wooden beam and rope tied to bullocks in their hands to guide the bullock cart through the water. The water turned out to be a bit too deep at one particular spot, and the bullocks managed to break free and ran away. Both the men clung to the bullock-less cart and took charge. Maa had to get down in the little-more-than-knee-deep water, holding me in her arms, and cross the stream. The two men pushed the cart to the safety of the other bank along with my siblings. The positive side of this incident was that my father soon purchased a Chevrolet car which would run about seven to eight miles on a gallon (4.5 litres) of petrol.

Talking about the behaviour of bullocks, I am reminded of an incident during my father's Allapalli days. Mr Buit, who holds the record of holding the topmost post in the Maharashtra Forest Department for some thirteen years, was my father's boss when the incident had taken place. Mr Buit was passing through a dense forest in a bullock cart, followed by my father's cart just about a furlong (an eighth of a mile) behind. Mr Buit's cart was passing through a depression, a tiny pass, and he was carrying a loaded gun with him. Suddenly, his bullocks started feeling nervous and refused to budge an inch. At that moment, sensing danger, the cart man jumped out of the cart and ran away and climbed a tree nearby. Mr Buit realised that the bullocks had smelt a carnivore and was reaching out for his gun. At that moment, a tiger that had been eyeing the bullocks from the embankment made its charge. The bullocks broke the rope and ran for their lives. Mr Buit fell on the ground with his gun on one side and his tiffin on the other. He quickly picked up his gun and walked away to safety. The tiger, meanwhile, had set off after the bullocks.

In a matter of about five minutes, my father's bullock cart, along with the RFO's cart, reached the spot. They saw the cart without bullocks, saw the tiffin box lying on the ground, and heard the cries of the cart man from a treetop saying, 'Sahib ko sher ne maar dala!' (The tiger has killed the master!) After a lot of coaxing, the cart man got down from the tree. Everybody made concerted efforts and reunited with Mr Buit, the RFO organised a new cart for him, and my father joined him in his cart and took him safely to his destination. A big search party was organised to look out for the runaway bullocks, which, amazingly, had escaped unhurt and were ultimately rescued.

Hats off to all the foresters of yesteryears who did their duty under such challenging circumstances with all sincerity and courage! Hats off to their better halves too, who stood by them through such a challenging time! Hats off to Maa!

27

BEING A FORESTER'S SON

In 1957, my father was DFO of the West Berar Division, in charge of the Akola and Buldhana districts. It was the year when the entire nation was celebrating the first major patriotic event after Indian independence, the centenary of the War of Indian Independence in 1857. Pandit Jawaharlal Nehru, our prime minister then, had come to Akola. I was a 5-year-old kid. Clad in a white *churidar* and *sherwani*, sporting a white *khadi* Gandhi cap, I was given the privilege of welcoming Chacha Nehru at the airport with a red rose. I remember that he had accepted it gleefully and picked me up in his arms. He travelled in an open car through people lined up by the roadside to greet him. He was reciprocating the greeting by throwing garlands back at them.

The DFO's bungalow was substantially big with huge premises. We stayed there from 1957 to 1959. Incidentally, I came to stay in the same house again from 1986 to 1990 as DFO of Akola. It is still in good shape and continues to be the residence of the DFO of Akola even today. We had plenty of wildlife within our campus. I remember hunting was a popular sport then. My uncle Major Gaikwad used to come over from Mumbai to our place equipped with a gun and used to sharpen his shooting skills at the *titar*s (partridges) and *bater*s (quails) found on our campus. This campus also boasted of a large prominent variety of snakes. Some also strayed inside the bungalow, especially in the rainy season. Evening time was for a 'chorus-singing competition' for the *kolhe* (jackals). It was also the time for a full-grown *neelgai-rohi* (blue bull) to return home along with the domestic cattle gone for grazing. It was indeed a unique mixture of domestic life and wildlife. Night was the time for the *ullu-ghubad* (owls), *chippak* (nightjars), and *titawi* (lapwings) to start exercising their vocal cords.

Our next-door neighbour was Mr Dinkarrao Deshmukh, a collector. He was a tall, handsome, fair person with a very sharp nose. He was an avid hunter. He had a pair of hunting dogs named Raja and Major. These dogs were trained to hunt hares. I still remember an incident when these dogs had chased down a hare under a culvert in our compound and had sealed one end while we kept vigil at the other end. The poor trapped animal had to give up.

Those were the days when hunting was taken as a sport and an act of valour. In fact, collectors and forest officers could freely indulge in *shikar*. I remember a senior forest officer putting tiger hunting as a precondition for becoming a DFO. My father was a vegetarian and managed to be an exception to the rule and remained always miles away from *shikar* even in those days of plenty. My neighbour collector uncle, however, used to visit the Narnala, Dhargad, and Gullarghat areas of the Melghat forests for a tiger hunt. One such incident when he came back from a tiger hunt is still very fresh in my mind, even though six decades have elapsed.

We kids were eagerly waiting for the truck carrying the hunted tiger to arrive. When it arrived, I remember that the truck was a bit too small for the huge tiger, and its legs were dangling out. We had chased the truck from the gate to the collector's bungalow. The tiger was unloaded and carried upside down with its legs tied to poles. An appropriate open space was soon finalised for skinning. The skin, along with the claws, was to go to the hunter (the collector) as a souvenir of his valour. As the skinning progressed, the strength of the onlookers increased. Ranging from meat to organs to blood to bones (particularly the 'wish bone') to fat to whiskers, each body part was being eyed by the onlookers. Salt was applied to the skin as a preservative, which was then stretched and pegged. The length of a tiger is the distance measured 'between the pegs' from nose tip to the end of the tail. Elsewhere, this achievement was celebrated over a few drinks in the field beside a campfire. The oft repeated joke then was that 'the length of a tiger increases between the pegs'.

The above incident at Akola remained permanently etched in the memory of a young boy (me) who was destined to be the FD of Project Tiger and directly work for tiger conservation. From Akola, we came to Nagpur in late 1959 and shifted to a bungalow in Civil Lines on Ramgiri Road, where the Officers' Club stands today. During our six years' stay there, we visited Melghat – Chikhaldara, in particular – on three or four occasions as my father was particularly fond of it, and he wanted his six children to spend as many of their Diwali and summer vacations there as possible.

I remember a Melghat trip in the early sixties when my cousins too joined in, making it a full team of eleven children in the age bracket of 4 to 14. The rear seat of our Hillman car was removed, and we, 'the excited bunch', sat on the floor, with the baggage sent to the top of the car. As the ignition switch was not functioning, the car was crank-started. The drive on the plains was quite smooth, but once we hit the hills past the Bihali gate of Melghat, the engine started overheating. However, after a couple of hiccups, our Hillman made it safely to the high-point town: Ghatang. After a noisy meal of *dal-bati* prepared and served in the shade of a banyan tree (the tree is still there in the rest house premises), we descended to Semadoh.

At night, we took a post-dinner drive up to Kolkaz for seeing wildlife. During the seven-odd-mile drive, we all were hugely excited to sight a 'bear' which, on closer look, turned out to be a tar drum kept for road repairs. At FRH Kolkaz, we had another wildlife sighting: the fat ranger napping on the sofa, with his huge moustache fluttering with every snore. He was wearing his uniform for the occasion, including a leather cross belt, shoes, and sola hat. I can't forget the sight of his getting up with a start and saluting in the opposite direction of my father.

The PWD rest house at Semadoh was right in the middle of the forest, and at night, the 'cricket team' was expected to sleep on the floor in the veranda. Nobody wanted to sleep on the veranda edge for fear of the wildlife. I was just about 9 years old, and our team leader, my sister, was all of 14. Nobody messed with her. Her *firmaan* (order) was that my cousin Jayu and I were boys and should therefore be brave and be responsible for the safety and welfare of the entire gang. The 'bravehearts' had no option but to pull their bed sheets over their heads and rough it out. Every rustle was a snake crawling around and every grunt a carnivore closing in.

The next day, it was Chikhaldara, where we met the CF, Mr J. C. Sarvate, at Braeside, the summer residence of the CF. Some excellent local varieties of mango were planted by the British in the Amzari nursery, Peach Grove, the FRH, Braeside, and the garden managed by the Forest Department. The CF had free access to these mangoes during the entire summer. We relished the juice of *laddu* mangos with ghee for lunch with the CF. It was more than fifty years ago that I had tasted those mangos, but the taste lingers. Undoubtedly, they were the best and the sweetest local mangos I'd had in my life.

After seeing the usual tourist points, it was time to say goodbye to Chikhaldara. We children were quite upset at the dream outing coming to an end without sighting the Melghat tiger when lo and behold! There stood one right on the main road, in broad daylight, a little beyond the Amzari garden. We got down from our cars to admire the king of the forests disappear behind some lantana bushes and got a good licking from my father for risking our lives. One of my father's colleagues was a good *shikari,* and he cursed his luck for not carrying his gun and missing out on a golden chance of hunting a tiger. Those were the days of plenty. A book written by an enthusiastic *shikari* mentions the sighting of seven tigers on the Chikhaldara plateau in one day. This person had driven down to Chikhaldara in his car from Srinagar (J&K) in the mid-1920s.

Today we have come a long way in tiger conservation. Tiger hunting, which was an act of valour about half a century ago, is a serious crime today. Also, hunting those days had some ethics, at least for some of the hunters. Tigers were neither snared in foot traps nor electrocuted or poisoned near a waterhole. 'Progress' has resulted in 100 per cent electrification of villages and even brought with it pesticides. These two boons (?) continue to be generously used by poachers to massacre tigers. Indeed, the animals have paid a heavy price for this 'progress'.

28

THE CHHOTE SAHIBS

In those days, the Indian Forest Service officers had to complete a probation period of three years before getting confirmed in service. The break-up of this period was two years of professional training at Dehradun, four months of the foundation course at Mussoorie, and eight months of fieldwork during range charge. I was doing the last leg of my probation period when the news of my posting to Dharni came. I did my range charge at a remote tribal village called Tarubanda and completed my probation period there. The regular RFO at Tarubanda was an enthusiastic person by the name of B. U. Ingle. He would not hear of letting me proceed to Dharni without attending a small 'send-off' organised by the range staff. I remember all my field staff had come, some walking twenty-odd kilometres. They were wearing uniform and sat on the floor, cramped up in the rather small office room. These twenty-five-odd persons had worked so closely with me during the last eight months that they had become almost my family members, and I felt sad while bidding goodbye to them. They had very affectionately contributed money to buy me a gift – a fountain pen.

While handing over the gift on behalf of the staff, Ingle had commented, 'Sir, you are beginning your long journey towards occupying the highest chair in the Forest Department from this tiny remote tribal village called Tarubanda. We expect you to use this pen always for a good cause.' The pen remained with me only for a few months, but Ingle's words of wisdom still ring in my ears and have come in handy on numerous occasions in service.

It was March 1980 when I had landed up at Dharni. I had now graduated from a *naye sahib* (new master) to a *chhote sahib* (junior master). This terminology was popular in the erstwhile CP for referring to the ACF or the sub-DFO. I was to remain a *chhote sahib* for about two years before graduating to a *bade sahib* (senior master), i.e. DFO. Dharni is a tehsil place in the Amravati district, located sixty-odd kilometres from my earlier place of posting, Tarubanda. The interstate border with Madhya Pradesh is not very far away.

I was required to supervise work in three or four ranges and manage a timber depot and a logging unit comprising some twenty trucks and ten tractors. Our trucks basically brought teak timber to the depot from the neighbouring forests. This timber was separated by girth, length, and quality, arranged in lots, and then sold by auction. Interested buyers came near the lots of their liking to bid. For big-sized good-quality teak lots, the initial bid used to be in multiples of ten thousand rupees. For an increase in bid, the buyers communicated by signals/gestures. It could be the movement of a finger or a paper or pen in the hand. A slight movement of the head or batting of an eyelid would mean a formal but secret communication between me and my buyers. The batting of an eyelid meant a bid worth about my annual salary. I remember having sold timber worth more than ten million rupees in a single day. Ten million was a huge amount in 1980, when my monthly salary was just about one thousand rupees. (A four-figure salary was something that a marriageable bachelor could boast of those days.) The daily wage was just about seven rupees. Allumwar was my depot officer. He was an old stalwart who, towards the fag end of his service, had been promoted from forester to range officer. He had perhaps started his career during the British Raj and used to wear a sola hat 24/7. He would wear very thick glasses and was very fond of eating *paan* (betel leaf).

My logging unit was headed by a young forester named Gawai. (Remember? He told me to do *pradakshina* en route to FRH Tarubanda from the village.) The unit comprised basically a workshop, a spare parts counter, a servicing, and a petrol/diesel oil distribution centre. Our fleet of thirty vehicles was kept in excellent health by our mechanic Hanif, whose twin brother, Yusuf, was a truck driver with us. Hanif had perfected the art of smooth driving. If one closed one's eyes, one would not know when Hanif changed the gears. I have never seen a better driver than him in my life. He taught me the trick of reversing a tractor with a trailer. He also taught me the art of truck driving and also imparted some basic knowledge on automobile mechanics. This added qualification helped me take strong action against those drivers who cooked up excuses for not taking their truck to the forest on flimsy grounds.

I had very close supervision over the activities of the drivers. After more than three decades, I can still recall the truck drivers' names and their truck numbers. We basically had TATA, Ashok Leyland, and Leyland Comet models in trucks and had Massey Ferguson tractors. The best behaved of the drivers was one Abdul Sattar, Ashok Leyland truck number 5432. He would go out of his way to help anybody (especially the lower field staff) expecting a free lift in his truck. I remember once, in my absence, he rushed to the bus stand in his truck to pick up my friend Tasneem's mother. She had suddenly landed all the way from Faizabad (UP) with a lot of paraphernalia, including a big hookah. Sattarbhai is no more now.

Generally, drivers were professionally good and expert in driving loaded trucks on the hilly Melghat dust tracks. Driving such trucks down slippery slopes, especially after a shower, was the ultimate test. Once the truck starts skidding down a slope, it becomes very difficult to control. I never came across any drunken driving. Perhaps the drivers knew that they would lose their jobs if they dared indulge themselves. The nearest big town in Madhya Pradesh was Burhanpur, famous for Milan *mithai*. I longed to go to Burhanpur but did not get the boss's permission to go out of the state.

The cinema hall Melghat Talkies and the forest check post with a road barrier on the main Nagpur–Indore road were the most happening places in Dharni. The *chhote sahib* was a big shot in a small town like Dharni. I remember my batchmate and close friend Tasneem Ahmad had come down from Chikhaldara once. Chikhaldara had no cinema hall, and I boasted of one. Hence, we both decided to go for a movie to Melghat Talkies. This cinema hall was a dilapidated structure, a cross between a tin shed and a warehouse. In the interval, the manager invited us for tea in his office, and Tasneem, as was his habit, got busy chatting with him. We got so engrossed in the chat that we forgot that we were watching a movie. More than half an hour had elapsed when we suddenly realised the passage of time and wanted to rush to the theatre lest we lose some crucial part of the film.

Looking at our anxiety, the manager assured us, 'How dare we start the movie, sir, when Chhote Sahib is not in the cinema hall.'

When we re-entered, we were greeted with catcalls. The half-hour break had provided smokers with time to finish off a few additional cigarettes/*beedi*s. The smokescreen was impossible to penetrate, especially for the eyes of backbenchers like us. When the manager was apprised of our problem, he not only got all the doors of the theatre opened but also rewound the part that we had seen hazily and rescreened it for us. Such was the importance of the *chhote sahib* that no passenger bus could enter or leave Dharni without clearance from the *chhote sahib,* thanks to the forest check post.

At the check post, three forest guards were deployed on eight-hourly duty round the clock to keep vigil on the movement of forest produce, including timber. One such guard was Bairagi, who was old, frail, and ailing; perhaps he had tuberculosis. He just had a couple of years to go before retirement. Looking at his health, I would give him duty at a time convenient to him. Bairagi had two sons, namely, Somdas and Ramdas. Both were in their teens. I had taught the staff and their children how to play cricket, and both these boys were regular members of my cricket team.

One day Somdas came to me crying, saying that his father was no more. Bairagi had died inside the cabin abutting the check post while on duty. I went and consoled the bereaved family, assured the elder son, Somdas, of a driver's job, and proceeded to the field. I thought it was the end of my role in issues related to Bairagi's death. I took my time returning from the field and was surprised to see Bairagi's family waiting for me for the final rites. They could not think of taking Bairagi off on his last journey in the absence of the *chhote sahib*. I attended the last rites performed on Bairagi. Interestingly, in Bairagi's (nomadic) tribe, during the funeral procession, the dead body is carried in a sitting posture for being buried, and thus was Bairagi carried and buried. Somdas soon joined as driver and continues to work in his father's department – the Forest Department.

The incident of Bairagi's family waiting for me for the funeral had set me thinking. So far, I was thinking only about my official responsibilities. The incident made me think about the personal responsibilities of the *chhote sahib* too. Somewhere I got the feeling that I had been inducted as a senior member of the 'forest family' at a tender age of 27.

29

MAIDEN EXPERIENCES

When I had joined Dharni as *chhote sahib*, I did not have an independent jeep. I travelled in truck number 5432, driven by the kind-hearted Mohammad Abdul Sattar, who would gladly volunteer to carry me around. While Sattar loaded his truck, I would do my field inspection. We went empty but came back loaded and travelled at a snail's pace. We hardly had any jeeps for all the officers then. But looking at the nature of my work, my DFO, the *bade sahib,* had sent me battered, rattletrap jeep number 1201. When he got to know of my close encounter with a gaur off the Dhakna–Dolar road while travelling by 1201, he pulled authority, and one day a brand new Mahindra jeep (registration number 3913) arrived. It was a diesel vehicle with a soft hood and a four-wheel drive facility. About a week later, Tasneem too got a new jeep, registration number 3866. The new arrival was the talk of the town at Dharni. At the first opportunity, I set off on my maiden trip in 3913.

As the vehicle was brand new, I dispensed with any escort and thought of travelling alone along with my new driver Hasan. (I am still in touch with Hasan.) The best inaugural ride I could think of for my new jeep was naturally the Tarubanda Range, where I had only recently spent some great times; it also abounded in wild animals. My first stop was at Somji Patel's house at Tarubanda, where we toasted the vehicle with a cup of black tea (milk was then a scarce commodity). I then proceeded towards Kund. This village has now been translocated to make undisturbed space for wild animals. The sun had set by the time we reached the Sakhri River on this side of Kund. We had to cross the river at a point where there was water, and below the surface were biggish boulders.

Banking on the fact that the vehicle was new and had a four-wheel drive facility, I very carefully put it into the water and was halfway through when the axle hit a boulder, climbed over it, and lifted the rear wheels up. When I accelerated, the rear wheels happily spun at the same spot in the water. A four-wheel drive is designed for exactly such exigencies. But to my dismay, it refused to engage. The jeep moved not an inch forward or backward. We were literally stuck in troubled waters.

Just then, I heard a sloth bear call at a long distance, followed by a sambar alarm call in our vicinity, indicating the presence of a carnivore. The area was darkening by the minute, and our jeep was stuck in the middle of a waterhole where, in a short while, the wild animals would arrive for a drink. I was getting a bit worried when the superman in my companion, Hasan, came to the fore. He quickly removed his shirt and disappeared under the jeep. 'Dar lagey to gaana gaa' ('Sing when you are afraid') goes a Hindi song. I started singing loudly to keep fear as well as the wild animals away. He took the jack underwater, elevated the jeep, and removed the mischievous boulder. The earth once again found the rear wheels, and the jeep gurgled out of the water. It was in almost total darkness that we moved out of the problem spot. That was our maiden trip on vehicle number 3913.

After initial hiccups, 3913 adjusted very well to the Melghat terrain when I came across my second maiden experience about a *naka-bandi* (road block). One evening I got secret information that some timber smugglers from Madhya Pradesh had entered the Maharashtra forests via Bhokarbardi, the border town, and cut some teak trees. So I carefully selected a team of daredevil youngsters. The team leader was a young RFO, and the rest were forest guards. We left Dharni after dinner around ten on our maiden *naka-bandi*.

On that dark chilly night, we reached our spot around midnight, just about two kilometres from the Madhya Pradesh border. The path narrowed there, giving us the best chance of nabbing the culprits along with stolen material. Around three in the morning, we heard the loaded bullock carts coming. (Loaded ones make less noise.) When they were close enough, we all pounced on the smugglers and caught them with their booty: five bullock carts full of precious teak timber. The material was about half a truckload. Unfortunately, taking advantage of the darkness, one alert offender ran away. Thinking that this fellow would go to their village and return with reinforcements, we hurried through the job of preparing the preliminary offence report (POR) and rolled off – thieves, merchandise, and all – towards Dharni.

On each bullock cart, I had planted a forest guard. The RFO and I were in 3913, closely following and supervising the procession. We reached Dharni around daybreak. Our procession got an unprecedented welcome. Later, I learnt that the runaway had gathered an armed mob of about two hundred and had come chasing us but missed us by a whisker. This was our maiden *naka-bandi* experience, mine and of 3913. During the *naka-bandi*, another maiden experience got sandwiched inside, which deserves a separate paragraph.

While doing *naka-bandi*, I had hidden 3913 about a hundred metres away from the cart track. We were sitting by the roadside in two bunches: the five forest guards constituting one and the other comprising the ranger *sahib* and the *chhote sahib*. The forest guards were sitting about a hundred metres away from us. The RFO was about ten metres away from me. As it was very cold, we both had covered ourselves fully with *ghongdi* (rough blankets). As he recounted later, suddenly, the RFO heard something in front of him but could not see because of the pitch darkness. So he switched on his torch. Shiver or no shiver, he broke into a sweat when he saw an inquisitive tiger looking at him from just a metre away. My heart pounding hard, I was watching the spectacle from very close quarters. The tiger's curiosity was soon satisfied, and after pondering for a little while, it disappeared into the forest from where it had come. Phew! Talk of narrow shaves! I immediately went and hugged the RFO, who was visibly trembling, teeth chattering uncontrollably. Which set of teeth wouldn't after seeing death at such close quarters? I offered him a hot cup of coffee from my flask, and we continued with our *naka-bandi*. Imagine – our second group was totally unaware of our maiden wild animal encounter. After this experience, I increased our patrolling along the Madhya Pradesh border.

My fourth maiden experience was in the morning near a village on the Madhya Pradesh border. I was patrolling near the river Tapi along the border when I came across four tribal maidens running towards their village. They were obviously panic-stricken. I stopped my jeep and asked them what the matter was.

The girls just stuttered, 'Tiger, sir! Th-th-there's a t-t-tiger chasing us!' and kept running.

I went down the road. After just about two hundred metres, I indeed saw a tiger walking towards my jeep. It came as close as about five metres and stopped. My jeep had now effectively blocked its progress in the direction of the girls. The tiger didn't know what to do. Bypass my jeep? Turn and enter the forest nearby? It chose the second option and disappeared into the forest. I was quite puzzled at the whole sequence of events and, to satiate my curiosity, returned to the village. The village chief summoned the girls. The girls were hesitant at first, but slowly, one opened up, and the others soon followed. Soon, they were all speaking together. Through the cacophony, the story that emerged was this.

...a large pack of wild dogs had chased a tiger into the river.

That morning, the four girls had gone to the river to wash clothes. Halfway through their job, one of them noticed a tiger sitting about fifty metres behind her in the shallow part of the river. Jolted at first, she quickly recovered and noticed that a large pack of wild dogs had chased the tiger into the river. This courageous girl understood the tiger's plight and told the others to hold their ground till the wild dogs dispersed. A big enough pack of wild dogs can indeed chase and kill a tiger. Once the dogs had dispersed, the girls beat a hasty retreat. But the scared, grateful tiger kept following the girls at a respectable distance. That such a threatened tiger feels secure in human presence is a well-accepted fact. But hats off to the courage displayed by the tribal maidens and to the gratitude of the tiger! They together had provided me with a rare experience. It provided me with the platform to make a closer study of this unique relationship among the king of the forest (the tiger), the whistling hunters (the wild dogs), and the supreme predator (human beings).

30

THE SHOE SIZE
TURNS LARGER

First, it was *naya sahib* (probationer) and then *chhote sahib* (sub-DFO) and then *bada sahib* (DFO). After remaining *bada sahib* for a decade, I had joined Paratwada as the CF and FD of the MTR and was reunited with my beloved Melghat. From DFO to CF in those days was a quantum jump; the sphere of responsibilities increased substantially. Chalking out and attending to the CM's and other VIPs' tour programmes, coordinating with the divisional commissioner, attending meetings in Delhi, visiting other states, and so on were going to be my new responsibilities.

I stayed FD for a little more than four years. It turned out to be a dream tenure, and I enjoyed each day of my innings there. This tenure was roughly divided into two parts: half at the headquarters at Paratwada and the remaining half at the headquarters at Amravati. I was instrumental in getting the HQ shifted from Paratwada to Amravati by first making the proposal and later following it up with the governments, both state and central. There was a huge uproar in the media as well as on the floor of assembly about the shifting. However, the decision remained unchanged. This shift has withstood the test of time for the last quarter of a century and redeemed the value and attractiveness of the FD's chair.

For management purposes, the Project Tiger area was divided into a core area and a buffer area. The core comprised 361 square kilometres of total wilderness without any village. The buffer was a little more than 1,600 square kilometres, with a little over 50 villages nestled in it. The core fell exclusively under my control, while the buffer area was under the concurrent jurisdiction of the FD of the MTR and the DFOs of East, West, and South Melghat. When I took over, no felling of trees was allowed in the core area. With the passage of time, felling stopped in the buffer zone too. I had a skeleton field staff of about a hundred men – young, sincere, and courageous – who had been hand-picked by Mr Ghanekar, Mr Gogate's predecessor. A good number of guns and rifles were handed over too. They were meant for self-protection, but I found Melghat so safe that we were never required to carry them in the field.

In his send-off speech, Mr Gogate remarked that he was handing over charge of seventy-odd tigers and expressed the wish that they breed profusely during my tenure. Their number did not increase dramatically during my tenure but remained steady, hovering around seventy-two. Hilly terrain, limited water resources, fires, and the biotic pressure of the fifty-odd villages – all these factors contributed to limiting the number of herbivores and, consequently, the number of carnivores. The relocation of villages, it was believed, could do the magic. The process of relocation was started during my tenure, and so far (2016), fourteen villages have been successfully shifted. These areas are turning into beautiful meadows now. If the perennial waterholes are properly guarded, catering exclusively to wildlife requirements, and the meadows are religiously protected against fires, the tiger has a good chance of survival in the MTR's wilderness.

My official car was an Ambassador, but we soon purchased two Maruti Gypsy petrol jeeps: one closed and hard bodied and the other soft bodied. They were powerful, low-noise, four-wheel-drive vehicles suitable for the hilly Melghat terrain. Incidentally, they were the first ones of their kind in the entire state and a subject matter of envy from colleagues. We made some modifications to the soft-bodied Gypsy – a wireless set, camouflaged colour on the body, an additional battery for the searchlight, an additional petrol tank under the driver's seat, a VIP seat that could be raised, and a special toolkit for clearing a jungle path – and it was ready for any contingency in Melghat. Cover it up with a few twigs, and it became a mobile machan for observing carnivores returning to their kill.

The overall priority given by the territorial officers to wildlife management in the buffer area was, unfortunately, low. I recollect visiting the waterholes at Chamarudhada, Chaddupati, Kuvapati, and Pipalpadao in fading light. I was shocked to see that the areas surrounding these waterholes were encroached and occupied all over by cattle. Instead of sighting the majestic Indian bison, all I could see was the Indian *bhaisan*, the buffalo. The poor, shy wild animals had no chance of getting even a sip of water. The terrain was flat and, with a little effort, suitable for developing into tourism zone. Grazing as well as camping of cattle, therefore, had to be prohibited in the tourism zone area, and alternative sites needed to be provided.

The authority of regulating grazing was with the chief wildlife warden, and accordingly, a proposal was submitted to him, and he promptly approved it. Guarded gates at Chamarudhada, Kuvapati, and Pipalpadao kept the cattle out, and waterholes began being maintained. Anti-grazing patrolling on foot was started. Habitat manipulation activities such as the pollarding of edible fodder species were taken up. Viewing lines, salt licks, and wallows were created in the tourism zone area. These moves had a magical effect on wildlife sighting, and from November onwards, tourists regularly started seeing some large mammalian wild animals. The minibuses started moving around regularly in the morning and evening with the tourists.

As there were no villages inside the core, barring a couple of forest guards at Koktoo, no staff stayed there. Their patrolling meant just travelling a few kilometres from their headquarters inside the core and back. Not happy with this touch-and-go patrolling, we started a new *zopdi* (hut) system of patrolling. Making free use of local material such as poles, bamboos, and grasses, a series of huts were constructed at a distance of about twenty-five kilometres from one another. They were located about half a kilometre from a permanent source of water, and a two-metre-wide inspection path was cleared to connect the chain of huts. Each hut was equipped with a field toilet, a few indigenously made beds, bamboo relaxing chairs, and a place to burn firewood to keep warm and safe from wild animals. A register was kept for the head of patrolling parties to compulsorily make entries about his observations. A community ration box with the bare minimum necessities was kept locked in the hut; the leader of each patrolling party would carry a key to it. I started staying in these huts, and it really helped us tighten the security of the core area. In fact, the best outing of my lifetime was in November 1993, when, in a span of four days, I stayed in four different huts and, in the process, walked over a hundred kilometres in the core area.

The huts were so cosy and beautiful that the officers and staff enjoyed staying in them. In fact, there was a healthy competition among the staff to innovate and improve upon the huts. The then CM of Maharashtra, Mr Sudhakarrao Naik, visited our hut at Sadhukundi and expressed immense satisfaction at their erection, upkeep, and utility. VIP visits to the MTR had been quite eventful during my tenure, and to do justice to them, they need separate space. Though patrolling in the core area was quite a regular feature, patrolling in the buffer area was rare because it was in the charge of the territorial DFO, who reported to a different authority. Our first joint outing was thrilling, and I describe it below.

As FD, my major work lay, obviously, in the field. My first major outing was a reconnaissance of the buffer area with the territorial DFO. Our top priority was to visit the vulnerable areas along the Madhya Pradesh border and jointly work out anti-poaching measures. As we were passing through the bordering forests, I noticed a man moving rather suspiciously. I told Hasan to slow down, hopped out of the car, and got after the fellow, who now began running into the forest. My co-travellers, who had not sighted the man, wondered what I was up to. This chap was carrying something heavy in his hand, which was actually hindering his speed. Realising that I would soon catch up with him, he quickly hid the stuff under a bush and disappeared. I gave up the chase and looked into the bush.

...it was a gun, a loaded gun.

To my surprise, it was a gun, a loaded gun. The man was obviously moving around in search of some wild animal. I met my car mates and apprised them of the incident. As we had a long way to go, the DFO instructed his forest guard to carry the gun to the nearest range forest office where a POR would be filed, and we continued our journey. On our return, we got to know that five or six persons had mobbed the forest guard and snatched the gun away from him. The DFO felt very embarrassed and, in a fortnight's time, sent a big force to a village in Madhya Pradesh and arrested the poacher and confiscated the gun.

My FD's tenure was indeed a pleasant learning experience. My passion for walking around and covering each nook and corner came in very handy. I encountered a loner gaur while sleeping outside the Banaam protection hut, a leopard while walking towards a machan near Bitkilpaati, a large pack of wild dogs when I was walking alone towards the waterhole at Amrai Number 1, followed the Dunda-aam tiger on foot, and sustained a bear attack during an early morning walk near FRH Koktoo. What more could one ask for in the post-*shikar* days? This tenure put the stamp of a wild-lifer on a forester like me.

31

A RAMBLE THROUGH THE CORE

Melghat had a totally habitation-free core area. As there was no village in this 361 square-kilometre core area, the field staff generally stayed in villages on the fringe of the core. Also, as there had been neither harvesting of forest produce nor grazing in the core for a long time, there were hardly any cart tracks or cattle tracks or footpaths in the core. These two factors were mainly responsible for the touch-and-go patrolling of the field staff on the few existing main roads. Another factor was that a state highway passed through the core on which the cattle passed. These cattle were required to be immunised and quarantined and made to cross the core in the quickest possible time so as to prevent the degradation of the habitat and the spread of any disease from cattle to wildlife. I remember having caught Kathiawadi cattle near the Adhao village. When threatened with dire consequences, the owner, a very rich person, had removed his turban and placed it at my feet, indicating total surrender.

Besides this case, two other cases – one involving illegal fishing and the other involving the theft of forest produce, *kusum* (*Schleichera oleosa*) tree lac – had come to my notice. The thieves had come to our core area all the way from Madhya Pradesh because unlike at other places, where a sporadic tree grows here and there, making lac collection difficult, the core had gregarious patches of *kusum* trees. These experiences made me disbelieve the claim of the field staff that the core was generally inviolate. It was not so, and we had to pull up our socks.

I discussed this problem at the head office with my documentation officer, Ajay Pillarisett, and research officer Ravi Wankhade, and we worked out a simple model plan to combat the situation. We proposed to develop a chain of protection huts similar to the ones in which sages of yesteryears had stayed. For these huts, the concerned RFO was expected to use freely available poles, bamboos, and grass. He was sanctioned an amount of rupees, ten thousand per hut towards wages. The hut was to be located about half a kilometre from a permanent source of drinking water so that the wild animals could quench their thirst undisturbed, particularly at night. A temporary toilet and bath too was constructed. Innovative ideas could be tried for organising some sitting arrangement in front of the hut. The whole complex was to be enclosed by fragile bamboo fencing, which was to work as a psychological barrier for the wildlife. A register was to be kept in every hut for the remarks of the head of the patrolling party. Observations during patrolling, including biotic interference, were also to be noted. The absence of any such activity was to be certified too. Some RFOs had also kept a ration box with essential dry ration and multiple sets of keys. Huts were generally located at twenty-five to thirty kilometres' distance from one another, and a six-foot line was cut between the adjacent huts for the free movement of patrolling staff. Also, this line would be useful as an internal fire line for restricting and combating fire.

To motivate my staff, I started staying in these huts. In fact, in the winter of 1993, I trekked for four days and stayed in four different huts on consecutive days. Generally, we walked from one hut to another between 6:00 a.m. and 6:00 p.m. On the way, we noticed, among various other things, the biotic interference, wildlife (if any), kills, and signs of wildlife presence: nail marks, pugmarks, droppings, calls, alarm calls, and so on. During our treks, the staff of the next round would welcome us at the spot where their area began. I would drag out field expert Ajay to accompany me on the trek. His expertise benefitted me greatly. We had given clear instructions at home and office not to disturb us unless it was an emergency. We carried a walkie-talkie with us just in case. Ajay would climb up a nearby hill every morning and evening to establish contact on the walkie-talkie with the main station.

We started our trek from Vairat (the highest point in Melghat at an altitude of about four thousand feet above mean sea level) along with the field staff of Chikhaldara. We travelled on a six-foot-wide footpath cleared for easy movement and reached the Punyang rock overhang overlooking a deep gorge. It resembled a typical rock shelter of the prehistoric man and was large enough to accommodate more than fifty persons. Our labourers sometimes stayed there. On one side of the cave, a perennial spring had formed a water screen. We stepped in very carefully as it was dark inside, and we wanted to ensure that neither bear nor leopard was resting inside the cave. Though we did not find these animals there, we saw plenty of evidence of their presence, mainly pugmarks and droppings. I remember Ajay telling me the story of a British *sahib* who, in the darkness, had accidentally landed too close to a sloth bear. The bear had charged and held the *sahib's* head in both its paws. The *sahib* had shown presence of mind to first free his head and push the bear away before shooting it. Had he shot the bear earlier, the dying bear would have tightened its grip on the *sahib's* head and crushed his cranium, thought the *sahib*.

Our first halt was in the Kalukundi protection hut, so christened because of its proximity to a waterhole by the same name. After a day-long walk, the stiff bamboo bed and the sleeping bag gave more pleasure than any five-star comfort.

On day two, we ascended a ridge completely covered by *karvi*, the shrub which flowers once in seven years, and descended into a valley called Chidi-rani, named after an attractive bird seen by the locals long ago. Chidi-rani was in a valley, and it was very cold. There are valleys in Melghat which have such frost holes, and we avoid such spots while selecting nursery sites. My torch was a five-in-one, and one of its functions was measuring the temperature. In the morning, when I saw Ajay taking a cold water bath in a nearby rivulet, I checked the temperature: it showed two degrees centigrade. I am an unabashed admirer of Ajay's qualities, and I wondered how well this Mumbaikar had adapted to Melghat conditions.

Day three involved another ascent to a ridge from where the nearby Bhopadeo and Rupaibhabla plateaus could be seen. During the rainy season, a double-streamed waterfall emerges from the Rupaibhabla plateau, one stream called Rupai and the other one Bhabla. Rupai, a Korkoo girl, and Bhabla, the boy, were in love and wanted to marry against the community's wishes. They were forced to leave the village. They stayed together on the plateau but could not pull on. Ultimately, they jumped together from the waterfall and ended their lives, hence the name Rupaibhabla. My staff visited the site from where the couple had jumped and found some very old household items like cooking utensils. In the evening, we descended into the Banaam valley and reached the Banaam hut. Banaam is a perennial waterhole which forms an important source of the Gadga River.

On day four, we left Banaam early in the morning and traversed cross-country to reach Sipna-khandi. This spot happens to be on the Koha–Vairat fair-weather road, which remains closed for four months in a year and is hardly used at other times either. But it gave us a feeling that we were near civilisation. We have a big enclosure there for the breeding and release of herbivores in the wild. We had kept pigs in the enclosure which were being used for experiments for fixing the dose of tranquilisers. Next to the enclosure, we had a silage pit for manufacturing vitamin-fortified fodder for the wild herbivores during the pinch period. We then passed by the dilapidated walls of FRH Rangrao, down the trail leading to the Sadhukundi protection hut for halt. This was our most popular hut, which we showed off to senior officers. We also housed the CM there, who visited us twice.

Near Sadhukundi is the shrine of Sadhu Baba. Near the shrine is a spring where green grass is found growing on the rocks even in peak summer. Locals believe that Sadhu Baba roams the area on horseback and uses this grass for his horse. The protection hut is on the bank of a *naala* which has deep perennial pools in the rocky bed. The food prepared in this water gives it special taste.

I must share an interesting duel that I witnessed in the Sadhukundi hut. This was not a fight between the mighty tiger and a wily bear or between a tiger and a leopard. It was between two lesser mortals: a centipede and a lizard (*Calotes versicolor*), *sarda* in Marathi. The lizard had committed the mistake of underestimating the power of a tiny centipede and was complacent. The centipede gave a nasty bite to the lizard's neck. The poison soon paralysed the lizard's body. After a couple of minutes, I saw the tiny centipede clinging to the lizard's neck and, with some effort, dragging the mighty lizard's full-grown body. The episode gave me as much excitement as I could get at the sighting of large mammalian wildlife. The lesson that I had learnt was that one must not crib about not seeing a tiger in the jungle but start observing smaller creatures to enjoy the magic of nature. They too need an appreciative eye.

Talking about lizards, I am reminded of another interesting incident that occurred during my stay at FRH Tarubanda. One night a senior colleague of mine and I decided to go patrolling. As usual, I took my khaki shirt off the wooden peg in the rest house, tucked my shirt into my trousers, and took the steering wheel to drive towards Harisaal. After driving for about half an hour, I felt some movement inside my shirt. I applied the brakes, jumped out of the jeep, and, to the utter surprise of my colleague, pulled out my shirt under the beam of the headlight. Imagine what I saw. A shiny snake-like creature, about ten inches long, jumped out on the road, remained dazed for few seconds, and hurriedly took shelter in a nearby bush. The animal which had taken a free ride in the jeep was the common skink (*Mabuya carinata*). In Marathi, we call it *sapsurli* or *sapachi maushi* ('snake's aunt'). Imagine the slithering guest stuck inside my shirt, close to my body, travelling peacefully for half an hour without biting me!

The presence of the centipede ensured that there was one more decentipedean operation in our hut by the insistent field staff before I became horizontal on my bamboo bed covered with dry grass. Incidentally, during my service, I realised that I, particularly my shoes, acted like a magnet for the centipedes. Very often, a centipede was neatly parked inside my shoes. By the way, while in the field, one had to watch out for ticks in winters and leeches in rains.

PATROLLING

Ready for patrolling

Patrolling in the rains

A typical road block in jungles.

Patrolling in the core area of MTR

32

OF DREAMS AND NIGHTMARES

It is the late winter of 1965, and you are the DFO of Melghat, on a tour of the Tarubanda forest village in your private car. You have taken a left turn just before Harisaal and are now off the Ellichpore (now Achalpur)–Khandwa tar road. About another eight miles on the dust track, and you will reach FRH Tarubanda. The fair-weather road and the two tiny *ghat*s make you believe that it would be almost an hour's bumpy, dusty ride, testing the shock absorbers of your Hillman car. But you are in for a pleasant surprise. It seems that the ranger *sahib* had leaked your tour programme to the Chikhali, Tarubanda, and Patkahu villagers, who voluntarily repaired the track and sprinkled water on it just before your journey to ensure a bump-free, dust-free ride. You land up in FRH Tarubanda in a happy state of mind.

In the evening, the villagers of Keli, Bhiroja, Kund, Adhav, Patkahu, and Tarubanda gather at the FRH, literally jostling to get a glimpse of you. The ranger *sahib* (RFO) – sporting khaki breeches, a khaki sola hat, and a shining brown cross belt – disciplines them and makes them sit in an orderly manner. The people's representative from each village gets to sit on the veranda floor, and the rest fend for themselves. Some have even climbed up trees to get a glimpse of their hero (that's you). You take to your *aaraam-kursi* to a thunderous applause from the gathering. Somji Patel, the *sarpanch* of Tarubanda, sits on your right, and on your left sits your camp clerk with his portable Remington typewriter. The ranger *sahib* is the only person standing. A nod from you, and he tells the *durbar* that initially, only community issues would be dealt with, followed by individual problems.

Somji Patel explains that the festival of Holi is less than two months away and that all villagers from Tarubanda and its neighbourhood need such work, which will give them money to blow. You know very well that Somji is hinting at the timber harvesting work. Rather than walking about five to six miles to and from the work site, a hard-working couple can stay in the forest in a temporary shelter, work day and night, and earn up to twenty rupees per day (the daily wage was only four rupees). You quickly check with the ranger *sahib* if the marking of trees to be felled has been done and the coupe roads for the carting of harvested material are ready and whether your office has sanctioned the coupe estimate. On a confirmatory signal from him, you announce that the coupe harvesting would start from tomorrow. You've bowled them over. This is perhaps their happiest moment of the year. As the applause dies down, a brief round of whisperings begins about the preparations for tomorrow's 'coupe opening', including who will arrange the 'cock plus bottle' for the forest guard. Somji Patel is quick to take advantage of the public mood and announces that from the payment of wages for coupe working, everyone has to shell out one rupee each for the construction of Dolar Baba's monument on Adhao road. They all agree.

The second community problem is raised by the *gaoli*s of the Bhiroja and Keli villages. The milk supply for the DFO's camp at Tarubanda and Semadoh comes from these villages. For a touring conservator, the rules provide for a buffalo for milk (yes, you've read it right; it's not 'buffalo milk') besides the establishment of a grocery and a barber's shop. Their problem is that the level of water in their community well has gone down and that the water is infected too. You immediately direct the RFO to prepare an estimate for deepening the well and putting an appropriate quantity of bleaching powder in the well to purify the drinking water.

Next, the villagers from the Adhao village request for the replacement of the thatched roof of the school building, which was blown away during the last storm. For more than a month now, the school is being held under the shade of a banyan tree. More estimates for the RFO to prepare. The RFO is also instructed to start the work of the survey and demarcation of the coupe and the construction of coupe roads and attend to the serious problem of crop raiding by wild animals. 'Get the culling done, RFO!'

As this dictation is finishing, there is a commotion in one corner of the gathering, where some drunkard is creating a ruckus. The embarrassed RFO catches hold of the troublemaker and is about to administer corporal punishment, but you prevent him from doing so. On enquiry, you come to know that he is a primary school teacher at our school at Kund. You take a serious note of the teacher's irresponsible behaviour and dismiss him from service on the spot. The order is typed and kept by your camp clerk to be served tomorrow. An eligible local youngster is appointed then and there as schoolmaster for the Kund school. On a signal by the RFO, three to four forest guards appear on the scene and arrange to move the drunkard teacher away from the gathering.

After community issues, it is time for some serious individual issues. Among the many other issues, two are remarkable. A landless man had encroached upon a two-acre piece of forest land for his sustenance. You verify the fact and issue a *patta* of that land to the needy. The second is the case of Somji's *lamjana* or *ghar-jamai*. As per Korkoo tradition, the girl brings the boy to her father's home after marriage, and such a son-in-law is called *lamjana*. He is a tall well-built person, fourth standard pass, and aspires to become a forest guard. A few minutes of interaction with him, and you are convinced that he knows the forest inside out and can walk sixteen miles alone in the forest at a stretch without a problem. You instruct the RFO to complete the formalities of confirming his eligibility and get the camp clerk to issue his appointment order as forest guard to be handed over to him by the RFO on the successful completion of the walking test. You can see the gratitude in his eyes when you tell him to join duty from the first of next month. Before you wind up your *durbar*, you appeal to all fathers of two and more to go in for vasectomies. After a brief discussion, five or six youngsters agree, provided the RFO remains present to hold their hands as they are being operated upon.

Fast-forward to the present, please, and let's look back and compare. There was a strong bond of trust between the Forest Department and the local forest dwellers. Both sides strongly believed that they would not be let down by the other party. Also, there was only one agency, the Forest Department, that was a panacea for all the problems of the forest dwellers. The relationship is in turmoil today; the trust stands shattered. It is not half a century ago that it was the age of 'heroes' and today is the day of 'villains'. So what's gone wrong then?

During the last fifty years, 'civilisation' (?) has encroached upon the wild, resulting in more pressure on scarce resources. The Wildlife Protection Act came into existence in 1972, which banned hunting. So no more sambar feast for the locals. The ban on tree felling in the MTR has deprived the locals of extremely remunerative work which they did for generations and in which they had expertise. The recruitment procedure for the frontline staff of the Forest Department has undergone many changes, making it more complicated, scotching the aspirations of local boys. The abolition of the forest village system deprived the local forest officials, with a well-spread-out network in remote forest areas, of revenue powers. This reduced their importance and inconvenienced the local population. Now they have to rush to the *taluka* for work, which the RFO did earlier. Issues like drinking water, health, and education in the remote forest areas ceased to be looked after by the Forest Department. Similarly, the village tanks abounding in fish got transferred to outside authorities, who now prefer to auction the fish to contractors who earn profits rather than feed the locals. The Forest Department now only redirects the needy forest dwellers to the 'appropriate authority'.

All these changes in a short time have left the local forest dweller high and dry. 'Nobody's baby' is the impression that he gets of himself. He wonders how a department that is supposed to look after them can now talk about relocating their village to convenience the tiger.

This shattered trust requires to be restored. Modest trust-building eco-development activities need to be initiated in and around the MTR. The skilful planning and implementation of these activities may be a step in the right direction.

33

REBUILDING TRUST

During my tenure as FD (1991 to 1995), the MTR had a core area of about 360 square kilometres, most of which was later declared as the Gugamal National Park. Though there were no villages inside this area, there were villages on its fringes which exerted biotic pressure on it. The MTR's total area is about 1,600 square kilometres, which was dotted with 59 villages. From the tiger conservation point of view, these villages were cancer spots, surrounded by their zones of influence, which would increase with time and ultimately engulf the entire buffer zone. This would be suicidal for tiger conservation. Therefore, shifting all these villages out was necessary. However, convincing the inhabitants, looking out for suitable alternative land for relocation, and organising the huge money required for rehabilitation made it impossible to relocate all villages at one go. Hence, villages on the fringes – like Bori, Dhargad, Koha, Kund, Vairat, Churni, and Pastalai – were to be given priority for relocation. In the other villages, eco-development activities were to be taken up, basically to minimise their influence on the neighbouring forest resources.

Eco-development was a much-talked-about term during the early 1990s. It would, however, first require a healing touch to the bruised relationship between the local people and the MTR authorities. The WII in Dehradun saw it as coming through the 'economic development of the local people by adopting measures which are ecologically sustainable'. In our context, it was a package of trust-building activities which would help them to live decently till the village was ultimately relocated.

In many other states, these activities included programmes of massive dimensions like, say, an irrigation project. In the MTR, we did not want big projects as we feared it would result in addition to local population, thus ultimately putting pressure on the already scarce natural resources. Rather than unilaterally deciding on the nature of the works to be taken up, we opted to get into consultation with the villagers in the fringe villages. These simple people had just one demand: water and food for themselves and for their cattle. Our eco-development plan thus primarily revolved round meeting these basic demands of the villagers by way of small works.

The work of providing potable drinking water was given supreme priority. Most of these villages had a community dug well, which became a small puddle during the pinch period, making both the quality and the quantity of water poor. It was proposed, therefore, that groundwater resources be surveyed, the existing wells be repaired, de-silted, and deepened, bore wells be constructed, and tanks be built alongside for drinking water for cattle. This would protect the waterholes in the core from infestation by the cattle and leave them for the exclusive use of wildlife. The immunisation of domestic cattle followed by ear tagging was also provided for.

To increase the productivity of agricultural land, terracing was proposed. A study conducted by IIM Ahmedabad in the Bori, Dhargad, and Gullar *ghat* region showed that terracing results in a 40 per cent increase in productivity. The MTR would create marketing facilities and also help in transporting the agricultural produce to Akot, a big marketplace. Reducing unproductive cattle and improving their progeny was proposed. Good-quality fish seed would be provided for the water tanks adjacent to the villages.

Crop raiding by wild herbivores has been a serious menace in almost the entire MTR area. Wild boars have been the biggest culprits. In seriously affected areas, the loss exceeded 50 per cent of the total production. To reach a solution, lot of experiments were tried. This included the construction of a stone wall or a trench between the forest and the agricultural land. The idea was twofold; one, it would be a crop-raider-proof fencing, and two, it would provide work to the locals right at their door steps. This was not feasible as both the wall and the trench collapsed after a couple of rainy seasons, and all the farmers were not prepared to maintain the structure.

The experiment of solar-energised fencing worked very well, though it had the following three limitations. All the farmers with farms abutting the forest had to take up the responsibility of weeding the grass below their part of the fence. Even if one person does not do the weeding, the weeds touch the fence, and voltage goes down. This results in an aggressive animal like the wild boar making inroads. So an individual farmer cannot take up a plea that his field was fallow, and that's why he has not done the weeding. Second, somebody had to take up the responsibility of battery maintenance, basically checking up the distilled water in the battery. Third, each village had at least one road passing through it. Someone had to keep the fence gate opened during the day and closed at night. Once the gates are closed at night, there has to be a warning signal to alert the passer-by about the energised fence. A bike-rider forester had badly got entangled in the live wires and was seriously injured. At Bori, I remember that a tiger had accidentally touched the live wire and was thrown off, partially breaking a claw.

Now about grazing issues. Owing to overuse, the area near the village was deprived of good-quality fodder and was encroached by an undesirable weed called lantana. These lantana bushes often harboured bears, sometimes wild boars and leopards in rare cases. There was a conflict situation when villagers went for answering the call of nature in the wee hours of the morning. So the work of uprooting lantana was proposed in the village surrounds. This activity was to provide the following benefits:

1. Employment at door steps is given
2. Relief from accidental attacks by wildlife is provided
3. Uprooted area provides space for fodder species to take over
4. Lantana could also be used for furniture making, as was done in Uttarakhand

The area in the village surrounds was divided into three sections, and only one was to be opened for grazing every year. This rotational grazing was to be coupled with harvesting the unpalatable grass before seed fall to give excellent results in two to three years. The plantation of fodder species was also proposed in suitable locations, preferably in village surrounds.

Now for a paragraph about the relocation of villages. During my tenure as FD of the MTR, we were seriously considering shifting Bori, Kund, and Koha in the first phase. I remember having seen a site near Rajurgirwarpur (in the Akola district) and sent villagers from Bori to have a look at their new village site. The positive features of the site were flat topography, good, deep black cotton soil, and an irrigation facility for crops. I had then told the villagers to decide fast; the one who moved in first would get the best patch. With the passage of time, Bori shifted there. Just out of curiosity, I recently visited Rajurgirwarpur. Each one having a bigger house and a productive farm, no crop raiding, a nearby school, a marketplace, public transport at door steps, health care in the vicinity, fruit trees in the compound, a Hanuman temple at the spot they desired – they all looked extremely happy. This was an exceptional case, and perhaps the villages that got relocated later were not as happy. The erstwhile Bori surround has become a huge meadow dotted with *bori* (Ziziphus) trees. The deserted village has been taken over by wildlife.

By the time I had vacated the FD's chair, the villagers were generally seeing the positive changes of the eco-development activities. People did want to contribute something positive to the MTR. In their enthusiasm, they sometimes went overboard; there were cases of villagers trying to save *cheetal*s (spotted deer) from leopards.

Some degree of lost trust was restored. But if the Melghat tiger has to survive, just eco-development activities are not good enough. Ideally, all the fifty-nine villages have to be happily relocated. Whether that materialises or not, only time will tell.

G

UNIQUE

This chapter includes eight stories related to certain unique characters of Melghat. The annual feature of devastating forest fires, certain rare birds and animals, unique species of snakes, the flash floods caused by the undulating terrain, the unusual floral diversity, and the gods and god-intoxicated persons all unique to Melghat appear in the form of individual articles. The penultimate article in this chapter is titled 'The Price of Progress'. It basically talks about the ill effects of electrification and the intensive agricultural practices respectively often misused in Melghat for the electrocution and poisoning of wild animals. We end the stories with a unique article about the Wednesday weekly market at Harisaal.

34

JUNGLE INFERNO

Forest fires in the Melghat area are a very serious problem. They generally start off sporadically by December, but the severity is felt more from mid-February onwards. In fact, that is the time when the fire season is formally declared in Melghat, and it stretches up to the onset of a monsoon. Once the fire season is declared, fire watchtowers are erected at vantage points. The watchtower staff, on detecting fire, pass on the information by wireless to the nearest field staff, who rush to the spot to combat and extinguish the fire. In fact, the wireless network got established in Melghat in the mid-seventies primarily for combating forest fires. To restrict fire, the forest area is divided into smaller blocks with the help of fire lines. Fire lines are long strips of earth cleared of any combustible material like dry grass or leaves, designed to starve the advancing fire of any fuel. The job of cutting and carving a fire line is done from November to December every year. Fire lines are regularly maintained by sweeping and keeping them clear of leaf litter and other debris. This job as well as the work of actually fighting fires is done by specially appointed staff called *angari*.

During firefighting, efforts are made to ensure that the fire does not pass from one patch to another by beating down the fire. An experiment to combat forest fire in Melghat by using modern technology was tried. In this experiment, a helicopter with big buckets was used. The helicopter would go to the water source, fill up with water, and throw it on the fire. This would reduce the intensity of the fire, and a well-equipped ground crew would douse it altogether. The experiment proved too expensive and was abandoned. The forest fires we have in Maharashtra are 'ground fires', where basically the ground flora, leaf litter, and some dried trees burn and the live trees get scorched. The scorched trees later die or develop hollowness. Wildlife is severely damaged, especially the ground-nesting birds. The fires that devastate the resin-rich coniferous forests of the Himalayas are called 'crown fires', where everything is turned to ash.

The causes of forest fire could be either natural or artificial. In the former case, it is an 'act of God'. In these parts, we do not have fires belonging to this category. Artificial or man-made fires could be caused by accident, negligence, or deliberate intention. Sadly, most forest fires are intentionally caused. The reasons are varied – wanting an early flush of grass, increase in the yield of gum or *tendu* (*Diospyros melanoxylon*) leaves, used for making *beedis* (country cigars), poaching and vandalism among them. From the middle of March to the middle of April, the *mahua* trees are in full bloom in Melghat. The succulent, creamish flowers are used for making the local brew. Picking these flowers in the morning becomes difficult because of leaf litter or the undergrowth. Once the area under the tree is burnt, it becomes black, and the task of collecting the creamish flowers against the black background becomes much easier. Such fire, if not doused properly, enters the forest.

Deer too shed their antlers in the summer. These antlers are used for making Ayurvedic preparations. There is a legal ban on collecting the antlers. However, unscrupulous elements set fire to the forest to burn up the debris on the forest floor. This helps in the easy sighting of these antlers. Such fires lit for small gains rage through the Melghat forests for days together. Revenge on the forest staff and/or hopes of getting employment as firefighters are other reasons for intentionally lighting forest fires.

Once, I remember doing night patrolling. Around ten at night, I saw a small fire by the roadside. My crew and I promptly jumped out and, in half an hour, got it under control. As we were boarding the jeep, we saw another fire about a kilometre ahead, which, again, we promptly extinguished. This got repeated till about four in the morning. I cannot forget that night when we spent the whole night extinguishing ten forest fires along the road. The culprit was walking about two kilometres ahead of us. His reason for this mischief? A tiger was supposedly staying in that patch of forest, and this was his way of keeping the animal from attacking him. During my range charge at Tarubanda, during my Dharni days, and later as FD of the MTR, I saw six fire seasons and combated numerous fires.

It was summertime again, around seven in the evening. I was three kilometres beyond the Kund village, patrolling the border of the core area of Project Tiger on the banks of the dry Sakhari River, when I spotted a small fire. This was quite near the spot where I had got stuck during my maiden trip on 3913. On this night too, I had a jeep with me along with a (purposely kept) trailer and, again, my brave driver Hasan as my only companion. Had we both gone on to Kund to collect a force to combat the fire, we would have lost precious time, and the small fire could well have become unmanageable. In fact, had it entered the core area, it would have become devastating. Since grazing was not permitted in the core area, combustible material had accumulated; the grass, particularly, had become very tall. So despite protests from Hasan, I decided to get down alone from the jeep to combat the fire and sent Hasan to Kund to fetch help. He promised to return in ten minutes, but I was prepared for thirty.

Before Hasan left, he had handed me a makeshift broom as a firefighting tool which could be used for both sweeping as well as beating down the fire. I occupied a fire line and got down to sweeping and clearing it of debris. The fire was still about half a kilometre away in a valley and emitted just enough light for me to see. The first thing that I saw was a shiny long snake slithering out from the fire and passing me at biting distance. Slowly, the intensity of the wind increased, and the fire got divided into three parts. One patch, about fifty feet wide, was fast climbing towards me and had flames about fifteen feet tall. I quickly cleaned up the fire line and stood firmly on it with a resolve to stop it.

Suddenly, a big hairy sloth bear rushed away from the fire, right by me. It was least bothered about taking cognisance of me; saving its precious life from fire was topmost on its agenda. Though the bear and snake had not threatened me in any way, the fact was that within a span of fifteen minutes, I had encountered two of the forest's most avoidable denizens. Feeling slightly nervous, I started praying for Hasan's early arrival.

As the fire came closer, the wind velocity also increased, resulting in the formation of a mini whirlwind which helped the fire jump the fire line which I had cleaned. I quickly rushed to the spot and extinguished that patch. The rest of the fire came up to the fire line and stopped, which gave me great satisfaction, and I quickly put it all out. However, my happiness was short-lived as it soon became totally dark, and I had no torch. My dazzled eyes refused to see anything, and I was forced to remain glued to a spot, listening quietly to various jungle sounds. I was hungry, thirsty, and very scared in the pitch darkness in tiger country. I prayed hard for help.

...I occupied a fireline and got down to sweeping...

At long last, I heard the faint sound of a jeep followed by some rays of (hope!) light. It had taken Hasan almost an hour to return with a mixed bunch of fifteen youngsters and oldies, a barrelful of water, and some food for me. We had the other two fires to attend to and got on to the job. Around one at night, the water was exhausted. We had no option but to drink water from a dirty pond after purifying it using local methods. Rehydrating ourselves was essential because I had the experience of my dehydrated firefighting crew members passing blood in their urine.

The firefighting continued till four in the morning. I reached Tarubanda around breakfast time, wondering about the person who would have lit the fire. Maybe he was merrily watching us struggle. I also thought about those unsung heroes who had got singed or who had lost their lives while fighting fire in some remote area of the jungle. Incidentally, there is a monument at Harisaal to commemorate the efforts of a RFO who laid down his life combating a forest fire.

35

FOR MY EYES ONLY

Shooting with a Camera

It is human nature to want to sight something which others have not seen or only a few have. In the context of a tiger reserve, one more category can be added – seeing what others have not seen over a long time. For succeeding in achieving something unique, one has to put in a lot of hard work, alertness, and patience, and most importantly, one has to turn lucky. While moving around in a wildlife area, it is always good to carry a camera with a zoom lens and to keep a tripod handy. This is necessary because when you share your 'breaking news', it should go with some evidence. When I recollect some experiences that I had during the early part of my service career, I still regret not having a camera on that crucial moment. One such celestial moment was missed by me during a very early part of my service when I stayed in FRH Tarubanda for a month, waiting for my residence to be readied in Tarubanda.

The Celestial Moment
Wish List

During my posting as FD of the MTR, my rather long 'wish list' of wildlife was the following: the Malabar pied hornbill (*dhanesh/ wayera*) and stork-billed kingfisher (*motha-kilkila*) under 'Avians' and the smooth-coated otter (*pan-manjar*), pangolin (*khavlya-manjar*), and mouse deer (*pisori*) under 'Mammals'. The Indian white-backed vulture (*pandharyapathiche gidhad*) and the long-billed vulture (*laamb chochiche gidhad*) were so commonly seen in the rural area of Maharashtra that I presumed them to be present in Melghat too, but that was not so. I never saw them. Some colleagues reported sighting the long-billed vulture on the ledges of cliff faces at Echo Point, Chikhaldara. From the wish list, I could not see the Malabar pied hornbill, the pangolin, and the otter. A colleague claimed he had seen the Malabar pied hornbill in flight and heard its call near the Chacharda waterhole below Vairat. He could not get a picture though.

The Amphibious Mammal

In the late 1980s, I was posted in Akola when an interesting incident took place at Karanja (Lad). On summer nights, people slept out, and often an animal would run through the sleeping group. One night they pretended that they were asleep, and when the animal came at night, they pounced upon it, overpowered it, tied it up with a rope, and brought it to me for identification. It was the smooth-coated otter. Its habitat was a lake on the outskirts of Karanja (Lad), but the lake had dried up that summer; hence, the animal had come out on land in search of food. With similar lakes in the MTR, I had expected to sight them, but there was no trace of them. Incidentally, this animal is on the verge of extinction in Maharashtra; the few specimens left are breathing their last in the Gadchiroli and Ratnagiri districts. A pangolin too was brought to me for identification. Ironically, I have seen wildlife creatures like vultures, otters, and pangolins only in 'non-wild' areas; they have always eluded me in their wilderness abodes.

Bambai Ka Dost

I kept looking out for the stork-billed kingfisher without success till I was told the exact location where the great ornithologist Dr Salim Ali had sighted the bird during his visit to Melghat. I was mistaking this bird for the common one: the white-breasted kingfisher. I sighted it in the loop of Rakhi-doh in the river Sipna in front of FRH Kolkaz. This was the fourth variety of kingfisher I had seen in the MTR, the earlier three being the small blue, the white-breasted, and the pied ones.

Fate had a special discount sale in store for me. It was a 'buy one, get one free' offer. Having seen the stork-billed kingfisher after a lot of effort, I was fortunate to see a new variety without any. In January 1995, an ornithologist from the WII in Dehradun, Prachi Mehta, was working in the MTR for her PhD. She sighted a kingfisher that was unheard of in Melghat. It had travelled all the way presumably from the coastal area of Mumbai. Normally, it was reputed to travel inland along the creeks for some distance – and definitely not deep into Central India. It was a great piece of discovery by the JRF of the WII. I was fortunate to view this rare sight on 21 January 1995. I visited the site again on 7 February and photographed the bird. By 28 April 1995, the bird had flown away from Melghat – forever. The name of this visitor is the black-capped kingfisher, my fifth.

The Diurnal Owl

It was the monsoon of 1992. As usual, a huge army of Kathiawadi cattle was gathering on the border of the core area of the MTR, and emboldened by local political support, it was threatening to enter at the hint of slightest complacency. It was also the season for the poachers to get into the jungles with their dogs. To safeguard against these threats and to boost the morale of my frontline staff, I thought of joining the patrolling party. We planned the programme on 20 August 1992 on the Dhargad–Pirkheda–Chiladari–Koktoo route. Ravi Wankhade and a selected bunch of uniformed persons were with me. It was a tough twenty-one-kilometre trek in undulating terrain.

We crossed Pirkheda and reached a spot where we paused because the silence of the forest was broken by an unusual bird call. In a flash, two or three binoculars came out, and we all had a good look at the bird and recorded our observations in our field notebooks. Broadly, the bird looked like a biggish specimen of the spotted owlet, but this one didn't have spots. A nocturnal bird active and calling at eleven o'clock in the morning surprised us. We saw and heard the bird to our heart's content and referred to the literature at hand and concluded that we had spotted the rare forest owlet, which was last spotted in India in 1914.

After reaching the office, I made a special report to the Bombay Natural History Society (BNHS) about the location, habitat, time of sighting, call, and description of the bird. Unfortunately, we did not have a camera with a zoom lens and hence could not get a picture of the bird. We were informed by the BNHS that in 1979, Dr Salim Ali had toured Melghat for fifteen days and had observed that there were no forest owlets in Melghat. Our team was convinced that what we had seen on 20 August 1992 was a forest owlet, and I still stand by it. The official records though show that the forest owlet was rediscovered in Melghat by someone else in 1997.

Supreme Agility

After our experience on 20 August 1992, I made it a point to carry a camera with a zoom lens whenever I travelled in the MTR. On 1 December 1994, I left Koktoo after lunch, crossed Dolar, and was on the Dhakna road. It was half past two in the afternoon, and I was seated on the rear seat of my Ambassador car with a zoom-fitted camera in my hand. Hasan was on leave, and hence, Neemkar was driving. We were in a dry patch of forest on the border of the forest, with some habitation around us.

Suddenly, we both sighted a big cat (much bigger than the jungle cat) by the roadside. Its colour was reddish brown, and it had prominent triangular ears. It went slightly into the vegetation and arched its body like a bow after sighting a peacock. But perhaps disturbed by my car's arrival, the animal gave up its aggressive posture and suddenly came very close to the car to investigate. It was so close that I could not get it in my (rather powerful and long) zoom-lens-fitted camera's viewfinder. In the next fraction, it disappeared.

We had seen a caracal. I had seen it in Sariska earlier and hence knew how it looks. I remembered that it can kill nine to ten feeding pigeons at one go before they can leave the ground. We stopped the car and got down to investigate in detail. I could photograph the pugmarks. We also saw feathers and other fresh remains of a green pigeon killed by the caracal. There were claw marks too on a nearby tree which the caracal had climbed for hunting the green pigeon. Neemkar was very keen to know what we had seen. So after photographing all the circumstantial evidence, we proceeded to FRH Dhakna, where I opened Prater's book of Indian animals and showed Neemkar the photographs of various cats and told him to point at the picture of the animal which we had just seen. He confidently put his finger on the right one. Neemkar recently told me that he saw the same animal near Ghatang while he was with my immediate successor Mr Patki. This is one sighting which gave me immense satisfaction.

Amrai Ka Ghuggu

I was lucky to see the *amrai ka ghuggu* from very close quarters. It so happened one night that I was sitting on a machan in a mango tree at a waterhole when an unsuspecting bird came and parked itself next to me. It was a huge specimen, a little less than two feet in height. I still cannot forget those shiny eyes staring back at me when I flashed my torch at it. An *amrai ka ghuggu* sitting at handshaking distance from you in an *aam* tree indeed calls for some luck. In fact, in all my exclusive sightings listed above, I was convinced that luck played an important role. Though initially unlucky with tiger sighting, I turned out to be a champion while sighting something unique, for my eyes only.

36

HOLY SNAKES!

As the son of a forester and later a forester myself, I have stayed in big old bungalows with huge compounds. I have also had the opportunity to visit most of the forest areas and occupy numerous FRHs in Maharashtra. So I have always been used to venomous creatures like ticks, spiders, leeches, centipedes, scorpions, and so on, not to talk about bandicoots, skinks, and lizards. Snakes, however, have come to occupy the pride of place in my list of wild friends. This wasn't always so. Few people thought then about their environmental role as rat-control agents. They were man's mortal enemies and, by inclusion, mine too. They had to be killed at sight and continue to be killed even today or, as a maddening contrast, worshipped once in a year on the festival of Naag Panchami, the chief among the worshipped being the most poisonous one of all, the cobra. The worship doesn't bring any relief to the beleaguered animal either. If caught, it is defanged and thus crippled from hunting its food. It is force-fed milk, which is not its food, and often dies of choked lungs.

One of my childhood hobbies during the rainy season was to zero in on a snake just by listening to the alarm calls of the *myna*s outdoors. Snakes are very active during the rains. The snake to suffer the most, ironically, was the non-venomous *dhaman* (rat snake). We generally had at least one expert snake killer in our servants' quarters. One such expert, a genuine multitasker, was Mohanlal Mehraulia, who occupied our servants' quarters about fifty-eight years ago. He was a railway employee and would clean our premises. He had a dark, serene, wrinkled face. Down with high fever? Call Mohanlal. Possessed by an evil spirit? Call Mohanlal. A snake in the compound or inside the bungalow? The short thin frame of Mohanlal would appear on the scene of 'crime' from nowhere. He took charge of the situation in no time and really put us at peace. For handling a snake found indoors, Mohanlal would pour edible oil on the snake, making its body slippery on the smooth floor and thus preventing escape. He had a special stick for killing snakes. Interestingly, Mohanlal's son, Arjun, also joined the railways but did not pick up any of his father's special traits. In my childhood, I remember seeing a gun being summoned to kill a cobra.

There have always been lots of myths about snakes, and that is why there has been a formal ritual of disposing of its body. The ritual, in short, includes burning the snake. During my childhood, a copper one-paisa coin (with a big hole) was put in the fire, and some mantras were chanted. The snake killer was suitably rewarded for his services. The specialist killer explained to us kids that unless the entire ritual were observed, the snake could come back to life and avenge itself by biting its killer to death. This revenge line applied particularly to the *naag* (male cobra) and *naagin* (female cobra). Further, we were to refer to snakes as *rassi* (rope), not proceed if a snake crossed our path, not whistle (especially in the evening) for fear of attracting them, and not go near aromatic plants as they could well be nestling there. The list of myths is just unending.

As a forester, I was required to carry out the inspection of plantations, especially in the monsoons. This work involved planting, weeding, soil working, manuring, casualty replacement, and such other activities and involved walking in rains over large undulating terrain, often through tall grasses and bushes. Encounters with snakes, therefore, were quite common. I remember one such inspection getting totally sabotaged because right at the beginning of the inspection, an extra-cautious staff member saw a snake in the grass and panicked. Later, every five minutes, he suspected a snake to be at his feet and screamed and leaped. Within a little while, some others started screaming and leaping too. Soon, it became an epidemic, a kind of contest at who could leap the highest. Things went so totally out of hand that the inspection had to be abandoned altogether.

The cobra is the most feared of all Indian snakes, and three close encounters during my Tarubanda days are still very fresh in my memory. The first one was when, in August 1979, my boss, the DFO, had come on tour. He was inspecting markings in Coupe Number 4 Adhao on the Tarubanda–Adhao road. During inspection, we had gone quite deep into the jungle and, as it was getting dark, were hurriedly returning to the jeep. The DFO was leading, and I was briskly following his footsteps. Suddenly, in the fading light, I saw a shiny thing slither past the boss's feet. He had narrowly missed stamping on a six-foot cobra. Since I was following him very closely, I had to apply emergency brakes as I saw the snake pass between his two feet. It was indeed a very miraculous escape for my boss.

The second encounter was rather comic and took place near Chikhali, a round headquarter falling in the Tarubanda Range. A tenth-standard tribal boy from the residential ashram school had gone to the river Sipna for a bath. Cycling back, he accidentally ran over a cobra. The snake reacted sharply and struck at the boy but missed. In the melee, the nervous boy fell down from the cycle. When I arrived at the spot, I saw a full-grown cobra that had wound itself around the cycle and had raised its hood on the handle. The schoolboy was reduced to being a helpless and patient onlooker. I got down from my jeep to help the boy but could not as the cobra was not prepared to leave its prized possession: the cycle. Bringing the jeep near at full throttle failed to shoo it away. Finally, I had to move the jeep away and take the schoolboy for a short walk. Finding everything quiet, the snake felt secure, lowered its hood, and slowly disappeared into the forest.

The third near encounter was of the closest kind. My residence at Tarubanda had a courtyard at the back which was a three-by-three-foot toilet. One early morning, around five thirty, I went for a loo in the toilet when it was still dark. Judging from the rustling noise, my orderly could guess that I had got up. After I returned, I could hear my orderly getting into the routine of filling the bucket with water and placing the lantern there for me. Suddenly, I heard a scream accompanied by the frantic flinging of the bucket and the lantern and the hurried patter of his footsteps. As I stepped out, I saw him dash towards my room. He was thanking the Almighty for saving the *sahib* as there was a full-grown cobra inside the toilet which I had just left. Indeed, I was fortunate. In the darkness, I could have easily stamped on the cobra, inviting a bite from it during my two-minute stay in the toilet.

Another important snake of Melghat is the python. My first viewing was when the jeep I was travelling in was following a truck, about five kilometres ahead, carrying teak poles. The jeep was suddenly required to be stopped for something which initially I thought was a teak pole negligently dropped by the truck driver. Actually, it was a python which was so huge that the full breadth of the state highway was inadequate to contain it. It took its own sweet time to wriggle past the road. Such snakes crossing the road often get run over by speeding vehicles. There is need to exercise restraint.

We had one more occasion in Melghat where, had we not exercised caution, we could have run over the snake. Between Semadoh and Kolkaz, I once saw a Russell's viper right in the middle of the road. Like many, I too initially made the mistake of thinking it to be a baby python. It was Mr Sawarkar of the WII who had identified the snake before we could get down from the jeep to rescue it from being run over. There is a growing tendency, especially among youngsters, of catching a snake and then showing it off on one's body. This has to be a big *no*. In one case, thinking that it was a non-venomous baby python, someone was flaunting a Russell's viper on his body – around the neck, to be precise. The flaunter got bitten and died instantaneously.

I have seen pythons swallowing big prey like monkeys or deer. After that, the python finds movement difficult for some time. If it is near a path, it often becomes the victim of sadistic passers-by: they push it, kick it, stone it, and sometimes even kill it. Such a harassed python then throws out the animal it has swallowed. I have seen one such python vomiting a monkey which looked as if it was still alive. Once, a python had swallowed a barking deer whose antlers had punctured the snake's gut while it was regurgitating. The ten-foot-long python had died, and the skeleton was kept at the Project Tiger Museum at Chikhaldara.

Another encounter was in October 1979. I was trekking around Sakhari on the border of the core area of Project Tiger when in the midst of the lush green forest, I came across a beautiful waterfall which had made a nice little natural swimming pool. The situation was so tempting that I could not resist swimming in that exclusive luxury which I thought no seven-star hotel could have offered. After swimming for about half an hour, I felt totally recharged, and I scrambled out of the pool from one side. As I did so, I turned round to see that a huge python was slithering out from the other. This incident taught me to keep away from unknown waters in jungles as pythons can remain underwater for fairly long durations (1685).

37

IN A FLASH

The Koha village is located on the Akot–Harisaal State Highway (SH 204). This beautiful winding highway takes one through the dense forests of the MTR. A day drive on this road, particularly during the monsoons, is an out-of-this-world experience. During the night too, there is almost no traffic on this road except a stray patrolling vehicle of the Forest Department. If one starts from Akot (a tehsil of the Akola district) and proceeds towards Harisaal, one has to enter Melghat from the Popatkheda gate, where we have a forest check post. Then the long and rather lonely drive starts.

After about half an hour, one reaches a spot called Jinbaba, where many passers-by stop to pay respect to a deity. The deity is in the form of a stone statue with a thin slit between the lips. The devotees have a unique way of paying their respect to the deity. They offer it a *beedi*, which they insert between the lips of the deity. It is believed that Jinbaba smokes the *beedi* overnight and that only a stub remains the next morning. I have seen the *beedi* stubs between the lips every time I have passed by. Whenever my vehicle passed by any deity, my driver used to display his respect in a unique way. He would slow down the vehicle, honk, and proceed. This practice, he religiously observed for

Jinbaba too. In the later part of my service, as FD of Project Tiger, I had a unique (and frightening) experience at Jinbaba while travelling alone at midnight. That experience is narrated in my article about the deities of Melghat under the title 'In God We Trust'.

While travelling towards Koha/Harisaal, after crossing Jinbaba, one reaches a spot called 'the highest point' from where one gets an aerial view of the city of Akot. Passers-by often take a break here. This spot has a huge steep rise on one side and a precipitous valley on the other side. One evening, as I, along with our driver Hasan, was appreciating nature's beauty from this point, my attention was attracted by the alarm call of a sambar on the uphill side behind us. This call was immediately followed by a sambar stag crashing down just behind us on the road from a height of about twenty five feet. To our surprise, it immediately scrambled back to its feet, looked dazed for a moment, limped across the road, and went crashing down into the valley. We were indeed puzzled. We got our answer when we looked up at the edge of the cutting from where the sambar had fallen: a pack of hungry wild dogs had come to a screeching halt. I wondered if I had messed up their dinner.

As one proceeds from the highest point towards Koha, before Belkund, one comes across a road going towards Khongda, and near this spot is located another baba named Rajdevbaba. One wonders why there are so many babas on this road. One explanation is that it breaks the monotony of a long journey and recharges divine blessings. Incidentally, the status of the Akot–Harisaal road is of a state highway, and though seldom used, it has been in existence for a long, long time. Such spots are immensely useful for a lone traveller on this road to keep up his morale. Some staff residents of the erstwhile Koha village would go to Akot for the market, while the majority visited the Harisaal weekly market. Such travellers would take a journey break at these shrines.

As one passes from the 'highest point' towards Koha, the watershed changes, and a new catchment begins. The road also goes continuously downslope till one crosses the Belkund PWD rest house to reach Koha. This rest house had the dubious reputation of 'housing' ghosts; hence, no officer generally went to 'rest' there. I stayed alone there overnight but did not encounter anything. Perhaps the resident ghosts had gone visiting friends.

As one gets out of the Belkund rest house and proceeds towards Koha, there is a hilly patch beside the road on the left side. The *murum* soil from this hilly patch is gouged out, perhaps for repairing roads. The excavated portion has resulted in a deep concave patch. At a later stage in service, I remember coming across a sambar stag in this patch. The sambar was perhaps running away from a carnivore. My driver and I got down from the jeep to look at the stressed animal 'trapped' in the arc. It did not try to run away. We could almost touch it. We remained with the sambar for almost fifteen minutes, after which it felt comfortable and left on its own. On the lower slopes, the road runs alongside the Gadga River, sometimes running parallel to it and at other places crossing over it. Incidentally, just below the Belkund rest house is a bridge on the Gadga with a plaque reading, 'Belkund Bridge — 1886 R. W. Swinnerton Esq.: AMICE Engineer, Babu Deonath Sahai Overseer'. From the highest point down to Koha is one continuous fall – connected by about twenty-five kilometres of winding road. The altitude difference between these two points is about two thousand feet. I had heard that such a situation in the hills results in flash floods.

During my range charge at Tarubanda, I often visited Koha. This village has now been evacuated and its people rehabilitated elsewhere to minimise biotic interference by the villagers and their cattle in the wildlife habitats of the MTR. During my Tarubanda range charge days (1979), Koha was the headquarters of a round officer (one level below a RFO), and substantial field staff was posted there. I remember Round Officer Sawalakhe, who was my trusted deputy there. With various departmental activities such as the marking of mature trees, plantation, thinnings, nursery, etc. going on in the Koha round, it had become a busy work centre in my range. Naturally, I had to visit Koha frequently (almost weekly) with heavy cash to disburse to the Korkoo tribals who did most of the work. Koha was a beautiful village which was divided into two parts by the Gadga and the Akot–Harisaal road. The round officer's residence was located on a hilltop at the highest point. I remember there was a permanent primary school building with the national anthem written on its wall. I was a regular visitor to the school as well.

As most of the Koha inhabitants used to go to Harisaal for the Wednesday weekly bazaar (few used to go to Akot), I had made it a point to disburse wages to them on Tuesdays so that they were fully loaded for the shopping spree. Only once did I land up in Koha in the early hours on a Wednesday morning and become witness to a very interesting event. Incidentally, most of the Koha village, including Mr Sawalakhe's office, was located on the other side of the river Gadga. That morning, I waded through the ankle-deep water of the Gadga to reach the office and started making payments to a sizeable bunch of tribal labourers. I estimated that I would require a couple of hours to finish the payment. After about fifteen minutes, Sawalakhe looked up at the sky towards the highest point and, pointing to the dark clouds and lightning, urged me to cross the river back to the safety of other side, i.e. towards the road. I laughed at him and ignored his suggestion as there was not even a drop of rain in Koha.

After another ten minutes, he drew my attention to a low roar and said, 'Sir, the flash flood is approaching.'

Yes, I too heard the roar; he was right. Immediately, we wound up, bundled up the cash and vouchers, and dashed towards the roadside across the Gadga. Along with us, the entire village was quickly taking a decision: which side of the river they would like to stay on for the next few hours. By the time we were halfway across the Gadga, a slight drizzle had started, and the roar had become frighteningly loud. As we reached the other bank, I could see the flood waters rolling in at lightning speed, making a deafening sound. In a minute, about three hundred feet of the width of the Gadga was flooded. We had narrowly escaped getting washed away.

Amazingly, the drizzle had stopped. I finished making the payments near the Akot–Harisaal road, and most of the people reached the Harisaal market that day, but the Gadga continued to remain in spate for a good three hours. Interestingly, it was just a local cloud burst, and it did not rain anywhere else in Melghat. That day, I got first-hand experience of a flash flood and how devastating it could be. We were all lucky to survive the fury of nature thanks to our stars and the wisdom of Sawalakhe. I remembered my forester father's words: '*Beta* (Son), do not ever underestimate the power of fire or water in a jungle scenario'.

38

THE FLORA OF MELGHAT

The term *melghat* means 'a confluence of *ghats*' (hilly terrain). As one traverses through Melghat, one climbs up a ridge and goes down a valley. Every ridge, every turn on the road offers a treasure of scenic beauty. Travel down the Akot–Harisaal road in the monsoon and see for yourself. Melghat wears a different look every week, and every day it changes its shades. One, of course, needs a decent eye for appreciating nature. I love Melghat and have spent more than six years there, and every time I have found it looking prettier and the ambience more refreshing than the previous time round.

Melghat's beauty can basically be attributed to the flora of Melghat clothing the undulating terrain in different colours each season. Sometimes it turns different shades of red with freshly sprouted *kusum* leaves or the flowers of *palash* and *sawar* (*Bombax ceiba*) around Holi time; at other times, *amaltas* or *labernum* (*Cassia fistula*) turns it flush with golden yellow flowers. In the winters, the bushes are enveloped by the white flowers of *raanjai* climbers, which bring the added bonus of their mild fragrance.

The forests here are dry and deciduous, with a predominance of teak. In the summer, the trees defoliate and begin to look like pencils sticking out into the sky. With the onset of monsoons, the foliage comes back. The Melghat forest thus looks impenetrable in the rainy season, translucent in winter and transparent in summer. In some areas, the bamboos push teaks to the second position. Various climbers such as *mahul vel* or *raankeli* (*Musa* species) and *arjun* cling to the precious soil on the slopes and stream banks, respectively. The overall beauty of the forest in the core is further enhanced by the sporadic presence of the beautiful 'fair maiden of the forest', the white-barked *kulu* gum tree. The beginning of summer in the Melghat jungles literally intoxicates you with the fragrance of *mahua* flowers.

Ghar Ki Murgi Daal Barabar!

The late Dr M. A. Dhore, an eminent botanist, has covered the Melghat flora extensively. He was as much a Melghat addict as I have been. Where he could not climb hills because of health reasons, he used to make his son, a trained botanist himself, do the climbing, verify the observations, and then make the recordings. He listed 648 naturalised floral species belonging to 398 genera and representing 97 families. *Leguminosae* is the largest family with 98 species, closely followed by *Gramineae* with 92 species. Teak is the predominant species, growing to an average height of twenty to twenty-seven metres.

British forest management was revenue-yielding teak centric. Gradually, the revenue-oriented forest management shifted to conservation management. No felling of trees is permitted in the core area of the MTR. There are eighty-six tree species in the MTR, out of which *haldu*, with its turmeric-coloured timber, and the crocodile-barked *ain* are the major tree species. Fires have been rampant in the MTR from time immemorial, and that has been a limiting factor for the floral diversity, but fortunately, most of the flora is pyrophytic (resistant to fires). Yet this floral diversity in just a part of the old Melghat tehsil is more than is found in many European countries. It is just that we have always had plenty and hence do not feel great about it.

The Ghost of the Forest and Other NTFPs

The collection of non-timber forest produce (NTFP) is prohibited in the MTR. The *tendu* leaf is used in *beedi* making. *Aonla* (*Emblica officinalis*), *hirda* (*Terminalia chebula*), and *beheda* (*Terminalia bellarica*) are three tree species, the fruits of which give us *trifala* (myrobalans). *Mahua* flowers are used for manufacturing a local alcoholic brew. The local tribals also dry and grind these flowers to make *rotis*. An edible gum used in confectionary and ice creams is extracted from the *kadhai* and *dhavda* trees. The *kadhai* gum tree is quite branchy, and it is shiny and white. The *kusum* tree is found sporadically in the buffer zone and in a couple of gregarious patches in the core area. Since *kusum* lac enjoys a high demand in the market, lac thieves take great risks and enter the core, where the collection of huge quantities is easy. The riparian flora is unique, comprising species like arjun and Jamun (*Syzigium cumini*). The *arjun* bark is used for tanning. The *agyamohol* (*Apis dorsata*) variety of bees build their hives on this tree. Bears love honey and, for that reason, climb up these trees. Such trees often carry bear claw marks.

Grass-eating Tigers!

There are about ninety species of grasses found in the MTR. Among the grasses relished by wild as well as domestic life are primarily the *pavnya*, the *sheda*, and the marvel. Plantations of these grasses have been tried on numerous occasions but without much success. Interestingly, when a tiger has an upset stomach, it goes for the same medicines as dogs do – it eats grass. In the field, I have seen that the tiger prefers the wild sugar cane grass (*Sachcharum munja*). In the dry *naala* beds of the MTR, one sees droppings and regurgitates of the tiger containing this grass. Another grass which has got Melghat on the bio map of the world is the *rosha* grass (*Cymbopogon martini*), locally called *tikhadi*. The *motia* variety of this grass has a high percentage of raw oil. The oil once had its buyers in the world-famous perfumery market of Paris. Once upon a time, the business of distilleries extracting raw oil prospered in Akot, which borders Melghat.

Raantulas Spreading like Wildfire!

Among weeds, the *ghaneri* or the *tantani* (*Lantana camara*) ranked number one in the MTR about twenty-five years ago. Now perhaps *raantulas* (*Hyptis suaveolens*), the wild variety of tulsi, might have grabbed the first position. The former, a member of the teak family viz. *Verbenaceae*, bears berries which are eaten by birds and by sloth bears, as seen in their droppings. *Raantulas* is more obnoxious as not only are its spiny fruits non-edible, but also, they get dispersed by attaching themselves to an animal's body. I have heard of graziers abandoning patches where *Raantulas* has arrived. *Tarota* thrives in areas with substantial biotic interference. Its tender leaves make a lovely dish for the locals.

The Climbers

Among the woody climbers, also called lianas, are the *mahul vel*, the *palasvel* (*Butea superba*), and the *malkanguni* (*Celastrus paniculatus*), just to name a few. The woody climbers are often used as rope by the forest dwellers. Also, the big leaves of *B. vahlii* are used for roasting the local bread, called *roti*. *Malkanguni* is a treasured medicinal plant that has been used for centuries in Ayurvedic medicine for sharpening memory..

Wow! Orchids!

The orchid flora of the MTR include *Vanda tessellate*, which is quite common. It occurs on a variety of trees in almost all areas. *Aerides macculosum* has very attractive flowers and occurs exclusively on the mango trees around Semadoh. The terrestrial varieties *Habenaria grandifloriformis* and *H. roxburghii* occur in open situations on higher elevations, whereas *H. plantaginea* is fairly common on moist hill slopes throughout the MTR.

Bamboo, the Wonder Grass

Bamboos are the fastest growing vegetation. Some bamboos (not found in the MTR) grow extremely fast – up to one and a half feet in height overnight. *Dendrocalamus strictus* is the main species in the MTR. It is found in gregarious patches on the sloped areas and in the valleys. It is said to be in sporadic flowering when only a few clumps flower. However, the main flowering is gregarious flowering, where the entire Melghat bamboo flowers together. Gregarious flowering occurs once in forty years. After flowering, the bamboo dies. It is said that after the gregarious flowering comes famine. The reason for this is that the rodent population explodes after it gets plenty of bamboo seeds to feed upon, and it, in turn, destroys the food stored for human consumption.

MTR — The Giver

If we try to enumerate the goods and services the MTR provides us with, the list would be unending. The MTR provides us with free oxygen, conserves soil and water, provides a habitat (snags, den trees, and down logs) for wild animals and birds, and provides food to wildlife. The core area of the MTR is a storehouse of wild varieties of many floral species. These varieties have evolved through long periods of adversity and have developed resistance to these adversities. In case the new improved variety, which is susceptible to adversity, gets wiped out, scientists will have to fall back on these wild varieties to restore the improved variety.

Bhulanvel: The Magical Plant?

The rough meaning of this term is 'a climber that makes you forget'. It makes one lose sense of direction. Once, my predecessor, Mr Ghanekar, and his team, along with our domesticated departmental elephant, had gone in a patch of forest in the core area near FRH

Koktoo. After the inspection, they could not find their way back to the FRH. They remained 'lost' for two days and one night in the core area of Project Tiger. Chau, who located them and got them back to the FRH, firmly believes (even today) that the team must have crossed a climber called *bhulanvel*.

I had been hearing this story from the time I joined as FD of the MTR. On a rainy day in 1993, while we were walking from Bori to Koktoo, Chau showed me this plant by the roadside. It was in flowering, and since it is a rare plant in Melghat, rather than collecting sample, I took photographs. I identified this plant as *Tylophora rotundifolia*, belonging to the family *Asclepiadaceae*. In the late monsoons in 2011, I saw it fruiting on the Koktoo–Dhondriaam road ahead of the Chipi anicut. Though my predecessor and party had got lost, it did not have any effect on me. Was it because both the times I saw it, it was on the main roads, where perhaps I could not have got lost?

The Greedy Bear

Readers may recollect my story written elsewhere of the greedy bear I had seen on the Dhakna–Dolar road who had overfed itself on *mahua* flowers and turned tipsy. It was indeed a comic situation to see the bear staggering through the forest. I have also seen a bear crash-landing from a height of about sixty to seventy feet and dying because it wanted a lick of honey and the branch of the *arjun* tree was too delicate to take its weight.

There are two types of biodiversities, one faunal (animals) and the other floral (plants). Unfortunately, we are heavily biased towards faunal biodiversity and totally ignore the floral part. We have good reason for thanking our stars and Mother Nature for giving us something that the less fortunate ones in the rest of the world do not have. So the next time you visit the MTR, spare some time for appreciating plants too. The easiest way of appreciating the floral beauty of Melghat is to imagine Melghat without flora, and you will know its value.

THE VEGETATION
(CONTINUED 2)

A lofty *Haldu* (Adiana cordifolia) tree

Flower of *Kal-lavi* (Gloriosa superba)

Clematis, the fragrant climber

Desmodium species(*Lepati*), the Jungle velcrow

39

IN GOD WE TRUST

Having faith in a deity/god is a universal phenomenon, and the Korkoo tribals of Melghat are not an exception to this general rule. There seem to be various ways in which deities come into existence in the MTR. One way is that the followers of a noble human being erect his monument after his death. After some years, these monuments become deities. Monuments could also come in existence when villagers come together to commemorate an unusual event or discover an unusual spot where someone gets divine help. Sometimes an important person in the bureaucracy – say, an RFO – establishes a Hanuman or Shiva temple, and local devotees and tourists start visiting there. Such holy spots later get sanctified and come to be known as this baba or that dev. Baba in Melghat is equivalent to God, unlike other places, where 'baba' connotes a living person in whom devotees have faith. Babas in Melghat are generally left unattended and get special attention during annual fair time.

The monument is visited for various reasons. Some visit it because it happens to be on their way to the market. A short halt at the baba gives the traveller a breather. Sometimes the entire village turns up to Baba, demanding community relief from a drought or an epidemic.

Specific pleadings to God broadly include demands such as (a) a child, (b) relief from the ill effects of dog bites, (c) a cure for mental illness, (d) safety from wildlife attacks (especially bear attacks) while travelling in jungles, (e) a cure for chronic diseases and blindness, (f) protection to domestic cattle from diseases and from wildlife attacks, (g) fulfilment of other personal wishes, and, in a few cases, (h) the right number for placing bets (*matka*).

If a vehicle is passing by a shrine and the driver cannot get down and pay his obeisance to the deity, then he slows down and honks. I have seen all my Melghat drivers do that. Various offerings are made to appease the deity, which generally include offerings in the form of tobacco, *beedi*s, and oil as a goodwill gesture. However, on fulfilment of a major wish, sweets or a chicken or a goat is offered. There is a place at Ujjain in Madhya Pradesh where the deity is offered liquor. Generally, there are some auspicious days in the year when *pooja* can be performed. So also, once a year, around an auspicious day – say, on full moon – a large congregation of devotees takes place. Telya Dev and Mahadev Baba are particularly popular deities, with three spots each in Melghat by these names. I have a list of about thirty deities in Melghat, a few of which, for convenience, I have visited and will describe.

Kula Baba

Etched on a rock, about half a kilometre away from FRH Tarubanda, is a life-sized imprint of a tiger pugmark. This place is called the Kula (tiger) Baba and worshipped by the Korkoo tribals. The tribals believe that the etched pugmark actually belongs to a big tiger. I have visited this spot on numerous occasions in 1979 during my range charge. I visited it again in 2015; the pugmark continues to be as sharp. There is almost no erosion in the last thirty-six years. Even now, I could see the evidence of earthen lamps lit and coconuts offered to Kula Baba. It is nice to see the local tribals worshipping a tiger pugmark, in consonance with the spirit of tiger conservation. It helps to keep the tiger in focus in a tiger reserve.

Kandri

On the Tarubanda–Kund road, about five kilometres from Tarubanda, in the middle of a dense forest is a spot called Kandri. A tiny Hanuman temple was built here in the heart of the tiger land sometime in the 1960s. I remember walking down to the spot late on the Dashera festival evening in 1979 with a couple of bravehearts, viz. Hiralal, a labourer, and Phansalkar, the wireless operator who was of the rank of a police sub-inspector.

I remember it was getting dark, and we were almost at Kandri when a worried Phansalkar commented that we were passing through the tiger's jaws. These comments were soon followed by the deafening roar of a tiger from close quarters. You can very well imagine our plight. We hurriedly finished our *seemolanghan* (a ritual of offering obeisance to Hanumanji on Dashera evening) and beat a hasty retreat. I visited Kandri again in 2015. It has grown by leaps and bounds. Lots of construction has come up. If no control is exercised, we may ruin the tiger habitat. Nowadays, terminally ill patients are brought here on Friday and kept in the temple chamber for twenty-four hours for treatment. Also, those who are deaf, dumb, and mentally sick are brought here for divine help.

Dolar Baba

About four kilometres away from Tarubanda on the Tarubanda–Adhao road is the temple of Dolar Baba. It was constructed in 1966; the local Korkoos visit it, particularly when the prospect of a drought looms large or a calamity like an epidemic breaks out in the village. Somji Patel, the village headman, told me that long ago, a man named Dolar Baba actually existed and that he would use a pair of tigers instead of bullocks to plough his agricultural fields. Somji alone had the privilege of performing the community *pooja* at Dolar Baba's monument. One of the walls of the Dolar Baba monument bears Somji's name. *Deep-pooja* is performed here in July. Special prayers are also offered here for the protection of humans and their cattle from wildlife.

Jinbaba

Jinbaba is located on the Akot–Harisaal State Highway (SH 204). It is a stone statue with a thin slit between the lips. The devotees have a unique way of paying their respect to the deity. They offer it a *beedi*, which they insert between the lips of the deity. It is believed that Jinbaba smokes the *beedi* overnight and that only a stub remains the next morning. I have seen the *beedi* stubs between the lips every time I have passed by! Unusually, this baba is approached for getting the right number in *matka*.

Kuttardeo

The deity which gives relief from dog bites is aptly called Kuttardeo. On top of the Narnaala fort, there is a lake called Sakkar Talao, a *dargah* (holy place of Muslims), and this deity. These three adjoin one another and attract people from far-off places for getting relief from dog bites. The sufferer is expected to take a dip in the lake followed by a prayer at the *dargah* and the shrine. A Prasad of jaggery and roasted grams is offered to Kuttardeo. After the circuit is completed, the team, comprising the victim of the dog bite and persons accompanying him, are supposed to walk away without looking back till they are out of the fort.

Mahadev Baba Dhargad

This is a typical Mahadev/Shiva temple on the outskirts of the now deserted Dhargad village. Mondays in the holy Hindu month of Shravan attract a big crowd of devotees here. Interestingly, this temple is located in a big colony of porcupines. Unfortunately, increasing tourism, along with poaching, has resulted in the emptying of this colony. Recently, human movement, sound pollution, and vehicular smoke have flushed the original inhabitants (the porcupines) out of the premises.

Other Deities

I have not personally visited these deities, but they are interesting all the same. The Telyadev deity is offered oil, and Rumaldev is offered a handkerchief for appeasement. The former is located on the Harisaal–Chaurakund road, whereas the latter is on the Semadoh–Raipur road. Khilyadev is located on the way to a weekly market. Small nails along with a stone for hammering the nails are placed there to mend the footwear of the market-going devotees.

The last one is interesting. Udharbaba is the deity's name, and the system is based on mutual trust and fear of the baba. Some coins are kept at the shrine, and those going to the market can borrow from here, free of interest, the only condition being of returning the amount once the person has funds. I am told the system still continues for very small amounts. The devotees believe that one who does not return the borrowed amount after the stipulated time is over and is in a position to repay is suitably punished by the baba.

The Goose Pimples!

An interesting experience at Jinbaba before I wind up. My government vehicle had, as a rule, been driven by my official driver. In the absence of the driver, I generally picked an escort to accompany me in the vehicle. One night I planned a surprise check on the forest staff at the Popatkheda check post. So I left alone on a rainy night after dinner from Paratwada. This time I had neither a driver nor an escort accompanying in the jeep. After about three hours of driving, when I came close to the Jinbaba statue, it was around midnight. Driving carefully on the winding road through thick fog, I was trying to locate the statue so that I could slow down and honk to pay my respect too. At last, in the fog-shortened beam of the headlights of my jeep, a hazy-looking Jinbaba emerged.. As I was about to honk, I heard somebody whispering something from the back seat of my jeep. I was so startled that I jumped in my seat and looked back, but there was nobody. I must have pushed all panic buttons. For the first time, I had goose pimples!

Dazed, I drove down the slope for about a kilometre before the fog cleared. I stopped the jeep, had a couple of gulps of water, switched on the light inside, and investigated. Not a soul around – and the whispering continued. I made a desperate attempt to reach the source from which the whispering sound was emanating. Suddenly, the whispering stopped, which resulted in another round of goose pimples. Drenched in cold sweat, I prayed. As luck would have it, the whispers resumed, and I realised that the sound was coming from the speakers of the audio tape. The culprit appeared to be the faulty tape recorder in the jeep, which had automatically sprung to feeble life when my jeep jumped in a pothole in front of Jinbaba. One side of the tape were songs, and the other side was some speech, and what I had heard as whispers was the speech on the other side of the tape. Soon, I began to breathe easy and continued my journey to Popatkheda. Every time I pass by Jinbaba, I am reminded of this unique experience.

40

THE PRICE OF PROGRESS

Each coin has two sides: a brighter side and a darker side. In real-life situations too, such sides exist. To appreciate in toto a situation, an event, a work, a project, or an area, it is essential that we examine both the sides. So far, I have generally written about the brighter side, the happy Melghat memories. Let us now try to see the darker side. An attempt would be made here to enlist the negative facets of Melghat's personality. If tigers have to survive in Melghat, then these factors will have to be kept in mind at both the planning and implementation levels.

Wildlife needs its space for propagation. However, there is an interesting irony about space. To provide an interference-free habitat for wildlife, the villages are getting relocated. On the other hand, the ever-increasing population pressure along with land hunger has resulted in the encroachment of forest land. If such a shrinking of land resources continues, a day will come when the tiger would be rendered landless. The government policy of regularising encroachments on forest lands at regular intervals has encouraged a prospective encroacher. In fact, an encroacher is not apologetic about his encroachment but comes to the forest office with a request to book an offence against him so that he can have proof of encroachment, which will help him get his encroachment regularised. The ill effects of massive encroachments are already seen at many places. During my days, the Dhakna–Dolar road boasted of all specimens of wild animals, including the elusive caracal; today there is hardly any sighting. Similar is the situation in the Raipur surrounds. In the latter case, it is poaching, besides encroachment, that has taken a heavy toll.

In the early 1960s, we had a massive programme called 'Green Revolution' to boost agriculture production and to make India self-reliant. Unfortunately, this programme, which propagated the use of high-yielding seeds and chemical fertilisers, also made available lethal poisons in the form of pesticides at every nook and corner of the rural areas of India. This poison was mixed in waterholes presumably to kill fish, and it poisoned the entire food chain. Dr Pradhan, a senior scientist from the Zoological Survey of India who had come to the MTR, said that he found it easy to collect specimens of certain very swift insects – butterflies, in particular – in Melghat because they were drugged. Poisoned waterholes killed numerous birds such as peafowls and grey jungle fowls and mammals too. Poisoning apparently resulted in the blinding of certain human consumers of poisoned fish. The poisoning of carcasses and the resultant deaths of big carnivores resulted in a massive depletion of their population. Indeed, we paid a very heavy price of 'progress'. Whether we can reverse the trend is a big question.

Early marriages resulting in early motherhood and malnourished children is a big bane in Melghat. In fact, Melghat has the dubious distinction of being known all over India more for its high rate of infant mortality and malnutrition deaths than for tigers. Immediate corrective measures have to be implemented with all seriousness if we have to see a healthy new generation of locals. Second, the consumption of iodine-deficient salt has resulted in goitre in women who carry a two-to-three-kilogramme lump around their throats. Third, the habit of chewing tobacco has seen an increasing trend in cases of oral cancer. I remember local tribal brethren losing their precious possessions because they pawned them for some grammes of tobacco.

The government machinery has to gear up to attend to these health and nourishment issues. In 1993, I had started a diagnostic and surgical camp with the help of the Rotary Club of Nagpur South. We had made our accommodation at Semadoh and Chikhaldara available, searched for patients, and organised to-and-fro travel by MTR vehicles. A field operation theatre, portable radiological equipment, lodging, a cheap food facility, post-operative care, and so on were also looked into by the rotary. After twenty-six years, this camp is still held annually at Chikhaldara and has a national recognition for complicated goitre cases. Dr Madan Kapre, a world-famous ENT expert, is at the helm of affairs, and all the credit goes to him for the upward trend that this philanthropic activity is showing over the years. Incidentally, the patients as well as their relatives do not have to spend a single penny for the entire procedure.

Some villages are relocated, and their abandoned sites are turning into beautiful meadows where nature is trying to re-establish itself. Such places have already become wildlife's hub of activity. However, biotic pressure continues to be exerted on the wildlife habitat by the villages which are yet to be relocated and the fringe villages of the MTR. The point of interaction is the water body, which happens to be still shared by animals, both wild and domestic. As domestic cattle are still not fully immunised, they act as carriers and spread diseases in their wild brethren. Worse still is when either the graziers or the labourers work in the jungle camp at the waterhole, thus depriving the shy wildlife to suffer in silence as they go thirsty during sizzling hot summer days.

The man–wildlife conflict assumes dangerous proportions when crop compensation or cattle kill compensation is disproportionately low and not paid in time. In such cases, the aggrieved party often takes the law in their hands and ruthlessly kills wildlife. Wild boars and blue bulls are the major culprits in the cases of crop raiding. The crop yield on the sloppy, poor quality of soil in the jungle area is very meagre. If more than half is polished off by wild animals, then the poor farmer has reasons to be seriously aggrieved. We must appreciate that if a bullock is killed, the poor farmer cannot till the land and has nothing to eat.

Generally, in bureaucracy, there is total apathy towards this important event in the poor farmer's life.

Electrocution is another important factor responsible for poaching precious wildlife. In one incident, several wild animals get electrocuted. Sometimes even the person setting up electrical traps gets killed. Another important factor which provides limitations on wildlife population is forest fires. The early detection and timely extinguishing of the fire can go a long way towards getting optimum wildlife population. A rigid control over forest fires is a condition precedent to an optimum tiger population in the MTR.

A forest dweller living in harmony with nature is a thing of the past. Nowadays, for getting honey worth a hundred rupees, a tree worth three hundred thousand rupees is felled where, earlier, the honey gatherer would climb up and get at the honeycomb. Similarly, for getting a couple of *aonla* fruits, previously, he would use his stone-throwing skills; nowadays, he axes down the entire tree bearing more than a thousand fruits. When I joined service in Melghat in 1979, during my meetings in villages, I would tell farmers to educate their children. Accordingly, some farmers sent their children for education in ashram schools. These children did not get a forest guard's job. These children are of no help to the aging parents towards the evening of their life. The number of such educated unemployed persons is substantial, and unless jobs suitable to their status are provided to them, they would be potential anti-social elements indulging in setting fire to forests or doing poaching with the help of dogs in the rainy season or the theft of camera traps and so on.

Wild animals or birds do not know any boundaries, but foresters know their boundaries a bit too well. This working in isolation results in saving one's area from, say, fire by sending the fire in somebody else's jurisdiction, maybe in the form of a counter-fire. This is indeed bad for tiger conservation. In my times, to pass any exam for recruitment to forest service, one had to pass a twenty-five-kilometre walking test. The idea was that a forester maintains that level of fitness throughout his career and walks that much frequently in the field. This would keep him in firm control over all the field forestry and wildlife activities.

With an overall increase in the standard of living, improvement in the road network, and scientific advancements, the tendency to travel on a mo-bike increased. This resulted in the unfortunate thinking that having passed the walking test once, there is no need to walk that much again.

41

HARISAAL-HAAT

The first time I had heard of Harisaal was in 1979. I was posted to Tarubanda for my range charge, and my batchmate and close friend Tasneem Ahmed was posted at Harisaal. I envied Tasneem, for he was posted at a place right on the Nagpur–Indore highway, whereas I was about twelve kilometres off the highway. The Wednesday bazaar at Harisaal was an important bazaar in Melghat and would attract shoppers from far-off places such as Borikheda, Koha, Kund, and Rangubeli. Other prominent villages within the catchment of the Harisaal bazaar were Semadoh, Mangya, Keli, Bhiroja, Tarubanda, Chikhali, Patkahu, Bod, Chaurakund, and Chopan, to name a few. Many of the villagers would leave their village around five in the morning and return by midnight, travelling to and fro for more than fifty kilometres through dense forests abounding in wild animals. To keep our workers in good supply for the Harisaal market, I had made an unwritten rule of making weekly payments every Tuesday. There were smaller bazaars at other places like, say, Semadoh. Invariably, these bazaars were held under a banyan tree, aptly named so by the British because under the thick shade of this tree, a person from the *bania* community would establish his shop and do brisk business.

Most of the major shopkeepers came from Dharni, the tehsil, to Harisaal and put up their shops by eleven in the morning. Every morning a fleet of our empty trucks would leave from Dharni, pass by Harisaal, and go to the field to load timber. These loaded trucks would reach our Dharni depot by late evening. Some vendors would take advantage of these timings and would get a lift to and fro in our trucks by 'managing' our truck drivers. Also, in the evening, some shoppers would precariously perch themselves atop the timber loaded in the truck by paying the drivers. Some drivers would load only six cubic metres of timber instead of the standard eight cubic metres, thus keeping two cubic metres of space for vendors and their goods. At a later stage in my service, I remember punishing some such recalcitrant drivers.

The two major festivals in Melghat are Holi and Diwali, and the Harisaal bazaar prior to these festivals is always special. Special stalls are set up for selling items required for these festivals: colours for Holi, special sweets for both festivals, oil lamps, cloth, and firecrackers for Diwali. A jewellery shop is, of course, a given. The ornaments are normally made in white metal but can be made in silver on advance payment. The jewellery is basically for women and includes items like toe rings, anklets, waist belts, bangles, necklaces, and so on. This jewellery shop would always be of special interest to my wife and my cousin from Mumbai.

On ordinary Wednesdays, the bazaar normally has vegetable stalls, banana stalls, and spice shops for onions, ginger, garlic, chilli powder, turmeric, and mustard seeds; all these ingredients are required for a spicy curry. This shop also sells tobacco for chewing. Then there is a general store which keeps some cheap trinkets and cosmetics, some basic tools, toys, and so on. The last time I visited the Harisaal bazaar, *jalebi*s (a popular sweet) were being freshly fried at the sweet meat shop. Then of course, there is the butcher's shop, selling chicken and mutton. But the most preferred food of the locals is undoubtedly fish, particularly roasted minnows, which the fisherwomen lay out in big and small heaps.

As with all bazaars, Harisaal is a great place for meeting old friends. On one such bazaar day, I was passing by Harisaal, and I came across such a friend. He lived at one end of the market, where he took me for a cup of tea. I was amazed to see a deer in his courtyard, which he informed me he was using to study its food preferences. We could then create plantations of the preferred food in the tourism zone and thus manipulate the habitat to improve the sighting of wild animals. Every day the deer was offered different kinds of vegetable matter. The faeces were then studied under the microscope. Stomatal structures in the leaves would clearly indicate the vegetation preferred by the deer. This simple study done at Harisaal proved immensely useful for choosing the species for fodder plantation in Melghat.

In one corner of the bazaar stands a proud monument which is a mute testimony to the sacrifice of Ranger Nasir Mohammed. On 16 February 1935, he had suffered severe burn injuries while combating a forest fire and breathed his last in the Amravati hospital on 23 February 1935. Thousands of foresters all over India visit this monument every year and derive inspiration from it. One must appreciate the British for the way they motivated their staff by highlighting courage and devotion to duty, the Gunga Din syndrome of being 'faithful unto death'.

The last halt for many is, of course, the *deshi daruche dukaan* ('country liquor shop'). The shop timings are from 10:00 a.m. to 10:00 p.m. While the maximum sale is in the evening, there are some who provide customers right from 10 a.m. One such person was DW, who was a class-four employee in the divisional forest office at Chikhaldara way back in 1979. When he met me last in the Harisaal bazaar after a gap of almost thirty-six years, he had retired from service. He sported long black (perhaps dyed) hair. It was just about 11:00 a.m., and DW was already tipsy. He recognised me from a distance and, conscious of being drunk, tried to duck away unnoticed. I felt bad for this talented boy who, in his heyday, was a master at catching snakes, the cobra in particular. He must have captured hundreds of them. For the entire time that I was at the bazaar, he orbited around me at a safe distance and saluted me whenever our eyes met.

En route to Harisaal, in those days, there were the two stoppages of Udharbaba and Khilyadev (nail god), discussed elsewhere in the book. Thus, with borrowed money and mended footwear, they would make their weekly trek to the bazaar across unimaginable distances through dense forests teeming with wildlife. And what would they buy? Oil, tobacco, salt, maybe some fish – they could easily have touched their neighbour for all this. But the Wednesday *haat* was a composite package of enjoyment that included a thrilling trek, shopping, meeting new friends, socialising, and, of course, imbibing the weekly quota of *siddu* (local brew). For some, it would be an ideal place for matchmaking. For others, it was a place for bumping into old friends. I was told by Mr Havetson (the last of the British foresters) that he had met an old tribal friend who recognised him as the *jungli sahib*. Similarly, I have seen Mr Indurkar, my then boss and the ex-DFO of East Melghat, suddenly seeing a tribal friend, a person called Patel.

Mr Indurkar said, 'Aarey, Patel, tum kitna Buddha ho gaya! (How old you have become!)'

Patel responded, 'Tera bhi to baal kitna safed ho gaya baba! (Your hair has turned white too, man!)'

I remember the case of a young Korkoo boy who was attacked by a bear. His face had become so badly mutilated that to dodge the unpleasant looks of young girls, he would cover the damaged half of his face with a handkerchief. With support from helpful MTR officials and philanthropic doctors from Nagpur, the damaged part of his face was restored. It was such a pleasure then to see the young man move around confidently in the bazaar. He now goes to the bazaar with his wife. One bad thing I have seen about the bazaar is that a lot of youngsters get attracted towards tobacco. Tobacco, whether for chewing or for smoking, is offered free of cost initially. Once a person is hooked, the same tobacco is sold at exorbitant rates. I've personally seen tobacco ruin so many tribal lives.

Driving in the five-kilometre radius of Harisaal becomes quite a tricky job after sundown for reasons of life sometimes going wild. Once, I had an interesting experience on the Harisaal–Chaurakund road. Generally, when people set off for the long walk back, they take a rather strong one for the road to give them company all the way. One such high bunch had formed a chain because they could not stand unsupported. I have narrated their story in one of my articles. There,

I have mentioned about warning a tipsy bunch of youngsters about an irritated bear round the next turning. Their condition was 'United, they stand. Divided, they fall'. The bunch, carefully listening to my warning, had taken the support of the bonnet of my jeep and later could not balance themselves and take off individually till we helped them join hands to reform the stable chain.

Harisaal *haat* – their heart, their soul, their solace in good times and bad, their weekly destination till as long their legs and a friend's helping hand can carry them.

UNIQUE
MACHANS

A farm machan

.......readying for the night vigil

Machan cum camping hut

A camouflaged machan at Amrai no.1

HARISAL MARKET

General view of the Harisal market

Essentials for spicy, delicious curry

The mouth watering stuff for the shoppers

The monument located in the market

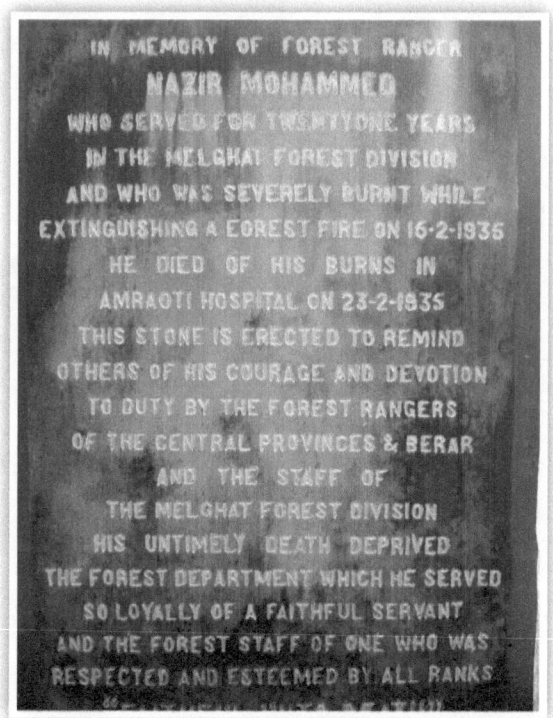

OH GOD!

Korkoo God akin to Jin baba . Observe the devotee's offering between his lips

Dolarbaba, It was believed that he would deploy a pair of tigers in place of bullocks for tilling his land

Kulababa. Devotees worship the Kula (tiger) pug mark on the rock

Local Gods of Adhao village are a witness to a dialogue with a village elder

EMINENT PERSONALITIES

Babulal, the fire watcher from Memna village shows the place where a drunkard was killed by a tigress with cubs

Jaju, the dare-devil tracker from Semadoh, sat alone perched on a tree top in the middle of a rainy night to ensure reunion of mother leopard (excellent tree-climber)with her cubs.

Surajpal, fearless tracker, who once boldly faced a bear attack and saved my field inspection party from imminent bear attack. An asset to MTR.

Prachi, the courageous ornithologist and a staunch Melghati

EMINENT PERSONALITIES (CONTINUED)

Giri an ideal forester, and an asset during a field excursion

Ajay Pillarisett, highly respected, sensitive Range Officer, dedicated himself equally for the cause of locals, staff and wlldlife. His paper on slothbears was much appreciated in an international conference

Ravi Wankhade ACF, a daredevil officer who once preferred camping in the forest knowing well that a pair of tigers were feeding nearby. just to ensure timely beginning of a field exercise

Chau who successfully searched out a contingent of officers along with our departmental elephant who were lost in the core area of MTR. He also rescued the FDPT from a precarious position while inspecting a porcupine burrow.

GLOSSARY OF UNFAMILIAR TERMS

SN.	The term	Meaning in English
1.	Aagya Mohol (M)	Big bees' honey comb
2.	Aam	Mango
3.	Aajibaicha batwa (M)	Granny's purse of ayurvedic medicines
4.	Aaramkursi	Relaxing chair
5.	Amraika ghuggu	An owl belonging to a Mango orchard
6.	Angari	A person specially appointed in fire season to detect and fight forest fires
7.	Avatar	Incarnation
8.	Baal	Hair
9.	Bailgadi	Bullock cart
10.	Bairagi	A Nomadic Tribe of India
11.	Bana (K)	Bear
12.	Banapoi (K)	Water point for bears
13.	Banakapar (K)	Precipitous slopes preferred by bears
14.	Bania	A business community in India
15.	Bater	Quail
16.	Beedi	Small country cigar filled with tobacco
17.	Besan	Gram flour
18.	Bhaisagaadi	Buffalo-cart
19.	Bhakri	Roasted country bread
20.	Bhaloo	Bear

21.	Bhoot	Ghost
22.	Bhootkhora	Valley of ghosts
23.	Bhulanwel	It is a climber which if crossed, one gets lost in the forest.(feel the locals)
24.	Bhumka (K)	A tribal doctor or black magician
25.	Bibtyacha-vavar (M)	Movement of leopard in a locality
26.	Bitkilpati (K)	A water-hole frequented by buffaloes
27.	Chatan (M)	Salt lick
28.	Chippak	Nightjar (A Bird)
29.	Chor	Thief
30.	Chudidar	A tight fitting pyjama worn in India
31.	Chulha	Hearth
32.	Dada (M and Bengali)	Elder brother or a bully
33.	Dal bati	A Rajasthani dish comprising lentils and hard wheat roll
34.	Darbha	Grass
35.	Dargah	Tomb of a Muslim saint
36.	Dashera	A Hindu festival
37.	Desi daru	Country liquor
38.	Dendrakhora (K)	Valley of crabs
39.	Dhaba	Wayside restaurant
40.	Dhaman	Rat snake
41.	Dhoti	Long loin cloth worn by men in India
42.	Doh	Deep water part specially in a river
43.	Dost	Friend
44.	Durbar	Crown Court
45.	Firmaan	Order
46.	Gaana	Song
47.	Gadwa (M)	A metal vessel for water
48.	Gawli	A cattle rearing community
49.	Ghat	Undulating terrain
50.	Ghongadi (M)	A rough blanket
51.	Ghubad (M)	Owl

52.	Gidhad (M)	Vulture
53.	Gofan	Sling shots
54.	Gorasaheb	Fair-complexioned master
55.	Gurgipati (K)	A waterhole catering to needs of horses
56.	Haat	Market
57.	Haath-chakki	Hand flour mill
58.	Haathkua	A well where water could be fetched by hands
59.	Jalebi	A circular Indian sweet made from deep fried maida casing and immersed in sugar syrup
60.	Khadi	Hand-spun hand-woven cotton cloth in India
61.	Khansama	A male cook in Government Rest House.
62.	Khus	Vetiver grass
63.	Kolha (M)	Jackal
64.	Korkoo	A majority tribe in Melghat
65.	Kula (K)	Tiger
66.	Kuladeo (K)	Tiger God
67.	Kulsund (M)	Wild dog(s)
68.	Kund	Waterhole
69.	Kurta	A long, loose, collarless shirt worn in India
70.	Kusal (M)	A grass variety with spiny fruits which on drying get stuck to the trousers or socks causing considerable discomfort.
71.	Lamjana (K)	A Korkoo son in law who stays at his wife's place.
72.	Langur	A type of monkey with long tail
73.	Lotan (M)	Wallow or a place frequented by some wild animals for a mud bath.
74.	Maa	Mother

75.	Machan	An elevated platform for observing the wildlife
76.	Mahavat	An elephant driver
77.	Mahulvel (M)	A common woody big climber seen in Melghats
78.	Makadi	Spider
79.	Mama	Maternal uncle
80.	Masan	Graveyard or crematorium
81.	Mashal	Torch burning at one end
82.	Matka	Earthen pot or gambling by betting on numbers.
83.	Mithai	Indian sweets
84.	Murgi	Fowl
85.	Nagin	A female Cobra
86.	Nag-Panchami	A Hindu festival of worshipping cobras
87.	Naka bandi	Road block
88.	Nalla	A small stream
89.	Nawami	Ninth day of the fortnight in Hindu calendar
90.	Nilgai	Blue-bull
91.	Paan	Leaf or Betel leaf
92.	Padao	Place for temporary storage of timber/firewood
93.	Palash	A tree, popularly called 'Flame of the forests.
94.	Pooja	Worship
95.	Pradakshina	Revolving round oneself or round a revered place
96.	Rassi	Rope
97.	Saahib/Sahaab	Sir or the master
98.	Sadhu Baba	Saint
99.	Sambar	Largest of the deer in India
100.	Sapsurli	Skink

101.	Seemollanghan	Ritual of crossing border of town on Dashera evening
102.	Shakkar	Sugar
103.	Shamshan-ghat	Crematorium or Graveyard
104.	Sherwani	A long coat-like garment worn by men in India
105.	Shikar	Hunt
106.	Shukla Paksha	The brighter fortnight in a lunar calendar
107.	Siddu (K)	The local intoxicating brew
108.	Shravan	A holy month as per Hindu calendar
109.	Sukli (K)	Wild boar
110.	Talao	Lake
111.	Tapal	Government letters
112.	Tarubanda	A parasitic plant
113.	Tawa	Hot plates
114.	Tembha	Same as Mashaal. A stick with fire at one end
115.	Tera	Your
116.	Titar	Partridge
117.	Titavi	Yellow or red-wattled Lapwing
118.	Ullu	Owl
119.	Varanda	Roofed, open-air porch, attached to outside of a building.
120.	Wawar (M)	Farm land
121.	Ye dekho	Look here
122.	Zopdi	Hut

N B-Most of the words are in HINDI
K-Korkoo and M- Marathi

ABBREVIATIONS

SN.	Abbreviation	Meaning
1.	ACF	Assistant Conservator of Forests
2.	CCF	Chief Conservator of Forests
3.	CF	Conservator of Forests
4.	CM	Chief Minister
5.	CP	Central Provinces
6.	DD ROAD	Dhakna-Dolar Road
7.	DCF	Deputy Conservator of Forests
8.	DFO	Divisional Forest Officer
9.	ENT	Ear Nose Throat
10.	FDPT	Field Director Project Tiger
11.	FRH	Forest Rest House
12.	FRI	Forest Research Institute
13.	HQ	Head Quarter
14.	IFS	Indian Forest Service
15.	IIM	Indian Institute of Management
16.	MPSC	Maharashtra Public Service Commission
17.	MTR	Melghat Tiger Reserve
18.	PCCF	Principal Chief Conservator of Forests
19.	POR	Preliminary Offence Report
20.	PWD	Public Works Department
21.	RFO	Range Forest Officer
22.	ST	State Transport
23.	UPSC	Union Public Service Commission
24.	VIP	Very Important Person
25.	WII	Wildlife Institute of India

ABOUT THE AUTHOR

Prakash Thosre, got into the world at Allapalli,(Gadchiroli district of Maharashtra), the Mecca of forestry in India on 18th August 1952. He followed his father's footsteps and joined the Indian Forest Service in 1977. He worked on important posts in Maharashtra including that of the Director, Social Forestry, MD of Forest Development Corporation and the Principal Chief Conservator of Forests, Maharashtra. Retired in 2012. As Member and later Chairman Maharashtra Public Service Commission he was responsible for recruitment of gazetted officers in Maharashtra. Similarly he had a role to play when he worked for UPSC for recruitment of IFS officers. He has been intimately associated with forests and wildlife for literally from the time he was born. He spent about seven years in the Melghat forest, including over four years as the Field Director of the Melghat Tiger Reserve. Thosre has been a regular contributor to newspapers on issues related to nature. He is also a popular speaker on the lecture circuit, and is much sought after for his slide shows and skills as raconteur. His pictorial book titled 'The wild mammals of Maharashtra' was released by Governor of Maharashtra and whereas the Chief Minister wrote the foreword.